Asghar Farhadi: Interviews

Conversations with Filmmakers Series
Gerald Peary, General Editor

ASGHAR
FARHADI

I N T E R V I E W S

Edited by Ehsan Khoshbakht and Drew Todd

University Press of Mississippi / Jackson

The University Press of Mississippi is the scholarly publishing agency of
the Mississippi Institutions of Higher Learning: Alcorn State University,
Delta State University, Jackson State University, Mississippi State University,
Mississippi University for Women, Mississippi Valley State University,
University of Mississippi, and University of Southern Mississippi.

www.upress.state.ms.us

The University Press of Mississippi is a member
of the Association of University Presses.

First printing 2023
∞

Library of Congress Cataloging-in-Publication Data

Names: Khoshbakht, Ehsan, 1982– editor. | Todd, Drew, 1970– editor.
Title: Asghar Farhadi : interviews / Ehsan Khoshbakht, Drew Todd.
Other titles: Conversations with filmmakers series.
Description: Jackson : University Press of Mississippi, 2023. | Series: Conversations with
    filmmakers series | Includes bibliographical references and index.
Identifiers: LCCN 2022031545 (print) | LCCN 2022031546 (ebook) |
    ISBN 9781496841056 (hardback) | ISBN 9781496841063 (trade paperback) |
    ISBN 9781496841070 (epub) | ISBN 9781496841087 (epub) | ISBN 9781496841094 (pdf) |
    ISBN 9781496841100 (pdf)
Subjects: LCSH: Farhādī, Asghar, 1972—Interviews. | Motion picture producers and
    directors—Interviews. | Motion picture producers and directors—Iran—Interviews. |
    Screenwriters—Interviews. | Screenwriters—Iran—Interviews.
Classification: LCC PN1998.3.F36 A53 2023 (print) | LCC PN1998.3.F36 (ebook) |
    DDC 791.4302/33092—dc23/eng/20220822
LC record available at https://lccn.loc.gov/2022031545
LC ebook record available at https://lccn.loc.gov/2022031546

British Library Cataloging-in-Publication Data available

Contents

Introduction   vii

Chronology   xiii

Filmography   xvii

A Reaction to Current Conditions   3
  Film Monthly / 1999

City of No Angels   6
  Alireza Motamedi / 2000

A Discussion with Asghar Farhadi, Director of *Dancing in the Dust*:
Snakes on a Plain!   11
  Omid Najvan / 2003

Which Part of the City Is Beautiful?   19
  Shadmehr Rastin / 2004

An Interview with Asghar Farhadi and Mani Haghighi: A Special Day   29
  Houshang Golmakani and Abbas Yari / 2006

The Autopsy of Elly   53
  Saeed Ghotbizadeh / 2009

Bitter Truth, Sweet Expediency, and Denied Redemption   70
  Massoud Mehrabi / 2011

The Butterfly Effect: Asghar Farhadi and Ali Mosaffa in Conversation
about *The Past*   97
  Hossein Moazezinia / 2013

An Interview with Asghar Farhadi about *The Salesman*: This Hidden Hell   121
   Massoud Mehrabi / 2016

No One Knows What the Past Holds   146
   Amir Pouria / 2018

A Country without Heroes   153
   Ehsan Khoshbakht / 2021

Index   159

Introduction

In a short span of time—just over ten years—every new film by Asghar Farhadi has become a major event, both in his native country of Iran and at international film festivals. But look back to his first interviews in the 1990s; the solemn talent behind a popular Iranian TV series showed no awareness of what was to come: directorial stardom. Still, the skill was always there, even if Farhadi was content working for television, producing various series of social significance. His weaving together of stories was at once deeply familiar to Iranians and yet something new. Those paying attention to Farhadi's early work would have seen indications that he was bound for cinematic glory.

Having won two Academy Awards for Best Foreign Film in a span of only five years, Asghar Farhadi has become Iran's most prominent director since the late Abbas Kiarostami. Around the world, there is a consensus that Farhadi is one of the great dramatist filmmakers of his generation. His reputation and influence in his home country have been even greater, where he has achieved a celebrity status that most arthouse directors can only dream of. His face is familiar even to those who have not seen his films. In spite of his private, cautious lifestyle, he is a fixture in highbrow journals and tabloids. At the same time, Farhadi's stature at home also has been prone to misunderstandings, controversies, divided critical reception, and, as of this writing, a backlash—the first among his own people—rooted in a rising dissatisfaction with the current regime.

By breaking onto the scene working for television, Farhadi did not follow the traditional path of state-backed arthouse films (many of which have been paradoxically banned or restricted by the state); nor did he work for the Center for Intellectual Development of Children and Young Adults (as Kiarostami and Amir Naderi did), or even for independent production companies. Instead, Farhadi wrote teleplays and then directed a series of successful urban dramas for home viewing, offering an uncharacteristically bleak portrayal of life in Tehran.

Farhadi's TV work was surely a challenge to its producer, Iranian national television (IRIB), known for steering clear of topical issues and of anything approaching a critique of Iranian society. Perhaps he escaped censure because all of his television work landed on the regional Channel 5, accessible only to people in Tehran province. This meant that Farhadi remained little known outside of a small circle of critics. It was only after writing screenplays for well-known Iranian filmmakers (Masoud Kimiai, Ebrahim Hatamikia) and making several underseen features that he had a breakthrough hit with his third film, *Fireworks Wednesday* (2006).

Farhadi thus became prominent while working within the system, distinguishing him from past generations of Iranian arthouse directors who were, generally speaking, left-leaning "outsiders." Even as a screenwriter, Farhadi acted as an intermediary between irreconcilable worlds in Iranian cinema: on the one hand, he wrote for Masoud Kimiai, one of the most popular prerevolutionary directors, whose work in the 1970s married new wave and mainstream, while on the other, for the unapologetic, regime-endorsed propagandist Ebrahim Hatamikia. (Farhadi has since disowned the latter script.)

Farhadi's first two films, *Dancing in the Dust* (2003) and *Beautiful City* (2004), belong in the tradition of Iranian social realism. They both star Faramarz Gharibian, an esteemed actor of an earlier generation, and both offer gritty, contemporary settings: *Dancing in the Dust* follows poor Azeri[1] migrants in Tehran, while *Beautiful City* is set at a detention center and prison. *Fireworks Wednesday* was the turning point, where Farhadi managed to merge social realism with modern melodrama and up-to-date elements of suspense. There was something else, too: youth. Farhadi's talents and razor-sharp scripts were fully realized when he found his team of actors, mostly people in their thirties. The new actors (Hedieh Tehrani, Shahab Hosseini, Taraneh Alidoosti, Peyman Maadi, Leila Hatami) brought with them an air of urgency and change to the universe that Farhadi was quickly expanding on. With his new acting ensemble, Farhadi saw his subject and setting shift dramatically. He opened a window on to the lives of the Tehran middle class. Amazingly, this was novel for Iranian cinema. Soon, Farhadi was championed by the very people who had become the filmmaker's subject of interest.

Mainstream cinema before the Revolution, known as *filmfarsi*, was mainly about tough guys, dancers, and prostitutes. Genre films privileged happy-go-lucky, working-class characters, and arthouse films mostly focused on rural areas, with very little interest in tackling the issues of the middle class in big cities. After 1979, the prerevolutionary model continued in both arthouse and popular Iranian films, with mainly villagers and the working class populating the screens.

So it was Farhadi who turned the camera on to the forgotten middle class. He depicted their lives with complexity and depth, masterfully situating their lives in the contexts of class wars that had been barely visible. He navigated the hidden tensions among the classes more meaningfully and accurately than any of his contemporaries.

Before Farhadi, "socialist" (or at least social-minded) filmmakers in Iran were known to show poverty and injustice in a style borrowed from Italian neorealism.

Since Farhadi's rise, the mantle of arthouse filmmaker has expanded to include nuanced forays into the lives of young bourgeois Iranians, their dissatisfaction and estrangement on full dramatic display—think Michelangelo Antonioni in the wake of Italian neorealism.

Farhadi's world is one of repressed, unpredictable, explosive emotions. His characters' search for identity can be understood by millions of Iranians going through the same agonizing crisis. His cinema reveals an Iran that has failed to meet the lofty ideals set by a revolution and instead, among those not suffering from poverty, finds tenuous comfort in the art of getting by. The mechanisms of this day-to-day survival are pretense, suppression, compromise, deceit. Farhadi's cinema has broken the dam in Iran, and a flood of films with similar subjects has followed.

The man known for making films about false and failed hopes suddenly became the new hope for Iran. On the nights of his two Oscar wins, joyous Iranians flooded the streets, an occurrence unwelcomed by the regime and typically reserved for World Cup victories. Farhadi is at once feted and under fire by his own government. In addition to making his recent films outside Iran, he has occasionally taken advantage of his celebrity status to offer statements of a political nature, on topics ranging from Donald Trump to poverty and capital punishment in Iran. In response to Trump's travel ban, which barred entry of travelers from seven countries, including Iran, Farhadi boycotted the 2017 Oscars. When his film *The Salesman* (2016) won the Academy Award that year for Best Foreign Language Film, Anousheh Ansari, the first Iranian in space, accepted the award on Farhadi's behalf and read aloud his statement, which did not mince words: "My absence is out of respect for the people of my country and those of the other six nations who have been disrespected by the inhumane law that bans entry of immigrants to the US." While this curried favor with Iran's regime, other actions by Farhadi have not. He expressed public support for his exiled filmmaker colleagues, Mohsen Makhmalbaf and Golshifteh Farahani, to return to Iran and continue their work. He also called for activist-filmmaker Jafar Panahi's threatened jail sentence to be revoked, prompting the government to temporarily withdraw permission to shoot *A Separation* (2011).

In a police state such as Iran, which has become increasingly fraught with anti-regime activism and political discontent, any amount of engagement in the highly controlled public sphere of national cinema is at once insufficient and yet too much. Jafar Panahi and Mohammad Rasoulof, both previously arrested and currently banned from filmmaking, still dare to make films in Iran about taboo subjects and have them distributed internationally. State-sanctioned cinema, instead, risks being written off as propaganda by Iranians. Farhadi has built his career on deftly straddling these two extremes. That he has done so without getting into (significant) legal trouble with the authorities is a testament to his popularity and to the subtlety of his craft.

More recently, however, Farhadi's cinema has been a source of contention and controversy within Iran. With his recent work outside Iran, a number of Iranian critics have gone so far as to call him evasive. If there is any truth in that accusation, then we may liken Farhadi's international films to a kind of antidote to the pressures of working and living in Iran—fine projects, yes, but also extended holidays, with a French (*The Past*, 2013) or Spanish (*Everybody Knows*, 2018) film as the outcome. The latter film, shot entirely in Spain with Spanish-speaking stars, was not approved for theatrical release in Iran, though it was widely distributed on the country's black market. Farhadi's latest film, *A Hero* (2021), shot during the COVID-19 pandemic, marks the filmmaker's return to working in his native country. It premiered at Cannes, where it won the Grand Prix (in a tie with the Finnish entry, *Compartment No. 6*), but this time Iranians were not celebrating in the streets—not so much for what the film says as for what it avoids saying. Word quickly spread back home that *A Hero* does not acknowledge the growing sentiment of disillusionment among Iranians with the current regime. Without having seen the film, disgruntled Iranians flocked to IMDb.com to give it low ratings.[2] Not even Farhadi, it seems, can fully escape the well-documented difficulties and pressures placed on Iranian filmmakers. The filmmaker addresses these controversies in an exclusive interview with coeditor Ehsan Khoshbakht and a blistering Instagram post, both of which are included in this volume.

Up until making *A Hero*, while Farhadi was abroad there were many filmmakers busy making "Farhadi films" in his absence. Some of the wave of Farhadi-inspired films were intended for the international market and festival circuit, but an even greater number were aimed at Iran's domestic market. BBC Persian has called this a "syndrome of Farhadism," an explosion of unhappy themes, including lying and infidelity, taking viewers on a suspenseful ride that shakes and rattles domestic structures.

"Farhadism," alternately, has meant the production of a good deal of literature in Persian on Farhadi's cinema. This is particularly remarkable if one contrasts the first twenty years of Abbas Kiarostami's filmmaking career, for which only one slim monograph appeared in Iran. In his first two decades working in film and television, Farhadi has instead been widely embraced: the scripts of seven of his films have been published in glossy editions.

Maziar Eslami offered the first study of Farhadi's cinema in *Asghar Farhadi: Poetics of Disintegration* (2016). Saeed Aghighi is the second Iranian critic of note to analyze Farhadi's oeuvre from a critical perspective in *The Secrets of Separation: The Cinema of Asghar Farhadi* (2017). A book called *Trauma* (Seyyed Majid

Hosseini and Zanyar Ebrahimi, 2016) maps the major sociopolitical events of Iran between 2009 (the year of the stolen election and massive street protests) and 2015,[3] all through the lens of Farhadi's cinema. A book of interviews appeared that was titled *Face to Face with Asghar Farhadi* (Esmaeil Mihandoust, 2018). And finally, in English, *Asghar Farhadi: Life and Cinema* (2014), a small volume composed of one lengthy interview and a brief analysis by Iranian-Canadian Tina Hassannia.

This volume offers a unique perspective into Farhadi's career in several key respects. Unlike most studies on this filmmaker, this one begins with his TV work. Just as Farhadi's background in theater informs his dramatic filmmaking, so too does his early and important work in television, which is unknown outside Iran. This volume also charts a parallel path, chronicling Farhadi's rise from theater student to Iranian dramatist to celebrated international filmmaker. Most important, to provide those in the West with an Iranian perspective on Farhadi, we located interviews conducted in Persian and had them translated here for the first time.

Farhadi speaking openly on an array of topics in his native tongue has several built-in advantages. He has in his command the power to express himself naturally and to the best of his abilities. He is not constrained by the inevitable questions from Western interviewers trying to satisfy curiosity about life in Iran rather than to magnify his work. These interviews also put a much-needed spotlight on Farhadi as television writer and director, before he became internationally successful.

The majority of these interviews were published in *Film Monthly*, Iran's leading film journal and one of the longest-running publications in the country. Known for its critical, in-depth engagement with filmmaking, *Film Monthly* ensures not only quality but also a sense of coherence, since the journal followed Farhadi's career from his early days in television up to his last film, always providing him with the space to reflect upon his methods and ideas.[4] His first films, which are socially his most daring and brilliant, did not receive the critical attention they clearly deserved. The *Film Monthly* interviews correct that slight.

The tradition of Iranian movie criticism is fortunately a rich and rigorous one that illuminates the complexities of filmmaking in Iran. The interviewers do not shy away from hard questions; and both the questions and answers tend to be long and challenging. Critics at home have been increasingly divided over Farhadi, especially since *The Salesman*. The Iranian interviews appearing in this volume will help readers better understand these fissures. They also cover important themes central to Farhadi's career, including the influence of theater and past filmmakers, and what he sees as his role and responsibilities as an Iranian filmmaker in a global age. Finally, they illuminate Farhadi's particular craft of scriptwriting and turning the written text into images, in this way offering the pleasure of a unique and in-depth guide to filmmaking.

EK & DT

■ ■ ■

EK: I should thank the interviewers and translators of this volume, half of whom now live in a country other than Iran. What made them (and me) live elsewhere—any Farhadi film made in Iran could give you a sense of that. So, I dedicate this book to those who stayed.

DT: Thanks go first to my coeditor and friend, Ehsan Khoshbakht, who is as gracious as he is knowledgeable. I am grateful to the interviewers and translators for making this volume as rich as it is, let alone possible; to the editors and staff at University Press of Mississippi, who have been consistently helpful and supportive; and to San José State University for its grant support of this project. I dedicate this volume to my parents—both introduced me to movies and, as importantly, thinking about them.

Notes

1. Azeri refers to Turkish-speaking Iranians from the northwest province of Azerbaijan that borders Turkey and the country Azerbaijan.

2. In an unprecedented response to this, IMDb.com disabled the ratings option for this movie's listing until the time of its theatrical distribution.

3. Although these major events are absent from Farhadi's films, one could argue that the psychological aftereffects are omnipresent.

4. In a Farhadian twist that reminds us what lies behind the seemingly stable facade of things, the owner of *Film Monthly*, Massoud Mehrabi, who granted us permission to publish his fine interviews in this book, passed away during the summer of 2020, at age sixty-six. After his death, the tension between his son, who "inherited" the journal, and the real creative force behind *Film Monthly*, particularly its editor in chief, Houshang Golmakani (who also has an interview published in this volume), became so hostile that it made the news and nearly put an end to the forty-year-old magazine. Golmakani and his team launched a new journal called *Film-e Emrooz* (Film Today). It is always sad to see good things come to an end, but this one was particularly unexpected and lamentable.

Chronology

1972   Born in Homayoun Shahr (renamed Khomeini Shahr after the 1979 Revolution) in Isfahan province, in central Iran.

1987   Joins the Iranian Youth Cinema Society, where he directs amateur films in either Super 8 or 16 mm formats. Titles include *The World of Walls, Radio,* and *The Adventures of Mr. Filmmaker.*

1993–94   While still collaborating with the Iranian Youth Cinema Society, the publication of the Society publishes some of Farhadi's very first scripts. Farhadi then moves to Tehran to enroll at the College of Fine Arts of the University of Tehran, studying theater. After obtaining a bachelor's degree, he continues studying theater at the conservative Tarbiat Modares University in Tehran, where he earns his MA.

1997–98   *The Kind Moon,* the very first series produced by the newly launched Tehran Channel (or Channel 5), is written by Farhadi. Right after, he not only writes the twenty-six-part *The Expectant* for the same channel but he also directs and produces it.

1999–2001 Cowrites and directs *Tale of a City.* The success of the series leads to a second season, which this time is written by Farhadi only.

2002   Writes the script of *Low Heights* for Ebrahim Hatamikia, but later disassociates himself from it; in his anthology of screenplays, later published in Iran, this script is not included. Nevertheless, *Low Heights* marks Farhadi's first work in the world of cinema.

2003   Directs his first feature, *Dancing in the Dust,* which is shown in only three cinemas. Nevertheless, he wins the best film award at the Fajr Film Festival in Tehran, and the film is then screened in some Asian film festivals, winning the best film award at Busan.

2004   *Beautiful City* is distributed in eight theaters in Iran, and for the first time a film by Farhadi is shown in the West (Warsaw).

2006–7   Mani Haghighi encourages Farhadi to cowrite the script for *Fireworks Wednesday,* which is then directed by Farhadi and stars the popular actress Hedieh Tehrani. The film becomes the biggest box office hit of the year in Iran and wins Farhadi the best director award at the Fajr

Film Festival. The film also wins at the Chicago International Film Festival and is shown at Locarno.

2008   Spends the year mostly writing scripts for others, including *Canaan* for Mani Haghighi, *Dayere Zangi* for his wife, Parisa Bakhtavar, and *Trial on the Street* for Masoud Kimiai.

2009   After some controversies regarding its actors (and an initial rejection by the Fajr Film Festival, resolved only when someone from the Ministry of Culture lobbied for the film), *About Elly*, directed and, for the first time, also produced by Farhadi, is screened and heralded as one of Iran's most important postrevolutionary films. The film gains wide attention at the Berlinale and is distributed in France (though not the United States until 2015).

2010   His permission to shoot *A Separation* is revoked after defending—and then protesting the filmmaking ban imposed on—fellow director Jafar Panahi. The Ministry of Culture restores permission only after Farhadi "explains" himself to the Ministry.

2011   *A Separation* wins the Golden Bear at the Berlinale and later the Academy Award for Best Foreign Film. The Farhadi phenomenon takes Iran by storm. His picture appears on every Iranian newspaper and magazine, even those unrelated to film or art.

2013   *The Past* is made in France with French and Iranian actors. In the same year, the annual *Time* 100, a list of the most influential people in the world, includes Farhadi's name.

2014   Cheshmeh, an Iranian publisher, publishes Farhadi's scripts in *Seven Scripts by Asghar Farhadi*. A year later the book wins the best book prize at the Annual Book Awards of the Islamic Republic of Iran.

2016   *The Salesman* premieres at Cannes and wins the best script and actor awards.

2017   Farhadi wins his second Oscar, this time for *The Salesman*. Due to Donald Trump's ban of Muslims traveling to the United States, Farhadi declines to appear at the ceremony and instead sends Iranian scientist and inventor Anoushe Ansari (also the first Iranian who traveled to space) to read his statement.

2018   *Everybody Knows*, shot in Spain with an all-Spanish-speaking cast and crew (with the exception of the editor), premieres at Cannes.

2021   *A Hero* premieres at Cannes, where it wins the Grand Prix in a tie with the Finnish *Compartment No. 6* (Juho Kuosmanen). This time, Iranians do not celebrate in the streets, and Farhadi, facing the biggest backlash of his career, is criticized for not using the film to support antiregime movements. IMDb, noticing that many Iranian users are giving the lowest rating possible to a film they had not yet seen, temporarily blocks the rating function for *A Hero*.

2022   In early April it is reported that a legal case had been brought against Farhadi by his former student Azadeh Masihzadeh, who accuses him of plagiarizing her idea (which later became a documentary) for his latest film, *A Hero*. Even though the Western media widely report that Farhadi has been found guilty, at the time of this writing the case is still being investigated. Nonetheless, the unprecedented wave of media coverage, often in a less sympathetic light, is another indication of the change in attitude toward Farhadi among fellow Iranians.

Filmography

MAH-E MEHRABAN (THE KIND MOON), TV series (1997)
Director: Behrooz Baghaie
Writing: Asghar Farhadi
Broadcast on Tehran Channel
Video, color

PEZESHKAN (DOCTORS), TV series (1998)
Director: Masoud Keramati
Assistant Director: Asghar Farhadi, Farhard Aslani
Writing: Asghar Farhadi
Cinematography: Hassan Emadi
Editing: Shirin Vahidi
Production Design: Shahrokh Forotanian
Music: Aria Azimi-Nejad
Cast: Davoud Rashidi, Farhad Aslani, Behnaz Nawzi
Broadcast on IRIB's Channel Three
Video, color
650 minutes (13 episodes)

CHASHM BE RAH (THE EXPECTANT), TV series (1998)
Producer: Asghar Farhadi
Directors: Asghar Farhadi (artistic director), Mahtaj Nojoomi (technical director)
Writing: Asghar Farhadi, Mohammadreza Erfani
Cinematography: Mansoor Nazmi, Ali Shahverdi
Editing: Morteza Jahanmehr
Cast: Akbar Abdi, Ahmad Aghaloo, Reza Babak, Mahboobeh Bayat, Gohar Kheirandish, Biuk Mirzaie, Fariba Motekhasses, Zhaleh Olov, Hassan Pourshirazi, Reza Shafi Jam
26 episodes, broadcast on Tehran Channel
Video, color

MOJTAME-E MASKOONI-E FARAJ VA FARROKII (FARAJ AND FARROKH RESIDENTIAL BLOCKS), TV series (1999)
Director: Asghar Farhadi
Writing: Asghar Farhadi
Editing: Majid Mirfakhrai
Cast: Zhaleh Sameti, Ebrahim Abadi, Esmail Davarfar, Saeed Aghakhani
Broadcast on IRIB's Channel Two in March 1999
Video, color

ROOZEGAR-E JAVANI (TIME OF YOUTH), TV series (1998–99)
Producer: Asghar Tavassoli
Directors: Shapur Gharib (artistic director), Asghar Tavassoli (artistic director), Hossein Ahmadi (technical director)
Writing: Asghar Farhadi (only the first season), Ali Akbar Mahloojian, Farhad Naghdali, Fariborz Kamkari
Cinematography: Houshang Babai, Seyyed Hossein Sotoudeh, Ali Mohhamdzadeh, Ali Shahverdi
Editing: Ali Sabokroo, Mohammad Albeigi
Production Design: Maria Hajiha
Music: Sasan Jamalian
Cast: Amin Hayaiee, Keyhan Maleki, Nasrollah Raadesh, Behzad Khodaveisi, Mehdi Sabai, Zohreh Fakkhor Saboor, Sahar Sabbagh Seresht
38 episodes, broadcast on Tehran Channel
Video, color

DASTAN-E YEK SHAHR (TALE OF A CITY), TV series (1999–2001)
Producers: Asghar Farhadi, Parisa Bakhtavar (executive producer)
Director: Asghar Farhadi
Writing: Asghar Farhadi, Ali Bazrafshan
Production Design: Jalil Fotouhinia
Cast: Faramarz Sadighi, Ateneh Faghih Nasiri, Ali Ghorbanzadeh, Ali Soleymani, Saeed Aghakhani, Reza Iranmanesh, Mani Kasraian, Mahtaj Nojoomi, Bahareh Rahnama, Kambiz Shabankare, Afshin Hashemi
Made in two seasons (each twenty-six episodes), broadcast on Tehran Channel
Video, color

YADASHT-HAYE KOODAKI (CHILDHOOD'S NOTES), TV series (2002)
Director: Parisa Bakhtavar
Writing: Asghar Farhadi

Cast: Sirus Gorjestani, Hamideh Kheirabadi, Mehraneh Mahintorabi
26 episodes, broadcast on Tehran Channel
Video, color

ERTEFA-E PAST (LOW HEIGHTS) (2002)
Producers: Manouchehr Mohammadi (producer), Parvaneh Partow (executive producer)
Director: Ebrahim Hatamikia
Writing: Asghar Farhadi, Ebrahim Hatamikia
Cinematography: Hassan Pooya
Editing: Hayedeh Safiyari
Production Design: Abdolhamid Ghadirian
Music: Mohammad Reza Aligholi
Cast: Hamid Farrokhnezhad (Ghasem), Leila Hatami (Narges), Gohar Kheirandish (Atieh), Mohammad Ali Inanloo (Pilot), Amir Aghaee, Mehdi Saki, Reza Shafi Jam
35 mm, color
115 minutes

POSHT-E KONKORIHA, TV series (2003)
Director: Parisa Bakhtavar
Writing: Asghar Farhadi (final revision), Mohammad Reza Fazeli
Cinematography: Bijan Mo'meni
Editing: Ahmad Vafaie
Production Design: Reza Dargazi
Music: Hamid Reza Sadri
Cast: Reza Davoodnezhad, Borzoo Arjmand, Ramin Nasser Nasir, Ali Abbasi Sadeghi, Sima Gorjestani
25 episodes, broadcast on Tehran Channel
Video, color

RAGHS DAR GHOBAR (DANCING IN THE DUST) (2003)
Producer: Iraj Taghipoor
Director: Asghar Farhadi
Writing: Asghar Farhadi, Alireza Bazrafshan, Mohammad Reza Fazeli
Cinematography: Hassan Karimi
Editing: Saeed Shahsavari
Music: Hamid Reza Sadri
Cast: Faramarz Gharibian (The Old Man), Yousef Khodaparast (Nazar), Baran Kosari (Rayhaneh), Malek Hadpour Seraj (Amri)

35 mm, color
95 minutes

SHAHR-E ZIBA (BEAUTIFUL CITY) (2004)
Producer: Iraj Taghipoor
Director: Asghar Farhadi
Writing: Asghar Farhadi
Cinematography: Ali Loqmani
Editing: Shahrzad Pouya
Art Direction: Keyvan Moghaddam
Music: Hamid Reza Sadri
Cast: Taraneh Alidoosti (Firoozeh), Faramarz Gharibian (Abolghasem Rahmati), Babak Ansari (Ala), Hossein Farzi-Zad (Akbar), Farhad Ghaemian (Mr. Ghafouri), Ahu Kheradmand (Abolghasem's Wife)
35 mm, color
101 minutes

CHAHARSHANBEH-SOORI (FIREWORKS WEDNESDAY) (2006)
Producer: Jamal Sadatian
Director: Asghar Farhadi
Writing: Asghar Farhadi, Mani Haghighi
Cinematography: Hossein Jafarian
Editing: Hayedeh Safiyari
Art Direction: Hossein Majd
Music: Peyman Yazdanian
Cast: Hamid Farrokhnezhad (Morteza Samie), Hedieh Tehrani (Mozhdeh Samie), Taraneh Alidoosti (Rouhi), Pantea Bahram (Simin), Sahar Dolatshahi (Mozhdeh's sister), Hooman Seyyedi (Rouhi's fiancé), Matin Heydarnia (Amir Ali)
35 mm, color
98 minutes

DAYERE ZANGI (TAMBOURINE) (2008)
Producer: Jamal Sadatian
Director: Parisa Bakhtavar
Writing: Asghar Farhadi
Cinematography: Morteza Poursamadi
Editing: Hayedeh Safiyari
Production Design: Keyvan Moghaddam
Music: Amir Tavassoli

Cast: Baran Kosari (Shirin), Saber Abar (Mohammad), Mehran Modiri (Abbas Razzaaghi), Amin Hayaiee (Ahmad Jafari), Mohamad Reza Sharifinia (Sorkhi), Gohar Kheirandish (Parvin), Bahareh Rahnama (Sholeh Kajoori), Omid Roohani (Abdullah Zadeh), Hamed Behdad (Driver)
35 mm, color
107 minutes

CANAAN (2008)
Producer: Mostafa Shayesteh
Director: Mani Haghighi
Writing: Mani Haghighi, Asghar Farhadi
Cinematography: Hassan Karimi
Editing: Mastaneh Mohajer
Production Design: Amir Esbati
Music: Christophe Rezai
Cast: Mohammad Reza Forutan (Morteza), Taraneh Alidoosti (Mina), Afsaneh Bayegan (Azar), Bahram Radan (Ali)
35 mm, color
106 minutes

MOHAKEME DAR KHIABAN (TRIAL ON THE STREET) (2009)
Producer: Masoud Kimiai
Director: Masoud Kimiai
Writing: Asghar Farhadi, Masoud Kimiai
Cinematography: Tooraj Mansouri
Editing: Mostafa Kherghehpoosh
Production Design: Reza Mehdi-Zadeh
Music: Farzin Gharahgozloo
Cast: Poolad Kimiai (Amir), Niki Karimi (Nasim), Hamid Reza Afshar (Abd), Mohammad Reza Forutan (Nekooyi), Hamed Behdad (Habib), Shaghayegh Farahani (Abd's wife), Negar Foroozandeh (videographer), Arzhang Amirfazli (Florist), Shabnam Darvish (Marjan)
35 mm, color
98 minutes

DARBARE-YE ELLY (ABOUT ELLY) (2009)
Producers: Asghar Farhadi, Mahmoud Razavi
Director: Asghar Farhadi
Writing: Asghar Farhadi (based on a story by Asghar Farhadi and Azad Jafarian)

Cinematography: Hossein Jafarian
Editing: Hayedeh Safiyari
Production Design: Asghar Farhadi
Music: Andrea Bauer
Cast: Golshifteh Farahani (Sepideh), Shahab Hosseini (Ahmad), Taraneh Ali-doosti (Elly), Merila Zarei (Shohreh), Mani Haghighi (Amir), Peyman Maadi (Peyman), Rana Azadivar (Naazi), Ahmad Mehranfar (Manoochehr), Saber Abar (Alireza)
35 mm, color
119 minutes

JODAEIYE NADER AZ SIMIN (A SEPARATION) (2011)
Producers: Asghar Farhadi, Negar Eskandarfar (executive producer)
Director: Asghar Farhadi
Writing: Asghar Farhadi
Cinematography: Mahmoud Kalari
Editing: Hayedeh Safiyari
Production Design: Keyvan Moghaddam
Music: Sattar Oraki
Cast: Peyman Maadi (Nader), Leila Hatami (Simin), Sareh Bayat (Razieh), Shahab Hosseini (Hojjat), Sarina Farhadi (Termeh), Merila Zarei (Ms. Ghahraii), Ali-Asghar Shahbazi (Nader's Father), Babak Karimi (police interrogator), Kimia Hosseini (Somayeh), Shirin Yazdanbakhsh (Simin's Mother)
35 mm, color
123 minutes

LE PASSÉ (THE PAST)* (2013)
Producers: Alexandre Mallet-Guy, Alexa Rivero (line producer)
Director: Asghar Farhadi
Writing: Asghar Farhadi
Cinematography: Mahmoud Kalari
Editing: Juliette Welfling
Production Design: Claude Lenoir
Music: Evgueni Galperine, Youli Galperine
Cast: Bérénice Bejo (Marie Brisson), Ali Mosaffa (Ahmad), Tahar Rahim (Samir), Pauline Burlet (Lucie), Elyes Aguis (Fouad), Jeanne Jestin (Léa), Sabrina Ouazani (Naïma), Babak Karimi (Shahryar), Valéria Cavalli (Valeria)
Digital, color
130 minutes
* In Iran: GOZASHTEH

FORUSHANDE (THE SALESMAN) (2016)
Producers: Asghar Farhadi, Alexandre Mallet-Guy, Olivier Père
Director: Asghar Farhadi
Writing: Asghar Farhadi
Cinematography: Hossein Jafarian
Editing: Hayedeh Safiyari
Art Direction: Keyvan Moghaddam
Music: Sattar Oraki
Cast: Shahab Hosseini (Emad Etesami), Taraneh Alidoosti (Rana Etesami), Mina Sadati (Sanam), Babak Karimi (Babak), Farid Sajjadi Hosseini (The man), Mojtaba Pirzadeh (Majid), Shirin Aghakashi (Esmat), Mehdi Koushki (Siavash), Emad Emami (Ali)
Digital, color
124 minutes

TODOS LO SABEN (EVERYBODY KNOWS) (2018)
Producers: Angélica Huete (line producer), Álvaro Longoria (producer), Alexandre Mallet-Guy (producer), Stefano Massenzi (associate producer), Andrea Occhipinti (coproducer), Cynthia Pinet (line producer, France)
Director: Asghar Farhadi
Writing: Asghar Farhadi
Cinematography: José Luis Alcaine
Editing: Hayedeh Safiyari
Production Design: María Clara Notari
Music: Javier Limón
Cast: Penélope Cruz (Laura), Javier Bardem (Paco), Ricardo Darín (Alejandro), Eduard Fernánde (Fernando), Bárbara Lennie (Bea), Inma Cuesta (Ana), Elvira Mínguez (Mariana), Ramón Barea (Antonio), Carla Campra (Irene), Sara Sálamo (Rocío), Roger Casamajor (Joan), José Ángel Egido (Jorge)
Digital, color
133 minutes

Asghar Farhadi is currently credited as the writer for a short film made in 2019: *Soledad* (dir: David Cordon)

GHAHREMAN (A HERO) (2021)
Producers: Asghar Farhadi, Alexandre Mallet-Guy
Director: Asghar Farhadi
Writing: Asghar Farhadi
Cinematography: Ali Ghazi, Arash Ramezani

Editing: Hayedeh Safiyarı
Set Design: Medhi Moosavi
Cast: Amir Jadidi (Rahim), Mohsen Tanabandeh (Bahram), Sahar Goldoost (Farkhondeh), Fereshteh Sadr Orafaie (Mrs. Radmehr), Sarina Farhadi (Nazanin)
Digital, color
127 minutes

IMDb has erroneously listed Farhadi as the writer for *Shab* (*The Night*), made in 2008.

Asghar Farhadi: Interviews

A Reaction to Current Conditions

Film Monthly / 1999

From *Film Monthly* (Tehran), Vol. 17, No. 246, December 1999. Translated by Amir Soltani.

A short conversation with Asghar Farhadi, writer and director of the TV series *Tale of a City* (1999-2001).

Film Monthly: What led you to use *In the City*[1] as a basis for the stories in your own TV series?

Asghar Farhadi: Reading the crime pages in newspapers always gave me a morbid feeling. About the environment around me, the people around me; it made me feel unsafe and instilled in me a sense of inevitability about everything around me. Ever since Adam's sons, Cain and Abel, began to fight, there has been oppression and oppressors. I had this sense that I couldn't do anything but observe this dynamic. It was a painful feeling, but, regardless, I bought newspapers day after day and read through the same pages. And it got me to start thinking about a TV series based on the incidents I had read about in the newspapers' crime pages. But there were two problems. First, that most of these crimes were not fit for broadcast on the five official networks on Iranian television. And second, how does one even approach such stories? There have been many series in the past few years that dealt with similar social problems, but the relationship between the characters and those subjects has never felt believable. For example, stories of journalists who follow a lead for no reason or become too involved with an event without apparent motives; the audience is left to wonder why the journalist was so invested. After a while, I developed this idea around a young group of producers for a daily television show who have to become involved in their stories because of the nature of their reporting. It was the director of Channel 5 on national television who suggested the central characters could be the fictional producers of *In the City*. And that's why I think the approach became very novel in this series. Nevertheless, the first problem still remained, and in the writing process, I had to change certain undisplayable elements of the stories to avoid censorship issues.

FM: In most episodes of the series, even though the primary plot is very eventful, there are secondary plotlines that often give us the feeling that we're watching two parallel stories. As an example, in episode nine, the story of the patient who is suffering from HIV and, in parallel, the story of Behzad's marriage. Or in episode six, the story of Shahab's poverty in parallel with familial poverty.

AF: It's my first experiment with this type of screenwriting. Usually, TV series with one plotline, where events follow one after the other in consecutive scenes, feel very naked and sparse to me. In successful TV series, even Iranian ones like *Once upon a Time . . .* , it is the multistory narrative that draws the audience in. Furthermore, I tried to draw lines between these plotlines, to expose connections between the primary stories and the secondary ones. In the episode you used as an example, Behzad's marriage breaks apart, and the HIV patient dies estranged and in solitude. I don't know. I wanted to draw a line between the loneliness of young people who remain single due to financial and social factors and the reasons behind the patient's condition. In this particular story, the secondary plotline was more important to me than the main one. My story was that of the HIV patient, but because we couldn't show many of its elements on TV, we relegated it to the secondary plotline. Some think the parallel threads of these narratives make them chaotic. I don't know. I think it's too early to judge that yet.

FM: It's the first time we see a TV series where the endings of each episode are very dark, particularly in the episode about the little southern boy. Did you have any issues with TV guidelines over this? And in any case, why so bleak?

AF: No, we had no issues with the broadcast authorities, but regarding why the stories are so dark, well, I'm blameless! When I begin to write a story, I don't know where it will end. The story carries me with it. I don't believe the endings are dark. I think the endings are authentic. The team behind the series did their utmost to make sure the atmosphere of the show is credible and realistic compared to the audience's daily experience.

FM: We've heard this show is going to continue.

AF: I'm not sure. On the one hand, I'm very happy that the show has found such a large audience that the network is interested in continuing with it. On the other hand, I'm worried about where these characters and their story will lead to.

FM: Have you learned from the unfortunate experience of your last show, *Time of Youth*?[2]

AF: I certainly hope that story isn't repeated again, otherwise all our efforts will have been in vain.

Notes

1. A reportage-like TV series on Tehran Channel focusing on the issues of the day in the city of Tehran. Farhadi used that as the framework of his fictional TV series *Tale of a City*, in which the makers of *In the City* interact with the subjects of their documentaries.

2. Neither of the editors has seen this series, but it seems that the second season of *Time of Youth*, which was aired without Farhadi's collaboration, could not meet the expectations raised by the first season and eventually flopped.

City of No Angels

Alireza Motamedi / 2000

From *Film Monthly* (Tehran), Vol. 18, No. 252, May 2000. Translated by Amir Soltani.

Tale of a City is one of the most successful TV series of recent years. Asghar Farhadi, who was previously known as the writer behind the show *Time of Youth*, claims to be only 30 to 40 percent happy with *Tale of a City*. This claim was enough to keep expectations—and anticipation for his next project—very high. One of his biggest wishes is to continue Kiumars Pourahmad's TV series *Majid's Tales* and build a show around Majid, who is now in his early twenties.[1] This is perhaps a nostalgic remnant of Farhadi's own adolescence, which was spent in the same city as Majid's city: Isfahan.

Alireza Motamedi: My first encounter with your work was through two plays: *Vagabonds* and *The Last Heroes on Earth*.

Asghar Farhadi: Before going to university, in the Youth Cinema Society, I made a few short and documentary films on 8 mm and 16 mm film, and it was then that I decided to learn cinema academically. Incidentally, I found that I enjoyed writing quite a lot and changed my mind to study theater instead of cinema. In university, I wrote a few plays and directed them myself, the last of which, *The Last Heroes on Earth*, went onstage last year.

AM: You've mentioned your interest in writing stories. One of the characteristics of *Tale of a City* is that, unlike other TV shows, you're not stingy about using stories and often tell two or three stories at once in a single episode.

AF: When I'm writing, I spend the majority of my time searching for stories. My interest in storytelling goes back to my childhood. I respect the TV audience enough to not overextend a single-episode story into a twenty-six-episode season's arc. I made my utmost effort to have secondary stories in each episode alongside the main line of narrative, to make the series more entertaining but also to complement the main plot indirectly with additional stories. As well, there are stories that one cannot tell directly as the main plot. For example, in one episode, the primary plot didn't have much depth, but the secondary plot was about an AIDS patient, which was important and new. If I'd switched those two plot-lines around, the episode would not have been allowed to air. Everyone asked me what the AIDS plotline had to do with the main story. My main goal was to discuss HIV, but because our society is still relatively unfamiliar with the phe-nomenon, if we had relayed a mountain of information to the audience in a single episode, they would have been overwhelmed. I had to relegate the topic to a secondary plotline. In some episodes, when the main plotline is too dark, I'll create a side plot, often a humorous one, to lighten the mood. Otherwise, the episode either would not get permission to air or would just depress the audi-ence on a Friday afternoon.[2] I've done my best to connect these plotlines in each episode delicately, though it is possible I've failed at times.

AM: Incidentally, these multifaceted plots have made the TV series more life-like. We don't deal with a single event at each stage of life, but rather we're facing an amalgam of happy and sad events.

AF: Yes, and those events might be unrelated to one another, too. What we never see in our TV shows is the daily minutiae of life. This is very important for me: going to the washroom, eating, making little jokes, crying . . . these are all im-portant. Developing these details lends a story authenticity. I gained this expe-rience while writing *Time of Youth.*

AM: As an example, Mohsen is stingy and an opportunist and takes advan-tage of others. I think these characters are developed very well. My only issue is with the character of Dr. Rafi, in part because of Ghorbanzadeh's performance. Although his performance has improved in recent episodes, I think, overall, the character is somewhat aloof and one-dimensional.

AF: I think two characters still have room for development: Moones and Rafi. I think the issue with Rafi, which I admit to, is that he is too young to be a doctor. This is really my fault, which is why in recent episodes I've pivoted away from focusing on his profession. What was very important for me from the begin-ning about this character was his loneliness—that his parents have left, but he's stayed behind for the same reasons we all stay behind. These reasons aren't very categorical. He has logical concerns about social issues. By contrast, Moones is very emotional, and I wanted that aspect of her character to be very exaggerated.

AM: Yet, this exaggeration stands in stark contrast with the realism of the other characters and that of your milieu. We all share these social concerns to some extent, but their reactions are melodramatic and unbelievable.

AF: The series starts with Moones's visit to the psychiatrist's office. In the final episodes of the show, we have another scene in a psychiatrist's office. Moones is not a stable character in essence, because she's been raised in a family that had sheltered her from major social crises. She's only been aware of social realities through books and magazines and the like. When such a person leaves the family and enters society, it is natural that their reactions are more pronounced than others. Maybe the audience doesn't like her very much because there aren't many Mooneses among us. A young person of Moones's age who has such concerns is rare. The other major problem is that because certain episodes weren't ready, the order of their screening was changed, and in the case of certain characters such as Moones, this really disturbed the natural course of their story.

AM: Wouldn't it have been better if Moones gradually developed social concerns as the show progressed?

AF: I was looking for something else in this series. I was looking for someone who had become familiar with social issues only at a distance and has now been thrown into them firsthand. So, instead of a gradual enlightenment, she suddenly goes from superficial awareness to a whole new vision. It's not just more awareness. As the show progresses, she doesn't become more knowledgeable but more negative, pessimistic, and disillusioned. I wanted the character to go from a romantic, idealistic vision at the beginning of the series, through a bleak and bitter one, to a more realistic vision by the end. I'm not sure how successful I've been.

AM: The strength of your show is that you don't offer solutions to problems. Avoiding cheap, deceitful simplifications in favor of simply presenting issues truthfully is a very worthy endeavor.

AF: The best gift for our crew would be to know that the audience is left contemplating the show for at least five minutes after it ends. I think that's the main responsibility of any work of art.

AM: Wouldn't it have been better if we knew more about the main characters' past, their backgrounds and families?

AF: That is something even my colleagues on the show pointed out to me, but because the stories and subjects of *In the City* were very important to me, I did not have the opportunity to develop the main characters of my show further, unfortunately. If all of them were also inflicted by their own set of social issues, the show would have been a bit unrealistic. So, I didn't really pursue characters who I didn't think had specific problems in their lives, like Mohsen.

AM: I didn't mean they should have all their own issues. Maybe their hassle-free backgrounds could have been the context in its own right.

AF: I admit that I've not yet reached the level of skill required to contextualize the massive cast of characters with so many guest stars and all the subjects. I'll try to be fairer to all my characters in future works. Unfortunately, in this show, it wasn't possible to devote equal time to all characters.

AM: I say this especially because people are so important to this show—much more important than the events and what happens in front of the camera. Because of the ambiguity of some characters, even an entertaining story can become irritating at times. Nevertheless, these stories, particularly their endings, are very bleak. Were you ever concerned that this bleakness, which I think is completely justified, would scare off your audience? Especially since television audiences have grown accustomed to happy endings.

AF: I don't think the stories or their endings are bleak; they're realistic and hence why I don't think audiences will be disappointed by them. I wanted to take this sadness and turn it into food for thought. We are melancholy people, but we aren't thoughtful.

AM: The majority of your guest stars, who aren't recognizable faces or even professional actors, are brilliant. For example, the drug addict whose phone has been stolen, or the girl in the episode about the cyberstalker, or especially the woman who played Christine. Where did you find these people?

AF: Like you said, most of them aren't professionals. The woman who plays Christine had recently come from Canada and wanted to live in Iran for a while. I don't think she was performing; she just immersed herself in the role. Whenever we needed professionals, we brought in actors like Mehraneh Mahintorabi and Shaghayegh Farahani. I'm very happy with all the guest stars on the show. Their presence was immensely helpful. For example, in Christine's story, the charlatan character who claimed to be her brother wasn't an actor. He was on the production crew and thought I was joking when I offered him the role. But eventually he agreed to play the role, and I'm so satisfied with the results.

AM: Have you seen the documentary *Christine* by Mohammad Jafari?[3]

AF: No. One of the sources that helped me a lot in finding stories was the crime pages of the newspaper *Iran*. I first came across Christine's story there. I had started working on a feature film screenplay based on her story when *Tale of a City* came about. I used that screenplay on this show instead. When preproduction was already complete, I heard that Mr. Jafari had completed a documentary based on this story, and so I became hesitant about finishing my version. Eventually I decided to proceed, but in order to avoid similarities as much as possible, I decided not to talk to Mr. Jafari about my story, even though he's a friend of mine. Actually, two filmmakers with different visions telling the same story from different angles is quite interesting, and I hope it becomes more common in our cinema and television.

The other point is, in approaching a real social event, must we remain faithful to the essence of the story and all its details? I hope one day we come to a point where we allow everyone to offer their own analysis of an event. For the episode on Christine, I did research, but at some point realized that the research was getting in the way of my critical thinking on the subject. I wanted to change the plot altogether, but it wasn't possible. I have been criticized enough for changing details in the actual story as it is.

AM: There is quite a wide gap in quality between different episodes of the show. Some are truly outstanding. Some are decent, and some are mediocre—although it must be said that even the weakest episodes are better than most other Iranian TV series, for example, the episode with Shaghayegh Farahani or the one where Reza Khandan played a cancer patient.

AF: I agree with you on the first account, but not the second. I made that episode based on an English poem. The poem is about a person who is trudging along in the brutal cold and snow and complains to God for having forsaken him, but a voice tells him to look behind himself. When he does so, he finds two sets of footsteps instead of one. The voice tells him that God is always walking alongside him and protecting him. Then, the snowstorm gains force, and the man loses the ability to continue. He looks behind him again and sees only one set of footsteps this time. He complains to God again for deserting him when he needs help most. The voice tells him that those footsteps are God's and He's carrying you on his shoulders. In this episode, I wanted to speak of miracles and faith, and I was actually very happy with the final outcome. It's ostensibly a story about healing, but beneath that, it's a story of connecting to God. In the end of the episode, Reza Khandan goes on the balcony and speaks with God alone for a few minutes. And we see an apple fall to the water from the tree, as though the healing process is complete.

AM: I like the theme. My issue is with the execution.

AF: Perhaps because it's the only episode without a secondary plotline.

AM: I don't think so. It's a different issue. You've explored a rhetorical idea here, but the form you've presented it in is old and stereotypical. These past few years, there have been many films made about faith and miracles that have all remained clichéd and generalized. And you've fallen victim to the same clichés. New ideas need new forms.

AF: Maybe that's the reason then. Because this episode is exploring spiritual themes, which is incongruous with the rest of the show. But the form has remained the same as the rest of the show. The risk, however, was to make this story feel distant, whereas by presenting it in formally similar ways, I wanted the audience to know that faith is attainable and miracles are possible.

Notes

1. *Majid's Tales* (1990), based on stories by Houshang Moradi Kermani, was an enormously popular TV series about an orphaned teenager who lives with his grandmother in the city of Isfahan.

2. Friday afternoon is the peak of TV viewing in Iran, as Friday is considered the weekend instead of Saturday and Sunday.

3. A documentary made about a woman born in Sweden and raised in North America who returns to Iran to find her biological parents, who had abandoned her when she was a child.

A Discussion with Asghar Farhadi, Director of *Dancing in the Dust*: Snakes on a Plain!

Omid Najvan / 2003

From *Film Monthly* (Tehran), Vol. 21, No. 310, December 2003. Translated by Zahra Khosroshahi.

This discussion with Asghar Farhadi took place on the final day of his shoot for *Beautiful City* (2004) and about two weeks after the limited screening of his first film, *Dancing in the Dust* (2003). For his debut film, he had encountered a new audience that had been witness to his touching realist television series, *Tale of a City* (2001). That same audience has now gotten to enjoy his strange experiment in leaving behind the city and taking refuge in a desert with only two inhabitants (an angry old man and an adventurous young man). For this film's setting Farhadi settled on the desert of Yazd by mere chance: "It was behind a hill . . . a village pressed into earth where the exposed domes of some of the houses were the only markers left, a village with no soul or life, with only streams of water where the snakes of the film's story could breathe with ease."

Farhadi's first experience in film was working with Ebrahim Hatamikia[1] to write the screenplay for *Low Heights* (2002). Prior to that, he directed about fifty episodes of the *Tale of a City* series, which garnered a wide viewership in its two-year run. Farhadi previously also wrote the screenplay for a number of television series, including *Time of Youth* (in its first season), *Doctors*, and *The Kind Moon*. He studied dramatic arts and stage direction at Tarbiat Modarres University.

—Omid Najvan

Omid Najvan: The overlap of your first film in theaters and the final days of shooting your second creates an interesting symmetry. Contrary to most filmmakers who make films almost every year, but don't receive general release for their films, it appears that you are a lucky person.

Asghar Farhadi: In my opinion, the most important thing about the two coinciding is that it's allowed me to consider the reception of my debut film as I wrap up the next one. In private or festival screenings—where the audience is generally selective and professional—one can only receive expert, technical perspectives on cinema; but the truth is that one must watch the film with a general audience that goes to the cinema in hopes of enjoying the film, and this only happens at public screenings. This is because most people don't know the filmmaker and don't care about his or her name. If one day I make a film that doesn't receive a screening, it will most certainly negatively impact my next film. I know that some filmmakers have gained in reputation when their films have been denied a general release, but I don't think like this. In my opinion, a film is made for its audience, and the director's most important duty is to entertain and to create an enjoyable atmosphere for the viewer. Even though the screening conditions have not been ideal—the film has only gotten a limited release and was eliminated from one of the main cinemas originally slated to screen it—I am still lucky, unlike many others, to have my first film shown publicly at all.

ON: You mentioned that you made *Dancing in the Dust* for the general public, but your film was shown at specialized screenings. Did you always consider this type of audience?

AF: No. I never thought that and I never will think that. In my opinion, the concept of specialized or general audience doesn't even exist and this description is wrong at its core. We must first describe what a "special" audience means. Does this mean someone more educated? Does it mean someone who lives in a more urban area? We really can't create such distinctions. It may be that someone with a certain kind of degree has a better understanding about the film than a doctor or an engineer. For example, there are cinephiles who, in terms of credentials or social status, may not be of the elite, but they are wise and perceptive. For this reason, I don't accept distinguishing between an expert and a general audience, and because of this, I don't make my films for a specialized or expert audience. If I wanted to do this, I would plan my productions accordingly, for example, with a nonlinear plot arrangement or a more complex storyline. In an attempt to create a connection with the general audience, I have tried to maintain the notion of "once upon a time" in my storytelling.

I am not saying that *Dancing in the Dust* is without problems. I know better than anyone else the problems of the film. The presence of Faramarz Gharibian[2] as one of the main characters, the selection of the storyteller's tone, and the creation of comedic and romantic moments in the film are part of the arrangements that have been made to allow the audience to follow the plot. From the very start, the plan wasn't for *Dancing in the Dust* to be popular, but I imagined that it would stand up. Of course, when the film began receiving awards from festivals here and abroad, it unintentionally became a festival film categorized as a film for a specific audience, and in this sense, the awards hurt the film. These reasons caused *Dancing in the Dust* to get distributed to a narrow group of cinemas—which by chance included some good venues. In my opinion, there is no justification at all to assume that audiences of arthouse films only live in exclusive areas. It seems that the authorities program films in this particular group of arthouse cinemas when they actually want to get rid of the films and make them less accessible, less seen. Having this group of cinemas can be the start of a positive movement, but we're still a ways from that.

ON: Do you accept that *Dancing in the Dust*, in comparison to other commercial films, is more personal and experimental?

AF: Yes, I agree that *Dancing in the Dust* is very different from commercial films, and my purpose in making this film wasn't chiefly financial. In the same way that my intention wasn't making an experimental film for a specific audience. In my opinion, films that try to bridge the gap between various tastes, that try to tell impactful stories, are always successful. In prerevolutionary cinema, some filmmakers used this method to make good films while creating a good connection with the audience. We've had this kind of filmmaker after the Revolution, too, such as Rakhshan Banietemad or Kiumars Pourahmad. My entire effort in making *Dancing in the Dust* was to place myself on this path.

ON: You've hinted at the issues with the film in creating a connection with its audience. Did you notice these problems at the film's public screenings, or did you know from the very beginning?

AF: The film's editor[3] and I were aware of these issues before the film's screening at the festival. The film's most important problem is that it has a few extra minutes. We weren't able to cut those extra minutes, because up to the night before the festival we were still occupied with problems related to the editing suite, and so our plan was to eliminate those extra scenes after the festival. Unfortunately, after the festival, despite my attempts, this problem was forgotten. A few minutes were eliminated in the new edit, but for some reason the edits didn't make it to the new version, and the film remained the same. This happened because of a lack of time, and it hurt the film.

ON: Does this mean that by eliminating those scenes, the film would have worked better?

AF: I believe that as it stands, the film connects with its audience. I say this based on the feedback of the audience at screenings both inside and outside of Iran. I have pretty much knocked on every door. I saw very few audience members who left the screening unhappy, but if the problems that I mentioned were not there, I do believe a wider audience could have been attracted to the film.

ON: Probably the problem you had with the film has to do with the scenes in the desert, where Nazar and the old man interact with one another.

AF: Everyone seems to think this and believe that the desert scenes of the film are slow in rhythm, but no . . . the scenes I am talking about have to do with the urban parts of the film.

ON: In any case, the second part of the film has a much slower pace.

AF: The pace of a film is like the speed of a car. When you travel in a car, if the driver begins the journey at a speed of 180 km per hour and then continues at 120 km per hour, you'll feel as though the car now moves slowly. In the case that the reverse of this happens, you feel as though you have traveled the same distance with a lot more speed. The main reason the desert scenes seem slow is because of the film's frenetic opening, which prepares the audience for watching something fast-paced, but because there are only two characters in the desert—where the images are naturally more still—it takes this option away from the audience.

ON: In other words, you spoil your audience with those opening moments in the film. In those scenes, you even transfer the intended information to the audience through the credits.

AF: That's correct. For this reason, in terms of the film's rhythm, the scenes in the desert have no issues. Actually, the most eventful scenes of the film take place in the desert, and there is constant conflict between the main characters of the story; there is no repetition, and that's where the audience becomes closer with the characters. The feeling that is evoked from the audience results from the first few scenes of the film. If there was the opportunity for this, despite the great details and a fast rhythm—for any filmmaker who wants the opening of their film to be faster-paced—I would have eliminated a number of the scenes so that, psychologically, the audience could be better prepared for the rest of the film's slow beat.

ON: So, the extra scenes in the earlier parts of the film must remain.

AF: Yes, in fact, and, contrary to some people's opinions, I really like those scenes. But because of the film's rhythm they should be eliminated from the film. In my opinion, Nazar's working in the factory or, for example, the moment when he talks to his mother, can be shortened. Eliminating these scenes from the film can slow down the rhythm. Of course, it has become fashionable to say that a more fast-paced film is better and a slower one bad. A good rhythm is one that suits the film.

ON: It's precisely like this. For instance, you cannot use the fast rhythm of Jan de Bont's *Speed*. . . .

AF: . . . for a Tarkovsky film!

ON: In any case, it appears that the purpose of the film's entire story is to create the context for the scene where they are catching snakes and the presence of these two people, alone in the desert.

AF: Allow me to say right here that the initial idea for *Dancing in the Dust* was from Abbas Jahangir. Mohammad Reza Fazeli, who—along with myself and Alizera Bazrafshan—wrote the final version of the screenplay, is Jahangir's brother-in-law. Mohammad had intended for a while to make a documentary based on his research on the lives of snake catchers, but I asked him to use his idea for a screenplay—which ultimately became the screenplay for *Dancing in the Dust*. Unfortunately, Jahangir's name is not on the credits. He is a great person and he could have reacted badly to this, but he didn't, and I see it as my responsibility to thank him.

I have to say that the introductory section in the city is meant to lead to the desert. I wish that this opening were shorter and had functioned more as an introductory scene. At present it functions as an independent introduction to the film itself. I would have liked very much for the entire film to take place in the desert. With only a few flashbacks, it would have been possible to tell the entire story with just the two characters in the desert, but even when the screenplay was being written and friends had warned against having a polarized setting for the film, I liked taking the central character of the story from the loud, congested, modern city—that can potentially be dark too—to a scene that is quiet and calm, where we might get to know him better—this in a world with only two inhabitants. I liked the contrast between the two spaces and really wanted to juxtapose the two places. So, in the end, I don't believe that the setting of the film is polarized. It is intentional that all of the urban city scenes are loud. The houses and even the streets are louder than what you would normally see. There is constantly the sound of music and the murmur of people from afar. Now, from this loud setting one person goes to a place that is empty, quiet. If I had made *Dancing in the Dust* without the urban scenes, the film would not have been tangible or realistic and instead would have been very specific and abstract, at which point the audience would have thought to him- or herself whether this kind of world even exists? But when there is a context for the character of the story to slowly travel into a foreign and new place, the place becomes believable for the audience. The next point is that the central character of the story does not intentionally go on this trip. It is by chance that he takes this path.

ON: You take the audience on a journey with the hero, and they travel together to a place filled with anxiety, stress, and worry. Did you mean to use symbolism too?

AF: I like realism and have never had this idea. But I believe in an artistic work, whereby hidden colors and symbols can both conceal meaning and, in certain contexts, create meaning. In my opinion, the snake and ring next to each other don't suggest an allegory, but the contrast between the two conveys an emotion in the audience that I had intended. A chopped-up finger in a container filled with ice can similarly have different meanings, but this was not my consideration at all. While watching this image, a feeling is created in you that transfers to the latent and hidden sense of the film. Contrary to what is imagined, in our culture and in many other countries in the world, snakes have interesting meanings. One of its meanings is health. When it's said that someone is sick, its meaning is that they are somewhere where there are no snakes! The image of snakes on the banner of many pharmacies has been used, and it signals health and wellness, healing and treatment.

ON: This interpretation applies to dreams as well, where a snake is symbolic for wealth.

AF: Yes, but in this film the snake is a barrier for the story's hero to overcome and to beat in a challenge. I don't believe that the film's desert setting is filled with anxiety and tension. Actually, I have made sure to distance the film from this feeling by adding elements of humor. Like the duel between Nazar and the snake. I can say that my view of his childlike behavior was accompanied with a smile. For example, in the moment when he is collecting the bushes, I have an omniscient view of him—that is, I look at him from a godlike perspective. This is a joke. Or, for example, when the smoke rising from Faramarz Gharibian's cigarette in the car appears as though the halos produced by the smoke are joined in a dance. In the film there are a few scenes like this where I pass judgment on the characters of the story and smile at their interaction and their way of life. But in any case, the snake, the dry desert, the solitude—they're all symbols that may have created a sense of anxiety; though I never intended such a thing.

ON: An interesting point in the film is when the snake catcher's car itself becomes one of the main characters and has a dramatic function in the film.

AF: This is a holdover from my childhood imagination, when I'd always give cars their own distinct characters. For this character, I was searching for a car that had lost so much of its exterior paint, it would appear metallic, so that I could then conceal a color—for example, red—within the car: like the color of the dashboard or the steering wheel; and second, so that the car would have a rough appearance. Cars that exist within these parameters mostly have short roofs and at times make visible their curvy lines and edges. In pursuit of this car, I searched all the used car listings. I knew that I was looking for an old campervan, but I couldn't find it at all. Until finally I saw one of these cars in the streets and convinced its owner to sell it to us. He sold it to us at a very high price, and we worked on it for about three to four weeks. We spent that time further nicking up the car's paint and, to help with filming, disconnecting its doors to make them transportable. I knew how important the car would be throughout the shoot and how it would serve the film. The car, in terms of performance, helped the production team a lot. In my opinion, the most important feature of the car in the film is that it's real, and though it doesn't have color, it produces the sense that one day it did.

ON: The car represents its owner, and it's the most important and suitable vehicle for introducing the snake catcher. Faramarz Gharibian, by the way, performs the role of the snake catcher with confidence. It actually appears as though the screenplay was written with his traits in mind, to give him a comeback.

AF: Working with Faramarz Gharibian—that happened again in my new film *Beautiful City*—was my good fortune. Interestingly, I didn't think of him at all during the screenwriting process. Of course, I was always interested in his acting. In any case, we must accept that he, and others like him, have made us interested in cinema. Through watching him, we learned cinema so we're indebted to him. When the screenplay for *Dancing in the Dust* was being written, I was thinking of an amateur actor for this role, but I finally reached the conclusion that the person who plays this role has to be a professional actor, because his only tool is silence, and performing with silence is much more difficult than performing with words. Among all the actors I had thought of for this role, the only person who kept a world of hidden words behind his silence was Faramarz Gharibian. And this comes from his physique: Gharibian's eyes appear deep even when he is quiet, and there is no sense of emptiness behind his eyes. The state of his eyes has helped the film *Dancing in the Dust* a lot—his gaze, his silence, his charisma. In this film, Gharibian has a very good costume and makeup design. Of course, my view of him was of a professional actor who would come on the set, do his job, and leave. But he really thought about his role in this film, and as we might expect more from a young actor, he worked hard on this role. It may be interesting for you to know that his already strong work ethic doubled in my new film. He is a very strong actor and an equally noble person. With his presence on the set, he provides a sense of calm arising from a person from the past generation whose experience and wealth of knowledge give everyone on the team encouragement. On the same day that Gharibian received the screenplay to read, he called immediately after reading it to say that he would certainly play this role. During the entirety of the filmmaking process, I witnessed his effort and commitment, and for this reason he got the response he did: audiences liked his role, and he received awards both in and outside of Iran.

ON: There must be a compelling reason for an established TV director, who has drawn viewership in the millions for television and now makes films for a more limited audience. Is this not so?

AF: I will have to say with honesty that television is much more important to me than cinema. If I make a film for television, I do my work for an audience that is involved with the subject and unfortunately has no time or money for cinema.

It is a shame that at the moment television does not know its own value and has polluted itself with petty issues, where there is hardly anyone who finds joy in creating a connection with viewers through this medium. People have more or less lost their trust in this medium. During the past few years, they have seen things from television that society has rejected. Unfortunately, the situation in television is such that one can't really produce good work. Perhaps my presence in television would be more influential, but it's clear that, in terms of reputation, fame, and respect, cinema has far greater potential and also attracts much more serious criticism. In private and in my heart, I tell myself that the aim is for me to speak about people I know, and those people mainly watch television and rarely go to the cinema. But what a shame that the work can't be done. I really want in the upcoming year to make a series like *Tale of a City*, but a series where television gives me the freedom to be bold and where there is no condition from the very beginning not to critique any office, organization, or institution. Making this kind of "social film" has no meaning. In the years before the Revolution it was said that because of such problems, it was only possible to make films about some groups of people, and now, in some cases, our hands are even more tightly tied. Television tries too hard to not offend anyone with its programs. I hope one day the atmosphere in television is favorable enough that it's possible to return and work meaningfully.

Notes

1. Hatamikia is best known in Iran for making films that deal with the lingering effects of the Iran-Iraq War.

2. Faramarz Gharibian (born 1941) is a popular actor whose career dates back to prerevolutionary melo-dramas, some of which are cult classics in Iranian cinema.

3. Saeed Shahsavari.

Which Part of the City Is Beautiful?

Shadmehr Rastin / 2004

From *Film Monthly* (Tehran), Vol. 22, No. 318, June 2004. Translated by Katayoun Youssefi.

Shadmehr Rastin: What triggered the idea behind this film? Was it your choice of the subject matter, or character, or location?

Asghar Farhadi: The elements that helped shape the story of *Beautiful City* were in fact not directly connected to each other. In one case, it can be traced back to the second season of the TV series *Tale of a City*, when we were shooting in a courthouse. In those packed corridors and during my brief chats with people, the subject of retribution and blood money sparked my interest.[1] There were people rushing into different rooms to do the paperwork that would propel the execution of a sentence, while others were desperately trying to obtain the consent of the complainants and stop the execution from happening. Earlier, during one of my visits to a courthouse to choose the location for the same series, I noticed blood on one of the toilets. Apparently, a woman was trying to forcibly remove her ring after her divorce was issued. This image intrigued me. It was as if I was searching for a jacket that suited this button. And the subject of retaliation and blood money became that jacket. First, I wrote a sketch called *Acid*, which was published in an issue of the magazine *Filmnegar*. This short piece evolved over the course of three years. It changed considerably as I was conducting more and more research on the legal and criminal aspects of retribution, blood money, and capital punishment. The last version turned into *Beautiful City*, which I was supposed to make before *Dancing in the Dust*. But I felt that the script needed more work.

SR: In addition to the youth detention center, the other important location is Firoozeh's house.

AF: When I was a university student, I traveled to Tehran by train a few times. Each time the train passed these neighborhoods, I was thinking how suitable these alleys and houses are for my stories. Halfway through the script of *Beautiful City*, I came to the conclusion that Firoozeh's house could be located in one of these neighborhoods, where the freight trains carrying steel and iron and copper pass through while these families are trapped in poverty and misery.

SR: The issue of blood money developed into the primary theme of the screenplay, while each character had their own story. A good example is the man who has lost his daughter. Where did it come from?

AF: In my youth, I heard a story that, although true, seemed unbelievable to me. During the war,[2] a soldier of the revolutionary guard and an army officer quarreled over an insignificant issue. The soldier lost his temper and opened fire on the officer. He faced execution, and for several years his family did whatever they could to convince the officer's family to give him a pardon. Eventually, they asserted that the death sentence could only be dissolved on condition that the murderer marry the widow of the victim. I am not sure if this condition was met or not. Regardless, it is a shocking story. For a long time, I couldn't get it out of my mind: how the relatives of the deceased could lay down such a condition? It seemed extremely cruel to me. I thought about the widow and the situation that prompted the family to come to such a decision. In any case, this was a brutal contract. However, we may think otherwise if we know more about both families and the conditions in which they live. We may no longer consider the decision cruel. I always wondered how the woman could live under the same roof with her husband's murderer. In circumstances like this, we may have a totally different opinion when we examine the situation in close-up. Your judgment depends on which side of the conflict you are on. You see, it's all relative. Anyway, this true story developed into one of the main elements of the plot. Indeed, I did my best to make it believable. I had to tone it down to make it more convincing.

SR: You are piecing together separate subplots to create a coherent whole. Each one is convincing in its own right. But the way they're put together, and the way the plot unfolds, make you doubt their coherence—both in your previous film and in *Beautiful City*. In this film, however, when the family imposes a new condition for giving pardon, it seems as if the sequence of events is aligned in a way that lead us to this point.

AF: You can't deny that someone has pieced them together. But it should be done skillfully so that it doesn't show. I did my best to arrange them in a way that seems convincing and authentic—not only in the script but even in directing. There is a problem, though. Some audience's understanding of this social class and their mentality toward them come from the media. They have a stereotypical image of prison and prisoner and underprivileged families. When characters in a story don't fit these stereotypes, they simply blame the screenwriter for creating unreal situations that never happen in real life.

SR: So, you admit its dramatic layout but do not agree that they are realistic presentations of unrealistic situations, since they are true stories.

AF: Yes. I know many of these people. Sometimes I have encountered situations in their lives that seem impossible even if I were to represent them in a documentary.

SR: Your life experiences serve as a rich source for your films. We can track this in all your scripts, TV series, and feature films. Particularly after *Doctors*, we are dealing with a writer who has witnessed and sensed poverty and all it entails. Now, he is depicting details and yet defamiliarizing them, emphasizing the joy of life in the midst of poverty and misery. Although this may work on a TV screen, it is not the same in cinema, where we hold higher expectations. I think at this stage, Farhadi the director is still away from the writing side of his career. As an example, in this film the neighborhood is depicted only through the window of Firoozeh's house. It may seem okay in the screenplay, but what is the role of the director, after all?

AF: In the case of this example, I think it works the other way around. Portraying the neighborhood through the window of Firoozeh's house is not so much suitable for television as it is cinematic. If it was to be made for television, it would have shown the whole neighborhood. In *Beautiful City*, I deliberately avoided long shots as much as I could. I wanted to depict the pressure that this environment put on people and tried to do this with the use of close-ups. You could also see this at the very beginning of *Dancing in the Dust*: close-ups and the frames in which the characters are trapped. The environment is left out and yet we see its influence on people. The impact of these downtrodden environments upon people was the whole point, not poverty itself. I did not want to make poverty the main concern of the film by depicting impoverishment in long shots of the neighborhood.

SR: We also encounter few establishing shots, and we know how common they are in classical cinema.

AF: Oftentimes, yes. In directing this film, I imposed several terms on myself from the beginning, such as unfolding the story by using medium shots and close-ups, or not emphasizing the main characters when I first introduce them. Do you remember the shots that introduce us to Firoozeh? First, you hear her voice, then she briefly passes by the camera, now her voice is heard in an offscreen dialogue, then she is back to the frame, and finally we see her. We are introduced to Abolghasem in a similar way. We first hear a woman's scream coming from his room. We realize that he is to treat her broken arm, and then we see Abolghasem in a long shot.

SR: So, we first encounter the effects of their presence before seeing them on-screen?

AF: Yes. This was one of my preconditions.

SR: It seems to me that in both films you are trying to create a situation for the characters to talk, hence the sequences with people having a meal together (or something similar to this). This may be seen as a flaw, since we are not witnessing any action. You intentionally design these scenes for people to just sit and talk.

AF: In a realist film, where the film attempts to capture reality, these are quite natural. In real life, we talk while we are eating in a restaurant. Or when we are riding a bus, we pass the time talking to a fellow passenger. Nothing extraordinary. I do not see these situations as artificial. For example, in the restaurant sequence, the dialogue was not meant to be a source of information. The content of conversations is not all that important. Rather, it provides a setting for developing a relationship. Gestures and glances should be the subject of scrutiny, not the words.

SR: You have mentioned in an interview that although the theme of misery and poverty may appeal to foreign audiences, you do not intend to please this group. On the other hand, domestic audiences tend to like feel-good movies, which are a far cry from your films. Are you opposing these two groups, or do you not care about meeting audience expectations in general?

AF: Cinema owes its meaning to its spectators. Each director, depending on his or her viewpoint, focuses on a particular audience. Some aim their films at the general public while others seek a smaller, more "elite" audience. Some address international viewers and others only Iranian audiences. I do not believe that there exists any director who does not consider viewers while making a film. Consequently, either they may conform to stereotypes (both popular and festival stereotypes), or it may result in a richer work that respects its viewers. I hope to be among the latter group and be able to attract the viewers without any compromise, no matter where they may come from. You mentioned international audiences; I do not believe that their enthusiasm for Iranian cinema is because of the misery depicted in Iranian films.

SR: So, you do not suspect any conspiracy?

AF: This conspiracy theory is outdated. Festivalgoers are savvy viewers with a firm grasp of cinema. When they encounter poverty in one or several films, they do not generalize it to the whole country where the story is taking place. Do you conclude from Indian films that mansions and cutting-edge cars are all you'll see in India, or that everybody there dances and sings spontaneously in large groups? What I do worry about is the seemingly realist movies that do not shy away from lying in order to attract attention and arouse pity for Iranians. The effect of these films will be revealed in the long run. They will hardly become influential.

SR: Which elements did you use in *Beautiful City* to attract an Iranian audience?

AF: The story. Film has a story, with many twists. Also, having professional actors such as Faramarz Gharibian and Taraneh Alidoosti.

SR: How close is Ala's part to what you had in mind?

AF: His role turned out different from what I had in mind while writing the script, but in a positive way. I think he is completely convincing now.

SR: How is it different and why?

AF: Unlike *Dancing in the Dust,* I tried to be more open in directing *Beautiful City.* I wanted to leave room for revelations. In the previous film, I had a clear picture of everything in my mind before shooting, from performances to decoupage. But in this film, I didn't limit myself to that image and let the environment and people around me have an impact on the film. Whenever it would benefit the film, I used it to my advantage, otherwise no. That included the actor who played Ala.

SR: What about the rest of the actors? The social worker or the actress who played Abolghasem's daughter. . . .

AF: Farhad Ghaemian, who played the role of one of the social workers, is a professional actor and knows very well how to approach the part and make it his own. The other social worker, Mehran Maham, had never acted before, although he was completely familiar with the idea of cinema. Abolghasem's daughter was also a first-time actor.

SR: Is it easier for you to work with amateur or professional actors?

AF: Professionals. No doubt a nonprofessional actor needs more time to learn the basic principles and connect with the group, and this takes a lot of energy, whereas with a professional actor you can put this time and energy into other necessities, provided that you find the suitable professional for the role. I do prefer, however, a nonactor who is fit for the part to a professional who, in terms of age and physical appearance, is not right for the part. Then again, mixing nonactors and professional actors can be risky in that performances may lose coherence. Here, it is the professional actor who should adapt.

SR: Does this mean that Taraneh Alidoosti's performance was affected by her fellow nonactor?

AF: For this film, she attended the shooting of almost all the scenes, even the ones that did not involve her, just to observe everybody's performances, especially Ala's—because we had discussed early on that the viewer shouldn't notice this combination of professional actors and nonactors. Both Taraneh Alidoosti and Faramarz Gharibian adjusted themselves to the nonactors who played opposite them. This had happened before to Gharibian in *Dancing in the Dust.* He really put effort into adapting to his fellow actor. A professional actor knows how to capture the essence of a nonactor's performance and incorporate it into his own performance; but a nonactor can hardly act like a professional. I was lucky, in both films, that I worked with nonactors who were extremely clever, which made everything easy for us.

SR: Don't you think that your method of working with actors is rooted in your experiences as a TV director? The new generation of directors has a different method; they use nonactors and narratives in a documentary style.

AF: No, it has nothing to do with TV. I think I had learned this in theater, where I worked with actors who were knowledgeable about their profession, expression, mise-en-scène, and stage. They would practice vigorously, even for the minor details.

SR: This is exactly one of the criticisms leveled at *Beautiful City*: that it tends toward theater. A case in point is the way you create the backdrop for dialogue, as we discussed earlier. If it really is your intention, can't we find examples where it didn't work in the film?

AF: I don't agree that any face-to-face conversation between two people is automatically "theatrical." This is a wrong approach to theater. Even when an actor is delivering a poor performance, they call it a "theatrical" performance. The fact is, you don't see any exaggeration or over-the-top gestures in our good productions; because the architecture of theaters has minimized the space between actors and audiences, there is no need to exaggerate. I have studied theater and have worked in theater for a while, and I will always cherish it. However, I never really tried to make movies that resemble theater in any way. Having said that, I have always wished to employ theatrical tactics for directing actors, methods such as practicing prior to starting to work on set or constantly polishing the roles.

SR: The ways you reveal information in the course of the film, both in *Beautiful City* and your previous film, have an element of surprise, such as the celibacy of Firoozeh and the family's condition regarding the marriage, as if you are trying to keep your viewers hooked. It seems to me adding these twists prevents us from thoroughly exploring the characters. If the viewers had all the necessary information from the beginning, they would be less confused. Some people even say that the film changes direction every ten minutes, that they cannot follow characters and do not know how characters finally deal with situations.

AF: Storytelling is an important aspect of this film. Of course, as a writer, I should avoid foreshadowing. I admit that *Beautiful City* involves too many twists and turns. But when the film claims to be a storyteller, I should keep the audience from guessing the end. When the story carries little weight in the film, it may be better to reveal everything at the outset and readily expose the characters. But this is not the case with *Beautiful City*. The film's main content lies behind this primary story.

SR: *Dancing in the Dust* was not a box office success. Did this experience affect the production of *Beautiful City*?

AF: The films had the same producer, and he already knew that the poor distribution was the main culprit. So, it did not have a negative effect.

SR: You started the production of *Beautiful City* when *Dancing in the Dust* was still in movie theaters. How does a producer agree to work with a director whose previous film did not sell?

AF: His motivations go beyond generating profit. Thankfully, he is more interested in the cultural side of it. From the beginning, we knew that *Dancing in the Dust* wouldn't be a box office hit. We believed that, under normal exhibition conditions, it could only cover its own costs. Unfortunately, the film was shown in three small cinemas that were not major movie theaters of the city, with almost no publicity. Despite that, it was able to earn a revenue of twenty million tomans,[3] which meant that its audience was proportionate to those particular cinemas. Having witnessed this situation, Mr. Taghipour accepted the proposal of *Beautiful City* and did all he could to improve the film.

SR: This could also be a successful economic approach: making low-budget movies with modest revenue instead of costly productions aiming to be high-grossing hits.

AF: I do agree. You can find many successful productions, both among audiences and critics, that have used this approach.

SR: I think *Under the Skin of the City*[4] was a pioneer in this respect, after which more and more low-budget productions appeared—films that were socially conscious and emphasized story. This way, directors don't find themselves in crippling debt after the film.

AF: Personally, I am more interested in this type of film. This does not mean that you can make a film with a budget that is too tight. You cannot avoid some basic costs. I much prefer having an engaging script that applies professional criteria to a large budget.

SR: How did your career as a writer influence the film at the stage of editing? For example, as a director you may encounter a scene that slows down the pace of the film and that requires some change. Jean-Claude Carrière has a famous saying that when shooting starts, the evolution of the screenplay stops; a whole new work is being born. How strictly did you follow your screenplay in *Beautiful City*?

AF: We closely adhered to the screenplay. But everybody was encouraged to comment, and this brought about some change. On the set, I wanted to look at the screenplay from the point of view of the director rather than the writer. In the case of *Low Heights*, I remember that when I handed in the final draft of the script, I tried to restrict my involvement with the work afterward. I did not want to disturb the director. I would sometimes visit them on the set and have a chat, but not to have control over my script. We should accept the fact that the director owns the screenplay, and everything should reflect his point of view. It is unreasonable to expect that the film must follow the script word for word.

SR: Was anything changed in the process of editing?

AF: Yes, some scenes were omitted, and some shots were moved here and there, including the ending.

SR: Tell us more about these two different endings.

AF: I liked the original ending a lot. But it would have changed the film's mood and atmosphere. The current ending is similar in terms of content and what the film wants to convey. Only the form is different. In the first one, the film ends on a shot completely separate from the previous sequence, which is different from what we see now.

SR: Can you elaborate on this shot?

AF: When Ala returned from Abolghasem's house, knowing that he wouldn't give his consent, he walked along a street, stopped every passing car, and asked for a ride back to the detention center. No one would do that, and the image faded. It was powerful, but it would have set a different tone compared to the rest of the film.

SR: What was your rationale behind this ending?

AF: I think this film couldn't have a firm and definite conclusion. In other words, the story is to be continued. Whether Akbar would be released upon Abolghasem's consent or be executed, the story will continue. Akbar is not the last one. After him, there is Shahin, and other detainees at the youth detention center, who await execution. A sense of closure is only possible when the act whereby these youths were sentenced to death is repealed. I could never convince myself to imagine a closure for such a grim story, be it a happy ending with Abolghasem's consent or Ala's marriage to the disabled girl out of sacrifice or a sad one that concludes with the execution of Akbar. The convicts in the detention center who are sentenced to death live in limbo. They live in a state of disbelief and do not know whether the sentence is real or not.

SR: How about the second ending?

AF: After the festival, we came up with another ending that differs from the previous one only in editing, with the addition of several shots. It did not change the general direction. It just resulted in a more coherent film. In the second one, the shot with him stopping the cars appears slightly earlier. Here, the film ends with Firoozeh lighting her cigarette in her room while a passing train blocks our view of Firoozeh's home and Ala. Firoozeh's decision concludes the film.

SR: And her decision is very important. Everybody else has made up their minds.

AF: Yes. She is the one who should choose. Despite the love she still feels for Ala, she chooses not to see him again for the sake of his brother. This is conveyed by lighting the cigarette.

SR: But Firoozeh and Ala had such an impact on each other.

AF: Of course. The film is not a closed circle. At the end of the film, people are back to where they began, but they have influenced each other. This experience has evolved them. Ala is a different person when he is back in prison. Experiencing love has changed Firoozeh as well.

SR: I think at some point this influence becomes the main goal of the film. As you said, the subject of blood money points to the issue of uncertainty and doubt. We ask ourselves which side we should take. Our judgment will be different depending on the side we take, and all that is left for us is constant doubt: what is right and what is wrong? We see the clergy in the mosque saying that prayer is more crucial than saving somebody's life. It leaves the audience with doubt. There are numerous situations like this. It seems that the film talks about distrust of conventions, people's behavior, and laws.

AF: In addition to doubt, you can point to judgment. I think the film is about judgment.

SR: Yes, and after all, right and wrong is not always absolute.

AF: For example, Abolghasem is a believer whose religious beliefs grant him the right of retaliation. Islam even promises him a reward for implementing the retaliation. On the other hand, the people around him discuss granting a pardon over and over again. When he seeks guidance in the word of God, the Quran advises pardon. Now he is faced with a contradiction. Islam has given him the right to retaliate while the clergy is encouraging him to pardon.

You see this kind of contradiction in other characters throughout the film, such as Abolghasem's wife, who does everything for her daughter. Her daughter's happiness is all she yearns for. When she brings up the subject of Ala's marriage, she still doubts whether it would be unjust to Ala. She even asks the uncle, "Isn't it unfair to him?" She is faced with the dilemma of choosing between her daughter and Ala. Firoozeh is not sure either. Should she sacrifice her love for Ala in order to save his brother or continue the relationship at the expense of losing her brother? There is a sequence in the detention center where these uncertainties surface indirectly in a dialogue between Ala and the social worker. The social worker recounts the story of Shahin, who was deeply attached to his mother. He murdered the guy who wanted to imprison his mother due to her debt. Did he do the right thing, or should he have passively accepted her imprisonment? All the characters are caught in these kinds of dilemmas and uncertainties. As viewers, we are also not sure who is right. We change our mind every minute. We back Abolghasem because he has lost his daughter, and one moment later we are on Akbar's side. He is a murderer, but he was in love.

SR: This is partly true. But you may ask why he killed Malihe if he loved her. Was it because of their decision not to marry anyone else? What about Ala and Firoozeh? The viewer is not sure about their relationship; their differences become very bold instead. The answer to all these contradictions and uncertainties could be love itself. But when even the subject of love is treated with doubt, the viewer loses trust. I am not saying they should have bonded at the end of the film, but I wish they hadn't denied this love. Firoozeh clearly did so.

AF: I don't see this as an end to their love. They will live with the memory of each other for many years and cherish this love. The way Firoozeh lights her cigarette shows her desperation, not the denial of love. I think their love for each other is the only undeniable fact in the film. Yes, they do not unite. But this doesn't put an end to their love for each other. Through the course of the film, we witness how they cultivate this love. Ala does not sacrifice his love for her to save his friend's life. The social worker's words become clear here: that the people who sentenced Akbar, Shahin, and the rest of the detainees to death have never fallen in love.

SR: I wish this had been highlighted. From the moment that some sort of bonding starts between Firoozeh and Ala, we are faced with an unpleasant side of Abolghasem's character. Our sympathy for him as a character fades away. We should also mention the other obstacle to this love: making the assumption that Firoozeh is a married woman.

AF: I agree with you about Abolghasem. When we are following Firoozeh and Ala's story, Abolghasem seems a very negative character to us. When we follow Abolghasem's story in the courthouse, we see him again as that innocent man we saw at the beginning of the film. Back to my main argument: your judgment depends upon which side you are on. About Firoozeh first being thought to be a married woman, I used this ambiguity to distract the viewer. When Ala knocks on Firoozeh's door early in the film, I did not want the viewer to predict their love. Now I think that I should have found a better strategy instead of coming up with a child and husband.

SR: I think you don't always need to stop the viewer from guessing what comes next; although here and with regard to form, nothing is definite for the viewer. My understanding was that you created all these situations to prompt Firoozeh to deliver an important line: "How do you think I live alone in such a neighborhood?"

AF: No, this dialogue was not the reason I wrote that sequence. In fact, this is the only scene in the film I wish I could change.

Notes

1. In Islamic law, these are two ways of dealing with a murder or intentional bodily injury: the victim or victim's heirs can ask for *qisas* (retribution), which is an equal punishment, or *diyeh* (blood money), which is a financial compensation. The third option would be that the victim or victim's heirs grant pardon to the perpetrator.
2. Iran-Iraq War, which lasted from 1980 to 1988.
3. Roughly equivalent to twenty-four thousand US dollars in 2002.
4. Celebrated realist Iranian film released in 2001 and directed by Rakhshan Banietemad.

An Interview with Asghar Farhadi and Mani Haghighi: A Special Day

Houshang Golmakani and Abbas Yari / 2006

From *Film Monthly* (Tehran), Vol. 24, No. 344, March 2006. Translated by Ramin S. Khanjani.

Fireworks Wednesday (2006) is meticulous and precise in script and direction and in both respects is regarded as an exceptional work in the last few years. It is the first collaborative experience of two totally disparate writers. In terms of directing, the film is exemplary of how a story with the capacity of easily lapsing into a conventional matrimonial drama of Iranian cinema has instead been turned into one of the most memorable films in recent years. We could have conducted separate interviews respectively devoted to the scriptwriting and the directing. Nonetheless, since one of the scriptwriters is also the director of the film, we decided to combine two interviews into one.

—Houshang Golmakani

Editors' note: Actor writer, and director Mani Haghighi (born 1969), the cowriter of *Fireworks Wednesday*, grew up in a family of film people—he is the grandson of Ebrahim Golestan, one of the founding fathers of Iranian New Wave, and the son of celebrated cinematographer Ne'mat Haghighi. He is one of the pioneering figures of digital filmmaking with his debut, *Abadan* (2002), and his recent films have often premiered at the Berlinale.

The original interview does not indicate which questions were asked by Golmakani and which ones by Yari, so we have used the initials FM (*Film Monthly*) for all comments and questions by interviewers.

Film Monthly: Let's start by discussing how you two found each other.

Mani Haghighi: I saw *Beautiful City* two years ago at the Fajr Film Festival and very much liked it. I had seen *Dancing in the Dust* before, which was a good film, but it didn't touch my heart as much as *Beautiful City* did. When I came out of the theater, I asked after its director. I was told that he was not in Iran at that time. However, I met his wife outside the theater, introduced myself, and told her that I loved the film and would like to know its director. Later we met and he watched my film *Abadan*, too, and told me that contrary to his earlier expectations, he had enjoyed it. Our overnight discussion of *Beautiful City* and *Abadan* led us to ask each other what we were planning to do next.

Asghar Farhadi: I described to him two of my ideas, one of which was *Fireworks Wednesday*. I had doubts as to which one to pick, because I loved them both very much. Mani suggested that we work on *Fireworks Wednesday*.

MH: He told me the story and I insisted on making it. He felt the story was still missing some parts. Right there, I started making suggestions.

FM: And you agreed to collaborate?

MH: By the end of the night we were convinced that we could work together, and our collaboration started thereafter. It was May 2004.

FM: What was the first story?

MH: The same thing. A story set on the eve of the last Tuesday of the year,[1] with a cleaning girl entering a home in which the wife suspects her husband is cheating on her.

AF: And she discovers the truth by making a plan with the assistance of the cleaning girl. The plan she devised was very different from the film and during our very first session we reached the conclusion that it must be changed. In that first version the wife plots to kill her husband and wants to use the girl as her alibi; she says that she's going to sleep but goes out, kills the husband, and comes back while the girl thinks she's been at home the whole time. A trace of this idea is still left in the film (when Mozhdeh puts on the girl's chador and steps out), but killing the husband was scrapped. That story was very undeveloped, and I had done less work on it compared to the other idea. When Mani suggested we work on this one, I said that it was very sketchy, whereas the other one was almost ready. We spent about seven to eight months working on the structure and details, and the script went through five revisions.

FM: What was your method of working together?

AF: We would discuss and take notes. Then we would part ways with some unanswered questions, to which we had to find answers. At night we'd go through them over the phone, and the next morning we would meet each other to go over our answers. Many times we couldn't find an answer the next day, but we knew what questions had to be answered.

MH: There have been very few instances of collaborative scriptwriting in Iranian cinema. When several scriptwriters have been credited, they were usually only responsible for revisions. Of course, the practice initiated by the Scriptwriting Workshop School was very fruitful and, as one of its results, collaborative scriptwriting has become something of a routine. Mani said that you two had totally different views on the details. Basically people can work together when they're on the same wavelength. How did you work together despite having different views? What were your differences?

AF: It's a complicated thing. In some respects, we are very similar; for instance, we have favorite films in common. But the nature of our work is different—meaning that *Abadan* is very different from *Beautiful City*, mostly in terms of the aesthetics and form. In the case of this particular script, the story itself dictated the form, so aspects of those differences were brushed aside. I also sometimes hear things about our differences, which in my opinion are ludicrous: things like, "Mani Haghighi is a haughty bourgeois, whereas I am coming from the depths of society!" This is not true.

FM: While writing the scenes, did you also discuss their execution?

AF: Yes. Since we knew that the film was to be directed by me, we also discussed how to do it. Our ideas on that differed, but we acknowledged this difference.

FM: What were the differences?

AF: Mani, for instance, envisioned many sequence shots as shorter and tighter shots. There were lots of differences in details. But the story itself was giving us some clue as to its essence, and both of us understood that. Even from the get-go we didn't have fundamental differences in writing.

MH: For me the most crucial aspect of our collaboration was our working method. We worked as if complementing each other. Asghar told me that his way of writing is to ponder over the story for a long time and then start committing it to paper from beginning to end. For me all the joy and pleasure of writing is derived from forming the primary structure. I feel that I need to make a template and determine the beginning, the middle, and the end of the story, even if not necessarily according to classic conventions. I need to be completely aware where in the film each event takes place. The framework of the story is very significant to me, and I enjoy building it. I imposed this predilection of mine on Asghar. A few times Asghar said, "For heaven's sake, let's start writing," but my reply was something like, "No, I still don't know at what time in the film Mozhdeh is heading off. I cannot start before figuring that out!" Asghar then would respond that we can write and discover that, but I didn't give in. This could have led to some tensions, because it felt like I was procrastinating. At last we reached the point when the whole structure of the film was drawn up. After sketching the overall structure, we felt that the characters were still not sufficiently developed. In other words, the pacing and the course of the story were clear, but we weren't fully clear on each of the four main characters' respective motivations. At that point, we spent a month shaping their backgrounds according to more classic conventions.

FM: In other words, adding the building material on to this framework. . . .

MH: Correct. For instance, now we know very well how Mozhdeh and Morteza came to know each other, who proposed and where. We know the stories of these four people very well, even if they are not depicted in the film. At the end of the two months spent on developing characters, we felt very familiar with these four people.

FM: The script for *Fireworks Wednesday* is akin to a jigsaw puzzle made up of small, delicate pieces, and one out-of-proportion piece would result in the entire structure falling apart. How much time and energy were put into this part?

MH: From May 2004 to January 2005 we met almost every day and were fully aware that it would be the details and intricacies of the story that would make it enjoyable.

AF: Sometimes they shouldn't be called details, because some of them are part of the main framework. As we were setting up pillars of this framework, small details such as the color of the walls in the apartment or the chador turned out to be crucial. We arrived at those details during the same process of shaping the framework. It was only after five to six months of discussion and notetaking that we finally reached the stage of adding color and filling out the framework. In other words, we discovered many things coming out of this framework.

FM: Did you write it scene by scene?

MH: After having the framework ready, we initially wanted to continue in the same manner and sit together and write. Then we realized that it would be very difficult to discuss every line when writing the dialogue. So, we switched our method, and Asghar went on to write the first draft. Normally it feels difficult to step aside at this stage and let the other party continue, but both of us knew the details of the script backward and forward, so I handed over the writing to Asghar without worry. I only pitied him for having to write down all of them! Then Asghar gave me the draft piece by piece, but the condition was that he had to stop writing whenever he didn't know what to write or didn't feel ready to proceed. There is one draft of the script that's missing seven to eight scenes. My task was to rewrite the scenes and fill in the gaps as he was moving forward. I used Asghar's draft as a basis and wrote what was in fact the second draft. Then it came to coloring, so to speak, in other words, polishing and adding details. Following that, we revised the script three more times.

FM: One remarkable aspect of this film, as with any great film, is its excellent rhythm, which is quite difficult to achieve. Did you consider the pacing during the writing stage?

MH: Very much so.

FM: How can the rhythm be discussed at such an early stage? How was this perfectly executed element addressed when writing the script?

AF: We were confident that by following classic rules in shaping the framework and details of the script, the right rhythm would be achieved. During the shoot I needed to carefully observe the chain of events and actions and reactions for each scene so as to not get stuck in one story event or too hastily move on from that event. Outside of the script, two things contributed to the film's pacing. One was the mise-en-scène, which at some point picks up and keeps the film from feeling slow. The second was the editing style. Watching Hayedeh Safiyari's[2] cut for the first time, I was shocked. I thought those bold jump cuts were very strange. At first, I was really worried, but after watching the edited scenes a few more times I sensed that Tehran feels the same on this particular day of the year. These two elements helped the pacing a lot. From the outset we knew that the story takes place in a limited location that could easily cause the story to stall. We kept reminding ourselves of this all the time and tried our best to keep the audience engaged.

MH: I looked at it in two ways. Reviews of Asghar's first two films refer to their slow pacing. For *Beautiful City* I thought the slower pacing worked. Anyway, we thought of rhythm in two regards. One was the order of the scenes, in other words, which scenes could be omitted and which parts of the story could only be alluded to later. This aspect wasn't that important to me, because it had been worked out through structuring the story. It was the inner rhythm of each scene that mattered to me more. We persistently tried to follow this eternal scriptwriting guideline: "Enter late and leave early." We tried to enter the events in their midst and then move ahead just before the spectator starts suspecting where it is going. At any rate, Asghar Farhadi is the director of this film and the film belongs to him. I felt what I had to do was to constantly make sure we weren't telling too much, moving on in a timely manner and without protracting the scenes too much.

FM: One problem with scripts of Iranian films lies in their dialogue. Your film has nice dialogue and the exchanges between characters work perfectly. What was your method for writing the dialogue?

MH: We never did things like putting ourselves in characters' shoes and start talking to each other.

AF: We sent the script to many people to read, and in one of our meetings we agreed that I was to write the dialogue. Of course, we were constantly revising the lines. The dialogue of the film is credible for two reasons. The most important reason is that the characters are full-fledged and we could see them as real people. We were in agreement even on the slightest details of their external features and we knew how each of them speaks.

FM: Had you selected the cast at that time?

MH: Actors playing the three main characters had been selected.

AF: From the first night I described this idea, we knew these three actors were going to play the main roles and fortunately they all came on board.

MH: Only Pantea Bahram, playing Simin the hairdresser, joined us later.

AF: I was very concerned about who would play this role. She had to have something about her that makes it look convincing for a family man with a wife like Mozhdeh to fall in love with her. She had to possess an inner quality, especially since the wife was to be played by Hedieh Tehrani.

Let's go back to our discussion of the dialogue. I knew that Morteza would be played by Hamid Farrokhnezhad, and I knew how he talks. I didn't know Hedieh Tehrani very closely, so I watched all her films. Mani knew her and clued me in on many of her traits. I knew Taraneh Alidoosti, who plays Rouhi, the help, from our previous work together. These considerations aided us a lot in figuring out how these characters have to speak. Most importantly, the realism of the script guided us not to write lines that we do not hear in real life.

MH: In my opinion, one key thing that we did during various stages of scriptwriting was watching films such as Abbas Kiarostami's *The Report* and Dariush Mehrjui's *Leila*.

FM: A common issue with the dialogue of most average Iranian films is that they don't sound like spoken language. Sometimes they come close to written language and sound forced, contrived, and slogan-like. Other times they morph into maxims or wisecracks. But in this film, we never get the feeling that these characters should have spoken differently. They don't deliver maxims or slogans. They are not supposed to only sound funny. I'm expanding on this just for you to tell us how this was achieved.

MH: We decided the characters should say things that they are supposed to, not that we want them to.

FM: How much was the dialogue changed by actors on set?

AF: Changes by actors had no impact on the course of the story or character development, and I was careful that they wouldn't affect the film's overall framework and direction. I asked actors to make it more real. I never forced them to deliver the lines verbatim. I even remember when rehearsing the scene in the bathroom, I asked Sahar Dolatshahi[3] to say her lines as if they were improvised. With all rehearsal on the sets, actors had a feeling that the dialogue belonged to them. At some point they were interrupting each other and didn't completely follow the written lines, and I preferred this realistic delivery. Such occasions demand a bit of selflessness. It does not really bother me that the film seems to have no script and feels like the outcome of a collective improvisation. I think it's in fact an accomplishment. Even the other aspects of the film were intended to be understated. I believe cinematography is the foremost example of this.

FM: Can you give an example of something that was not in the script and was added by the actors?

AF: For instance, one of Farrokhnezhad's first lines in the film, when he says over the phone: "Hawaii is for your aunt!"[4] The beauty of this line is that it makes us understand that the person on the other end has said, "Spending the New Year in Hawaii?" This short phrase both implies what is said and provides a response to it. This came from Hamid Farrokhnezhad. There are more of those lines that helped enrich the film. It's very much a characteristic of Farrokhnezhad to make tiny changes to the dialogue and make it his own.

MH: Fortunately, all the actors nailed their roles, each in their own way. We had some written dialogue, which to my regret is not in the film. All in all, however, I can understand why. Especially Farrokhnezhad was given a lot of leeway to change the lines, as long as the overall mood was correct.

AF: Compared to *Beautiful City*, not many lines were changed on the set. What made the actors' improvisation fall in line with the story was their full faith in the script. Everyone on the team was convinced of this by reading the script.

FM: How did you work with the actors before the shoot in terms of read-through and rehearsals?

AF: For each of them, it was different. I had some experience from *Dancing in the Dust* and *Beautiful City*. In both films Faramarz Gharibian played characters that were introverted and monosyllabic, so I was worried they would come off as identical. While shooting *Beautiful City* I realized that Mr. Gharibian becomes the character only after imitating his appearance. For *Beautiful City* all kinds of strange makeup tests were done on Mr. Gharibian, but one day he put on the character's costume and, after being quickly made up in the courtyard, came back to declare that he'd found the character's manner of walking. I realized that he works from outside to inside; in other words, he needs to find the character's external features first.

In *Fireworks Wednesday* actors had different methods. Ms. Tehrani is slightly like Mr. Gharibian in her approach and discovers her character very slowly and gradually. Ms. Alidoosti's approach is very logic-driven; she writes down every vague thing about the character and poses questions about them until she finds the answers. Mr. Farrokhnezhad attempts to bring out his commonalities with the role. It is a huge advantage for an actor to know themselves. We had a few sessions to discuss the script. We also had read-throughs, but not to discover the characters. It was for the three of them to know each other. Some scenes were rehearsed, such as the scene with Simin and Morteza in the car or the fight between Mozhdeh and Morteza at home. Rehearsals took a long time, and fortunately on the set I was not worried in the least about the acting. Makeup and costume tests also took some time.

FM: You said that Hedieh Tehrani embodied her character from outside to inside. Her hairdo aside, her appearance doesn't show much change, whereas Taraneh Alidoosti appears quite different from her real self. . . .

AF: I thought it was important for Mozhdeh to have a boyish haircut and not feminine long hair. First thing we did was to have her hair cut. Second was dressing her in a way that lacked delicacy and color. Also, with the exception of the penultimate scene, her face was not made up. I realized that for Ms. Tehrani to be able to deliver this high-strung performance, I shouldn't cut too often. This is one reason we have many sequence shots in the film. The way I saw it, the mise-en-scène had to serve and follow the performances; in other words, the scenes were blocked and rehearsed with actors and then the scene breakdown was adjusted correspondingly. It wasn't the other way around.

FM: What stood out in Ms. Tehrani's face is her nervousness and fatigue. It's as if she hasn't slept in days. To achieve this, did you resort to things like keeping her awake in some way?

AF: No, but she normally sleeps too little. When I said that Hedieh Tehrani will play this role, everyone was like, "Excellent, but she has already played sturdy characters." This worried me, but all the time I was telling myself that there's something in her face that makes her different from her previous roles. It's the fragility in her face, especially in her eyes. The blood vessels in her eyes are visible, just as in Gharibian's. It only had to be emphasized and brought out. Besides, Ms. Tehrani had subtly applied red eyeliner, which helped as well.

FM: Did you give actors any particular clues? Did you tell them to think of something or do something that could shape their performance? For instance, telling Farrokhnejad that he is a duplicitous character who pretends to be honest and innocent, and somewhere he should show his deceitful self, or instead telling him that he is an innocent guy stuck with an unhinged wife and so has every right to fancy another woman?

AF: I tried to impress upon each of them, privately, that their character is on the right side and they have to look out for themselves. So, everyone had the feeling of being correct without knowing the other two share the same feeling. As a result, they were all competing for their rights. To amplify this feeling, I also played some tricks. For instance, Mani and I were concerned about the kid in the film, because usually children in films come off as bland and mawkish. We thought that the real story of the film would not sound convincing to this child. Therefore, I told him an awful story and in fact lifted the blame from the dad and pinned unfaithfulness on his mum. As a result, he became excessively resentful toward Mozhdeh, enough to resist leaving with her in the scene in question. Up until the end, he was caring about his dad and adoring him. When calling his mum a "fool," he was really thinking that she is unfaithful and ruining their family. When he learned of the real story on the last day of the shoot, he was extremely annoyed with me, but I didn't think I had any other option. I did similar things to Ms. Tehrani, but she is very smart and such tricks didn't work for long, forcing me to think up new schemes.

MH: I tried to explain to Asghar that Hedieh Tehrani cannot be easily tricked. She is exceptionally smart, far smarter than one might assume. She understands that you are playing a trick on her to get what you wish but doesn't show it. Then she does what you need and says, "See, I nailed it without those tricks." This happened a few times during the shoot of *Abadan*.

FM: The acting in the film is great, but some people believe that Tehrani and Farrokhnezhad are playing themselves as Mozhdeh and Morteza, whereas Taraneh Alidoosti is an actor who splendidly embodies the girl.

AF: Obviously the gap between the self and the character was biggest for Ms. Alidoosti, and people probably wouldn't have had the same impression had she played Mozhdeh. It's obvious that Ms. Tehrani is closer to her role than Ms. Alidoosti; that's why I like her acting.

MH: It's extremely difficult to play oneself before the camera. When the camera is set up and the director asks you to play yourself, disaster looms. I mean it's terribly hard to self-imitate. So being closer to the role doesn't make it any easier for the actor. When an actor plays a role distinct from themselves and their world, this difference helps them observe their role better than if they were playing themselves. There are more difficulties when an actor has to play a role with whom they share social background and personal traits, because they are not given enough distance from the role to analyze and know it. That's why I'm wondering how Farrokhnezhad, despite this, has managed to completely transform in such a strange and excellent way.

FM: There are small, subtle details in acting, and I don't know how much of it was your instruction and how much happened on the spot. For instance, at one point, when Ms. Tehrani is in the bathroom, her voice cracks and cannot be easily heard. This adds to the feeling of that moment.

AF: I cannot remember exactly, but I recall that the main point of that scene was that the characters could be heard through the vent, so they had to whisper. Also, Mozhdeh has caught a cold, and with a stuffy nose she has difficulty breathing. On two occasions we see her using nose drops and it shows that she's breathing with difficulty. Chance had it that while shooting that scene Ms. Tehrani really did have a cold, and this helped. This shot was done in two takes and the first take was used. We shot the second take with the intention of having it slightly shorter. It was a still shot and everything had to take place offscreen. The second take was shorter, but it didn't give the same feel. For this shot we tore down the wall of the bathroom. Recording sound for it proved difficult as well.

FM: Somewhere else, when Mozhdeh's sister arrives and together they walk into the kitchen, Rouhi passes by. The sister asks, "Who is she?" and Mozhdeh quietly answers, "She's a worker!"

AF: This wasn't in the script, and we asked her to say that. Fortunately, our sound recordist was not very fussy about the line being clear and loud, and this gave us some flexibility.

FM: When Ms. Alidoosti finishes with her makeup, she looks in the mirror and moves her eyebrows. This gesture has a charm to it. Was it something added by her?

AF: There's a similar shot in *Beautiful City* in which she coquettishly looks into the mirror. When writing the script, I replicated that shot. The script describes it as "She looks into the hairdressing mirror flirtatiously and moves her eyebrows." Taraneh Alidoosti is very reticent, and no one knows what she's doing. When she shows up on set in the morning, it's clear that she's prepped a lot, but she doesn't discuss this. Only after shooting *Beautiful City* did I hear what she had done at home and in her own time to nail that role. She doesn't reveal what she has done to nail the role. The only thing I suggested to her was to hire some cleaners to work at her place. It appears that she did that.

FM: How did you choose the actors playing minor characters, such as the concierge and his wife?

AF: I had previously worked with the actor who plays the concierge. Directing some fifty episodes of *Tale of a City* has given me a wealth of resources. Many unknown actors came to test for that series, and I've handpicked some and continue to use them in my projects. The actor playing the concierge had played in one episode of *Tale of a City*, and I was happy with him. The one who played his wife is a stage actress. The actor playing Simin's husband had already played in *Beautiful City*, and I knew him from stage performances. He has a background in theater with plenty of experience.

FM: *Fireworks Wednesday* is one of the richest films of our national cinema in terms of the setting and background. In many films, characters come off as cutout figures pasted on a blank background. In this film, backgrounds exert their significance from the very beginning: like the street fish and produce market on the sidewalk, which is shown in passing. But the most important of all is the main location and the disarrayed home, which has already been painted and now has to be tidied up before they set off on a journey the next day. It symbolizes the chaotic relation of people in this home. Another director might have envisioned the home in a normal situation and not in such disarray. How did this find its way into the script?

MH: This is what Asghar emphasized from the get-go. We had to find elements around these characters that would reflect their relationship, such as setting the story on Chaharshanbe Suri, when there's bedlam on the streets. Or when the landlord of Simin arrives, it seems that everything—the city, the home, and the neighbor—are all in a transitional state. It's a common scriptwriting technique to make internal and external events echo one another. Chaharshanbe Suri in particular presented itself as an ideal occasion for the story.

FM: Chaharshanbe Suri provides a volatile and insecure backdrop for relationships that are on the brink of explosion.

AF: In selecting the main location, we took two essential things into account that helped build this atmosphere, and the cinematographer Hossein Jafarian contributed to this as well. I was looking for a location with many windows to give the impression of being empty and exposed. Several times in the film Mozhdeh says, "Shut the door. Why haven't you hung the curtains?" As if she's concerned about reestablishing their privacy as quickly as possible and finding solid ground to stand on. During renovation of the place for the shoot, a new window was added. Another thing that intensifies the confusion is the architecture of the home. As I mentioned, the apartment was renovated and its interior spaces were redesigned. For instance, Amir Ali's room didn't exist before and the kitchen looked different; now the drawing room is linked to another space with a set of stairs and doesn't look flat. The interior design of the apartment lacks character and is irritating. This helped a lot and gave me freedom in designing the shots.

FM: Was it Mr. Jafarian who suggested these changes?

AF: No, at that time Jafarian was in the States. He'd read the script. Over the phone I told him I was looking for an apartment full of windows and asked if this would cause him any problem with lighting. He welcomed this idea and said that he'd need a place that gets light simultaneously from inside and outside. Especially when curtains were not there, windows helped a lot.

FM: The film is full of rich details, for instance, the relationship of the concierge with other characters and his wife who is supposed to work for Mozhdeh but has been sent on an errand by her neighbor, in spite of the concierge claiming that she is barred by the building's management from doing jobs for residents. Later when Mozhdeh goes after Rouhi on the street and calls her, she, the concierge's wife, is seen coming back with a shopping bag. Mozhdeh goes to the neighbor's place and there's a delicate exchange. Without getting into an argument, Mozhdeh tells the neighbor's wife that she can get the concierge's wife to work in her place, just as the neighbor had sent her shopping. The concierge's wife has a one- to two-year-old kid and yet she is eight-months pregnant with a new child. When she hears from Rouhi about Abdolreza's love for her, she is compelled to say that her cousin used to love her.

AF: This naturally happens when we do not prioritize the characters and do not treat them in the script as significant or insignificant. The concierge's wife was only present in two or three scenes, but to me she is still an important character. The day we wanted to shoot that scene, I told Jafarian it feels so good to do it, because now there is a new character. To me it did not matter that she is only a minor character within the film's drama. When we give equal importance to every person in the frame, the result shows itself.

MH: A bow must be taken to scriptwriting gurus for their rules and principles, even if they are ignored as outdated by some. A very simple rule is to create an obstacle for every action. If you really make it part of your belief system—and don't just idly think about it—this becomes the stepping stone for details to take shape. A simple example is like when someone wants to step out but trips over the carpet, or when one picks a pot but cannot find its lid.

AF: This is the same thing that Kiumars Pourahmad[5] once wrote about and termed "knowing the ration book." I believe this has been applied in our film. It can be seen in Kiumars Pourahmad's films as well, and his *Majid's Tales* owes a lot of its beauty to it.

FM: True, he has added some details to every movement and action. A similar example in your film is the issue of improper car parking that escalates into a skirmish. Things of this nature enrich the film.

AF: This way the audience gets a clearer picture of the city and knows that the story world is not limited to this family; there are other people with their own problems, but since they don't serve the story of this family, their stories have not been told.

MH: This has to be emphasized; during creation of the framework for the script, which we already discussed, we had already planted seeds of a narrative process. So, for instance, the concierge enters the story in order for us to create certain developments in the film. When this stage is finished, and we feel that the narrative is pieced together well, a whole new world opens up. Now you start thinking of them not as roles with a narrative function but as humans who need identity and character depth.

FM: So all these backgrounds are calculated?

AF: Yes, everything, the Chaharshanbe Suri scenes included. Some people think they are documentary footage captured on an actual Chaharshanbe Suri, whereas most of it is constructed. Only some of the shots recorded from inside the car are documentary footage. We orchestrated a Chaharshanbe Suri festival on two streets over two consecutive nights. On one of those streets a memorial service for a deceased resident was taking place, and we were not aware of that, or the scenes of Chaharshanbe Suri in the park, which were all reconstructed with sixty to seventy extras.

FM: In one scene in the advertising agency, Morteza says something about editing the ad, which in fact points to his hypocritical side. It's as if he's put on an act.

AF: There is in fact a common thread that runs through every story event in the film: characters are either lying or trying to make up for others' lies, or they tell others that they are aware of their lies. This happens at the school, at home when the woman's car tires are punctured, in the agency, etc. Our goal was to make this a constant presence, but in the background, without hitting the spectator over the head with it.

FM: An instrumental and pivotal aspect of the story is Taraneh's lie, which puts an end to the quarrel between Mozhdeh and Morteza.

AF: During that day you hear lots of lies. Of course, Morteza had lied and hidden things before, but Rouhi's lie is the biggest.

FM: But why did she make up that lie? A young woman who's about to get married might be expected to take the wife's side. Why does she do something that aids the husband?

AF: She doesn't aid the husband as much as she aids the other woman, Simin. Even when Morteza asks her, "Why did you lie?" she replies, "Just because," meaning she didn't have a very clear reason for that.

FM: So, she sympathized more with Simin than with Mozhdeh.

AF: That's right. Because Simin didn't even charge her for doing her makeup and Rouhi sees that she's about to be thrown out of her place. She believes that Simin is innocent and imagines that helping her is morally right. Only later does she realize that what she did is also morally wrong.

MH: We notice Rouhi's change of attitude toward Simin near the end of the film, when she sees the latter at the door asking her, "What's the matter?" When Rouhi lies for the first time, she believes that Simin is somehow worthy of protecting. Even with all the proof and evidence against Simin, she resorts to lying in order to vindicate her, even in the spectator's eyes. Later when Simin passes by, Rouhi knows that she's been guilty, too.

FM: One important formal element of the film is its cinematography. Jafarian's camerawork is outstanding.

AF: We had the same cinematographic style in mind from the outset, but I was a bit uncertain. We wanted to have many long takes, which is a risky choice: first, because it makes the shoot extremely difficult and, second, it limits the editing choices. Jafarian helped a lot and insisted on moving ahead with this idea, because during blocking and rehearsals we could see that the acting was right for it; it was clear to all of us that the same feeling couldn't be achieved with shorter takes. Jafarian's encouragement helped a lot. He did another equally significant thing. He had envisioned the apartment painted in light gray. In most Iranian films, midnight blue is used to convey the cold atmosphere of homes, to a clichéd degree. Jafarian said, "I've grown tired of lighting walls painted in midnight blue. What color are our homes in real life?" It's usually light cream yellow. Switching to this color helped a lot. With interiors in midnight blue, the interior disarray would not have had the same impact. It also helped a lot that Jafarian didn't feel compelled to keep things within the frame. It doesn't happen very often in shooting films to keep part of the character out of the frame. But we agreed that framing shouldn't be pitch-perfect. The other thing we agreed on was to use close-ups sparingly, and in imitation of a fair witness, not to get too close to one character and instead treat them all equally. There are only three close-ups in the films: one is in the last part when Abdolreza gets suspicious. I wanted his suspicion to be shown in his facial expression rather than conveying it through a spoken line. The other close-up was used to show Mozhdeh's reaction when she's at the door of the neighbor's apartment; the issue of Simin is raised for the first time, and she realizes that it has even been discussed in the board meeting. The third close-up is part of Mozhdeh's rejoinder to the neighbor, which we already discussed.

FM: Didn't you get any inserts to incorporate into the long takes?

AF: No, we didn't.

FM: So, you decided on editing during the shoot?

AF: No, many long take sequences were shot, but they were cut into shorter shots in the editing stage. For instance, there was a long and difficult long take for the scene at the beginning of the film when Taraneh goes to the cleaning services company. Rails were laid, and shooting this scene in a single take was a very difficult feat. Had it been used more extensively in the film, it could have shown off the cinematography more. But two things about it annoyed me: first, it felt as if we were showing off our ability to record, in a single take, a four-minute shot with lots of movement, which in my opinion was silly to brag about. During editing, Ms. Safiyari cut it short. Later on, when Mr. Jafarian saw it, he said that it was a good call and that it enhanced the rhythm. The scene with Morteza and Simin in the car was done in multiple shots. Most of the scenes containing some sort of tension were done in long takes. One instance is when Mozhdeh comes home to pick up her son and leaves without understanding that it's his playtime. Morteza arrives and tries to stop her, and the child doesn't want to leave. This is all shot in one long take with no coverage, which was of course a huge risk.

FM: At one point the rhythm of the film changes: it is when a few quick shots show the plastic covers are pulled off the furniture and the curtains are drawn.

AF: Our intention was to indicate the passage of time. Rouhi was supposed to pick up Amir Ali from the school at two pm. We had to go from twelve to two pm very quickly. It starts with the neighbor's son throwing a paper plane with a message and continues with those jump cuts.

MH: There is an important point about showing the passage of time, especially in films with stories set in a single day. This is my third script with a story taking place from morning to night. In such films we are dealing with two types of time, objective and subjective. In other films, it's more convincing to declare the passage of three weeks than to mention a lapse of merely five minutes. That requires a very different solution.

FM: But you mentioned that while writing the script, you had not envisioned any jump cuts so as to preserve the film's realism. How come for this particular occasion jump cuts were used?

AF: We had more jump cuts, but none of them was as drastic as this one. When there is lots of movement, jump cuts are more invisible, but here it is noticeable because the camera is not moving.

FM: One thing that I can imagine was difficult for you to desist from was showing the car passengers' reaction to what they see on the street at night. . . .

AF: I always loathed the shots taken from the front of the car, showing someone behind the wheel. I don't know why. I prefer the camera inside the car and not in a frontal position. Besides, on many occasions, showing the back of the head instead of faces creates a stronger feeling when the proper background is used. A good example of that is toward the end of the film when Mozhdeh is shown from behind, sweeping. We agreed on doing it this way at the writing stage.

FM: It's very Hitchcockian.

AF: There's a distressing sound heard over a static shot. You see nothing, but perhaps this allows the spectator to ponder the previous scene, just as Mozhdeh is doing. If we had moved the camera in front of her, the spectator would have become concerned with changes in her facial expressions. Sometimes, it's more effective not to show the actor's face, especially when she's veiled in headscarf or chador.

FM: One interesting part of the film worth discussing is its ending. Open endings have recently become very popular, both in Iranian and international cinema. The way your film unfolds could call for such an ending. The audience is now used to this type of ending, such that seeing Taraneh and her fiancé drive off on a motorcycle prompts us to think the film has ended, when, indeed, on it goes. It seems that such an ending could have been more logical and anticipated by the audience, so when the film continues it feels unexpected or, to some, redundant; or others might think the film has multiple endings. If so, this second ending has its own elements and suspense, but what does it add to the "first ending"?

AF: Had the film ended at that point, we couldn't have achieved the feeling of the final scene, specifically the shot of Mozhdeh and her kid sleeping. Mani and I discussed this for over a month before the premiere. We could have easily removed this last part, but I think we instinctively knew that the ending needed to capture the feeling inside the home. The editing was done, and one night we talked about what to do. Over the past year and a half, most of our discussions had centered on this issue. Then I convinced myself that this ending would definitely receive criticism, but would also keep the audience engaged with the film after leaving the theater, so it had to be the ending. Without this scene, the film looked as if it were pretending to have an open ending. With the shot showing a pensive Mozhdeh from behind, the spectator might think she's going to leave home before Morteza returns, but now we see her staying despite all these circumstances, because she has a kid whom she loves unconditionally and who from now on will be the man of her life. This happens a lot in Iranian families. Never before had I been so confident about one of my film's endings.

FM: I'm in favor of the present ending, but I still want to know how you arrived at this conclusion. In addition to showing Mozhdeh lying next to her child, which signals the persistence of her doubts (as a result of Rouhi's ambiguous words to her at the door and also as a natural outcome of the shot showing her from behind sweeping), it also shows Morteza looking up at Simin's window. Seeing no one in the car, he perhaps concludes that Simin's ex-husband is upstairs, only to find him sleeping inside his car. But even this ending feels as if it's missing something.

AF: No, but there is something that should solve everything. I think the music in the shot showing the motorbike driving off doesn't start at the correct moment. For the first one hundred minutes of the film you don't hear any music, so when it does come on it might signal the end of the film to many viewers. In fact, the music mistakenly starts five to six seconds earlier than it should have. When we showed the film without the music, spectators didn't have the same feeling and we believed that we were right. Mani said, "You see, no one was bothered by the ending. So, it is the correct one." It's the music that creates such a feeling, and that was a mistake.

MH: One thing that spectators do is imagine different turns of events and anticipate possible results accordingly, but there's a difference between imagining and seeing. Even we screenwriters and filmmakers imagine different things, meaning that we tried several conceivable endings. For example, we envisioned the film ending with Rouhi and Abdolreza setting off on the bike and found it quite crude and abrupt. This applies to casting, too. Now that the acting has turned out well and the actors have received awards or praise, it's clear that everyone is in the right place. But when we were talking about casting the actors, everyone was suggesting, based on their preconceptions, that Simin should have been played by Hedieh Tehrani. All the time we had to ask them to see the result of our choices. At one point, we seriously discussed doing something strange and having Mozhdeh played by Taraneh Alidoosti in order for this character to look younger and more innocent. Taraneh herself was interested in playing this role. This is the difference between imagining a scene and seeing it.

FM: Since the film starts with a motorbike, naturally some might expect it to end with the same vehicle.

AF: There is no rule that requires a film to start and end with the same character and element. Besides, it's wrong to view Rouhi as the narrator of the story whose point of view has to be followed. Rouhi is only a pretext for gaining entrance to a household. Once she enters the home, the first thing we did was reduce her presence. We consciously wanted to inform the spectator that she's only a pretext for entering this home.

MH: Probably due to this wrong assumption that Rouhi is the narrator of the film, there is a strange line of criticism claiming that the bathroom scenes and the encounter between Morteza and Simin shouldn't have found their way into the film. However, we had earlier shown Mozhdeh going to Mostafa's office without Rouhi being there, or in a few other sequences we see the concierge's wife and Mozhdeh together, after Rouhi had left. I think all this clearly shows that Rouhi is not the narrator.

FM: Your film is full of details that have been thoroughly thought out. However, at the beginning of the film we see a broken glass, and later we learn that Mozhdeh and Morteza had a fight the night before, during which Morteza cut his hand and had it bandaged. I was expecting this bandaged hand to be of some use later in the film. Now it's too late, but this is what I would have suggested: at the end of the film, when Morteza is sitting alone on the bed, he could have unwrapped the bandage and examined his wound. Even the film could have ended on a shot of this wound. Usually an injured person feels tempted to check on their wound, and he could have done it at this moment of solitude.

AF: It's a good suggestion. I remember that Ms. Safiyari also suggested that the beginning of the film show a hand being bandaged. I think I discussed it with Mani but found it gimmicky. But now hearing what you say, I wish Morteza had been shown doing that instead of smoking.

FM: A bandaged hand is analogous to the home in disarray and could have a similar function.

AF: It's an excellent idea. It could have worked much better than smoking.

FM: Smoking a cigarette is very commonplace.

AF: I think I should find a solution for having too much smoking in my films!

FM: One clichéd gesture for characters to show their despair, or to signal being in thought, is to put their hand on their foreheads. This is something that Morteza does quite a lot, for instance, when he is in his office and talking to his colleague.

AF: No, he did it only in the car.

FM: So it is there, too. But he does the same in the office and incidentally smokes as well. . . .

AF: Yes, Yes.

FM: After playing in *Verdict*,[6] Mr. Entezami[7] said that he arrived at a different view of acting. This different view might only concern a director's method. When I asked Mr. Kimiai about this comment, his answer was that he had asked Mr. Entezami not to move his head and neck while talking.

MH: Sometimes these details are achieved because of the tiniest instructions by the director.

FM: Or, another example, Saeed Raad said that during the shoot of *The Journey of Stone*,[8] for a while he couldn't get the role right, but Kimiai gave him the solution. Raad used to take short steps in his other films, to the point where this became his signature walking style and was even loved by his fans. Kimiai asked him to take longer steps, which solved the problem.

MH: The easiest thing to do to actors with an established style, especially those whose style of acting has won them fans, is to disrupt their habits.

FM: Let's go back to Morteza's bandaged hand, which is never explained and only alluded to as some kind of altercation or accident. . . . In *Escape from the Trap*[9] Davoud Rashidi slams the car hood over Behrouz Vossoughi's hand. The hand is bandaged. Later, during a fight, Behrouz strikes with the same bandaged hand and suffers the pain. With all the care you've shown in this film, it's odd that this bandaged hand elicits no reaction from any character.

AF: I remember that we were supposed to do a shot showing Morteza at home opening the bandage while talking to Mozhdeh, but we forgot to do it.

FM: Even in his workplace no one asks what has happened to his hand. Even Mozhdeh's brother-in-law doesn't ask.

AF: The only one who asks about it is Simin.

MH: So now it can be intuited that apparently she's the only one who cares.

AF: I don't think it would have been any better if everyone reacted to the bandage. It only had to be addressed at the end.

FM: Another remarkable scene is when Morteza goes downstairs to give Mozhdeh a beating on the street. Here the camera stays on the empty elevator as it goes up, and the rest of the fight is not shown. Was it written this way?

AF: Not in the same way. Mani was insisting on getting close to the fight. I had experiences with similar stuff in *Dancing in the Dust* and *Beautiful City* and generally don't like such scenes to be shown from a close distance. Here again I was looking for a way to not get too close to this scrap. I think that getting too close to the scene could have cast Morteza in too negative a light, which might have prevented the audience from ever forgiving him.

FM: In how many ways had you imagined this scene?

AF: Two ways. According to the first idea, the shot would have continued, but I scrapped it because it would have slowed the rhythm. The elevator was supposed to go up to the sixth floor and come down again, showing that Mozhdeh is no longer there and Morteza is surrounded by people. Morteza's friend would have come out of the elevator, taken him into the elevator, and together they'd have gone up. It would have been a very difficult shot to execute, and fortunately once again I resisted the temptation of showing off a complicated shot. The alternative idea was that as Morteza leaves the elevator, the camera follows him and gets close enough to the beating scene for us to see the chador getting lost in the commotion. We settled on this idea, but during editing I was worried that it might not transmit Mozhdeh's feeling and even considered redoing the scene. But when the film was shown to different people, their opinions and reactions greatly helped us get to the present scene. I believe even the best directors need feedback from the audience. If we make the film completely ready and then present it to the audience, part of the creative process is left unfinished. Even during the writing phase Mani was the first audience of my ideas; without him saying anything, I could read from his eyes whether parts left him excited or unimpressed. We handed the script to many friends to read, from our own neighbor to professionals like Mr. Hatamikia,[10] Mr. Tohidi,[11] and Mr. Mo'tamen. . . .[12]

MH: What's interesting is that they all made comments that we found useful and that we used, even if it was as small as a short line of dialogue.

AF: Now I regret that I didn't shoot that scene with Morteza's hand. When the film was edited, I showed it to various people in groups of four or five. Their reactions were important for me. Doing this demands a bit of selflessness, but at the end of the day it will be to the director's own advantage. What is the point of keeping everything under wraps? A surprise launch of the film results in missing out on reactions that could have been useful.

FM: The spectator is clearly surprised to see Simin getting into Morteza's car.

MH: This surprise is mainly coming from the spectator's presumptions and not our narrative. We attempted not to play tricks on the spectator and to hide nothing from them. All the clues to the relationship between Morteza and Simin have been sprinkled throughout the film one by one. At the end of the film the spectator doesn't discover something new to their surprise. They already know whatever they need and have witnessed Morteza's attempt to cover up all along. We had indeed relied on the judgmental attitudes that are dominant in society. It's in fact the spectator's preconceptions about the characters that hinder noticing and discovering the truth. Mozhdeh is worn out and jittery and constantly grumbles, while Simin is bighearted and well tempered. Spectators are so used to the clichéd image of the third party in a love triangle, they find it difficult to imagine Morteza is cheating on Mozhdeh. We don't lie, but rather show our characters' lying skills.

FM: Unfaithfulness is defined by social norms. When two people get married and bind themselves legally, religiously, and socially in a relationship, they are indeed making a moral commitment to each other. When one of them starts an affair, this is considered cheating, even if the cheating person makes some excuse.

AF: I have an issue with this. Morteza doesn't go after another woman; he suddenly finds himself amid something that didn't happen willfully. There's nothing dissolute about the affair in the film, and I tried to remove everything that could give such an impression. It's human nature that anyone, despite their moral and even religious commitments, might inadvertently get themselves caught in such a situation.

FM: Why do you think in recent years infidelity has become a common theme in Iranian films?

AF: The clear and frank answer is that infidelity has become very common in society. When I sent the script to the Ministry[13] for their approval, a good friend of mine advised me not to make the film, because there were many films being made with the same subject. I answered that it doesn't matter and more films on this topic need to be made. Believe it or not, during the first week of the screening, more than ten men and women contacted me to talk about this film's treatment of this subject matter, which, according to them, reflected their own lives precisely. Just this morning a woman phoned—I have no clue how she got my phone number—and asked, "The story of this film is based on my life; has someone told you about me?" She said that a similar thing happened to her on one Chaharshanbe Suri and that she left home together with her kid. I don't know if it is like this everywhere in the world, but it's clear that there are many cases of cheating in our country. So, this subject and this film clearly speak to many of our viewers.

FM: You said that the music at the end of the film starts a few seconds earlier than it had to. I also think that it is too loud.

AF: You're right. Even though we started the postproduction rather early, the sound mixing was left to the last moment and we didn't have time to do final fixes.

FM: Peyman Yazdanian's work is fine, but the piece he composed for the end of the film seems to have been made of a handful of notes that loop.

AF: They don't loop, in fact. The main idea was that the four characters are somehow similar and we didn't want a different tune for each. For each shot we have a melody, part of which doesn't repeat in the following shot. Yazdanian's idea was to use the same melody with small modulations for the rest, and I agreed. I think it would feel less like this if the music started playing later.

FM: Mr. Haghighi, did you go on set?

MH: Not at all. For several reasons. First of all, about ten days after the shoot, I had to start working on *Men at Work*.[14] But the main reason was that after this period of friendship and being close to the project, I had to part ways with it at some point. Probably one reason that I unconsciously rushed to shoot my film was to find a way to cut my ties with this film. During writing we had thought a lot about how to execute the scenes, and despite myself I was imagining how the scenes should be broken down. Naturally Asghar's style of doing the scenes is different than mine and seeing this difference on the set could have been annoying. So, the only way to save myself from this was not to show up on the set altogether. But I was still so curious that I ended up going to the shoot one or two times! Even those two times were so agonizing that I never did it again.

FM: What was the first scene you shot after the death of Taraneh's brother?[15]

AF: It is still a mystery to me how Taraneh was able to do an interview with me under the pretext of talking about her acting, which was published in the *Hamshahri* newspaper. I still haven't found out how, after such a tragic event, she managed to push it to the recesses of her mind and come to the set. Taraneh is extremely fond of acting. I even suggested changing the title of the film lest it remind her of that horrible accident, but she insisted on sticking with the original. What's interesting is that her dad was coming to the set and would sit next to me while we shot many scenes. The first shot we took after the accident is where she goes to the balcony and the neighbor's son throws a message for her. The last thing shot before the accident is the overhead shot showing her on the swing. I feel that she had a premonition about something awful about to happen, because since the previous morning she had a few minor, unlucky accidents. For instance, her mobile fell down for no reason and got smashed. Even a bit earlier she had a nightmare of losing all her teeth, which is usually seen as a very bad omen. While I was taking the shot of Rouhi and Abdolreza on motorbike driving down College Bridge,[16] I had a hunch that a terrible thing was afoot. Nothing happened then, but there was a tiny issue with the camera, and despite others insisting we continue, I decided against shooting it again. Then the next day—which was the tenth day of the shoot—that awful thing happened. It was one of the worst nights of my whole life. I called Mani and told him that I cannot make this film under any circumstances. It must not be made. The producer who noticed my distress agreed to that. Next morning something strange happened. Each morning the driver would pick up Taraneh at 6:30 a.m. and then me, and we'd be driven to the set together. That morning Taraneh called me at 6:00 a.m. and, trying to keep her voice calm, said, "My brother passed away last night. Can I take today off?" Neither of us could continue this conversation. To me it was incredible. I understood how cinema could be so valuable that even losing one's dearest in life wouldn't take away from their love for it. Something else happened, too, which Taraneh doesn't want me to speak about, so I can only touch upon it. She had been interviewed by many, and their very first question was always about that incident. She never responded to that question, until I interviewed her. She always insisted on not discussing this issue. Finally, when the Fajr Festival was over I asked her: why didn't you answer this question? She told me she didn't want this whole story to affect the way people view the film and her performance.

FM: Was this the reason Chaharshanbe Suri appears all the more horrifying?

AF: We shot the Chaharshanbe Suri scenes before that incident. Had we shot them later, they would have turned out even scarier. What's interesting is that this scene was supposed to be shot in the same place where the accident happened, but for some unknown reason I said, "No, let's do it in Tehranpars."[17]

FM: What happened during the editing, and how was the rhythm changed?

AF: The most important aspect of Hayedeh Safiyari's work on this film was that she didn't feel compelled to keep the sequence shots (which comprised 30 percent of the film) in their entirety, no matter how much effort was put into them. She cut them whenever she felt it necessary. I was resistant at the beginning, but after a few days I realized that she was right. Besides it wasn't done to the main sequences of the film. Aside from being a good experience, this collaboration also got me thinking about whether or not we are allowed to use jump cuts in a realist film. In my head I was thinking that it's not right, because by making it so visible, this technique can separate the audience from the intended real mood. But I realized that there is something more important than realism, which is to invoke the mood of that particular day and the rhythm of public presence. These jump cuts—which appear frequently—helped intensify the sense of chaos and step up the rhythm.

FM: You also worked a lot with mirrors.

AF: Mirrors were really important to me. I wanted them to be used repeatedly without being obtrusive. For instance, the small bathroom mirror at the beginning, or the reflection of the city in the side glass of the bus during the credit sequence, or the mirror in the elevator. . . . I was really worried about them standing out too much, so I had them shot so that they could be cut out if needed, but fortunately that wasn't necessary.

FM: There is also a remarkable use of the mirror inside the apartment. In fact, most filmmakers want their use of mirrors to be visible.[18] By the by, how did you cast Pantea Bahram?

AF: There were a few days left until the beginning of the shoot. All the actors, even those playing bit roles, had been selected, but no one was yet cast as Simin. I thought this role could be the Achilles heel of the film, so to speak. I thought of many people for this role, including nonprofessionals. Mani's judgment on actors is different than mine, because he is not watching TV. Many people were tested, but to no end. From the earliest stage of writing, Mani insisted that I meet Pantea Bahram, but I resisted the idea because based on her previous work for theater and television I couldn't see her fitting this role. Even when she came aboard and after four to five sessions of read-throughs, I told her that she might not be the final choice and she agreed. But she did well in read-throughs and understood my worries and kept the role from slipping into a potentially negative type. So I ended up choosing her for this role. In retrospect I see how good Mani's recommendation was. We tried to keep her makeup, dress, behavior, and manner of speaking very simple. Things that attract men to her had to be not in her appearance but in her character; something that Mozhdeh was missing. Things like forgiveness and generosity and traits that matter a lot to Iranians. All of this had to be displayed in the short scene in Simin's place. Things like not charging Taraneh or saying that Taraneh is her niece all relate to this aspect of Simin's character.

MH: We really had lots of discussion over this role. To me it was a given that Pantea would be the best choice for this role. But Asghar's argument—which I also hear from others quite often—was that when an actor has been seen a lot and established in a certain type of role, it's hard to change the spectator's mindset. But I believe that we should move away from this thought that the film is only to be screened in Iran and in February 2005. I prefer to think that twenty years from now someone in, say, Portugal will watch this film who has no idea about Pantea Bahram's previous films, or simply wouldn't care.

FM: But everywhere in the world filmmakers have such considerations, and they cannot overlook the immediate consequences of their choices the way you are suggesting.

MH: This is true, but I say that on these occasions we should also think about the future. If there is a skillful actor, they should be given the chance to break away from their mold. An example is Mahnaz Afshar in *Men at Work*. No one initially could accept her taking part in that film, but the same thing happened and she did well.

AF: The problem is that some people don't voice their concern out of courtesy, but without the issue being explained, no solution for it can be sought out. We clearly expressed our concern right off the bat. Ms. Bahram understood it and used all her skills, and now I'm really happy she's in the film.

FM: What is next for you?

AF: I don't think that I'll make my next film very soon. For the time being, we have two scripts on hand: one is a strange project that I'll say no more about; the other is a script by Mani called *Canaan*,[19] which we are currently working on.

Notes

1. Known as Chaharshanbe Suri, this ancient tradition celebrates the last Tuesday night before the end of the Persian year with bonfires.

2. She is the editor on this film and every subsequent Farhadi production, with the exception of *The Past* (2013).

3. Cast as Mozhdeh's sister.

4. This expression doesn't have a precise equal in English and so has been translated freely and simply in the English-subtitled home video release of the film. "Hawaii, my ass" would have been a more accurate translation.

5. Iranian filmmaker, probably best known for his TV series for children, *Majid's Tales*.

6. A film by veteran director Masoud Kimiai, made in 2005.

7. Ezzatollah Entezami (1924–2018), one of the most respected Iranian actors of all time.

8. A film by Masoud Kimiai (1978).

9. A film by Jalal Moghadam (1971), starring Davoud Rashidi and Behrouz Vossoughi, a superstar of Iranian prerevolutionary cinema.

10. Ebrahim Hatamikia, the filmmaker, who directed *Low Heights* (2002) based on a Farhadi script.

11. Farhad Tohidi, the scriptwriter.

12. Farzad Mo'tamen, the filmmaker.

13. Ministry of Culture and Islamic Guidance, the body that governs Iran's censorship laws.

14. The title of the film Mani Haghighi directed in 2006.

15. Taraneh Alidoosti's brother passed away during the shoot of *Fireworks Wednesday* due to a fireworks-related incident on, of all days, Chaharshanbe Suri.

16. A bridge in downtown Tehran under which traffic and pedestrians cross and the site of several recent protests against the Iranian state.

17. A borough in northeast Tehran.

18. Here, the interviewer seems to allude to director Bahram Bayzaie, known for using mirrors in his films.

19. Mani Haghighi's 2008 film, adapted from an Alice Munro story and also featuring Taraneh Alidoosti.

The Autopsy of Elly

Saeed Ghotbizadeh / 2009

From *Film Monthly* (Tehran), Vol. 27, No. 396, June 2009. Translated by Shahab Vaezzadeh.

Had there been more time, half of this interview could have been spent talking about how Asghar Farhadi was able to immerse his actors in the storyline of *About Elly* (2009). Some of the actors were so affected by the overall tone and atmosphere of the film that they had to make a lot of sacrifices just to continue working on it. Farhadi claims that if you compare the film's earlier scenes with its later scenes, you can actually see just how much grayer Mani Haghighi's [Amir's] hair turned. In fact, during the later stages of production, the film's makeup artist had to dye the gray hairs of several other actors for the sake of continuity. Farhadi told me that Taraneh Alidoosti [Elly] stayed away from the rest of the cast for several days at his request in order to make Elly's disappearance feel more palpable to them. And when she finally rejoined the group, Shahab Hosseini immediately, and very loudly, thanked God that she was still alive! Needless to say, every member of the cast and crew clearly put their heart and soul into the making of the film and had complete faith in what they were doing.

We could have spent half of the interview discussing all of the problems and other issues that surrounded the film from the first day of production to the day of its release. We could have talked about how Farhadi, a likable man with his thick beard and small frame, was never given the recognition he deserved in interviews conducted by critics while he was working on his television series *Tale of a City* (although *Film Monthly* did publish a favorable review and interview with him at the time[1]) and how he feels now, seeing everyone pay tribute to his latest masterstroke in film. We could have focused on all of the rumors surrounding the film and many other things over the past year. We could have talked in greater detail about the subtleties of the film's simple yet intricate production design; or about the full cast rehearsals, which included scenes not featured in the original script; or about the editing and cinematography, which added to many of the film's intricate details. However, I only asked Farhadi what I considered to be the most important questions, and I'm sure that a film as charming as *About Elly* actually merits much greater discussion than the topics explored here.

We conducted two interviews with Farhadi. The first was laid-back and recorded in his office, while the second took place at *Film Monthly*'s office and was much more formal. I had to perform two difficult tasks in order to finalize this article: one was to summarize our discussions, and the other was to make our language more formal and polite. The latter was necessary in order to prevent the intimate and friendly tone of our conversation from sounding like a private, informal chat[2] and also to ensure that the weight of Farhadi's words was not diminished by his friendly and ever-humble tone. We are proud to live in a time when outstanding individuals like Asghar Farhadi make outstanding films like *About Elly*.

—Saeed Ghotbizadeh

Saeed Ghotbizadeh: There is an important emphasis on the time and location of events that take place in your films, as well as your television series *Tale of a City*. It seems whenever you're trying to develop a new story, your first priority is to think about where the events unfold and the period of time that the story takes place in. I'm just asking you this to try to break the ice and get the conversation flowing before we move on to *About Elly*.

Asghar Farhadi: I confine myself to the basic principles of storytelling. I like to tell my story methodically, and that habit, or preference, or whatever you want to call it, presents me with certain restrictions—self-imposed restrictions that allow a methodical approach. Storytelling for me is a technical and calculated task, like the skill involved in designing crosswords or mathematical equations. Crosswords, for example, can be designed in a variety of ways. Those with words that only go down or across and don't intersect one another have two important characteristics: the first is that they're easy to solve, and the second is that solving them is not rewarding. Anyone is capable of designing such a crossword, but designing a crossword with intersecting words requires you to be methodical and also gives those who solve it a greater feeling of satisfaction. What I'm talking about right now has nothing to do with artistic intuition or creativity or anything like that. The idea of being bound by a certain framework or set of rules is one of the most basic principles of being a scriptwriter. One of those rules is time, one is place, and lastly you have the subject. The significance of all those things is, of course, more obvious in theater. I like to know when my story starts and how long it should last, likewise, where it takes place and what it's actually about.

SG: Are the confined locations and short timespans of your films a drawback or an intentional feature?

AF: I don't know why they're like that. I can see your point; looking back on it now, none of that was ever preplanned. It may stem from what I learned as a theater student and the influence of plays that I studied and enjoyed during that time.

SG: Do you have any desire to break that habit for your next film?

AF: Sure! I don't want to be confined to just one particular type of storytelling. But these things aren't always up to writers or storytellers; many of them are required in storytelling. I model my writing on classic films. In classic films, we have an extended narrative arc and certain turning points that need to have a clear place within the story. I've yet to find a better model than that. I don't have any overwhelming desire to break old habits by bending the rules of traditional storytelling. These rules and conventions have been tried and tested for many decades in the history of cinema and are now well established. It's like a chair with four legs—there may be chairs with three legs, but I like the ones with four!

SG: The four legs on your chair seem to have been a little wobbly before *About Elly*! In *Fireworks Wednesday* and *Tambourine*,[3] for example, the main purpose of the story is to surprise and mislead the audience. You enjoy playing with the audience's expectations about the characters and where the story is going before finally revealing that they had misjudged things and the truth was not what it seemed. *About Elly*, however, is more meaningful than that; it doesn't try to trick the audience, although the issue of belief and judgment is one of its major themes. It is much easier to judge the character of Morteza (Hamid Farrokhne-zhad) in *Fireworks Wednesday* or Shirin (Baran Kosari) in *Tambourine* by the end of the film compared to the many characters in *About Elly*. The film's twist is the death of one of its characters, which you warn the audience about several times before it happens. It's like one of those short TV shows where a title card pops up or a piece of music plays before a tragic event in order to prepare the audience for a distressing scene. Elly's death then occurs, and every character becomes embroiled in the aftermath. At that point, however, you're no longer trying to trick or deceive the audience.

AF: I have no doubt that *About Elly* is an evolutionary step forward from past endeavors in my career, and I'm glad that every one of my films has been an improvement on the last. But I disagree with your opinion that the point of the storylines in *Fireworks Wednesday* and *Tambourine* are centered entirely on their surprise endings. The story in *Tambourine* would not have been ruined or lost its backbone had Shirin never been revealed to be a thief or had I removed that whole scene from the film. The revelation of Shirin's true motive for being in that building is just another part of the script's greater narrative arc! The truth is unraveled at the climax of the film for greater effect. That's not to say that the core of the story is based solely on that one plot twist.

SG: I feel like most aspects of the *Fireworks Wednesday* script and its execution are intended to mislead the audience and are less concerned with exploring the characters, regardless of whether they're involved in the film's secret plot or not. In other words, all of the drama is essentially meant to serve that moment when the truth is finally unraveled. The story of *About Elly*, however, is about more than just Elly: it's about each and every one of its characters. *About Elly* is certainly a much better film than any of your previous works, but the point I'm trying to make is that there's a kind of mischief in the narrative of *Fireworks Wednesday* that is meant to mislead the audience, while the goal in *About Elly* is not about fooling the audience, and it feels like we are actually living with the characters.

AF: I agree with what you said about *Tambourine*; the script deliberately jokes with the audience because it fits the tone of the film. But I didn't leave any hints in *Fireworks Wednesday* to deceive the audience. In fact, there are several hints in *Fireworks Wednesday* that help the audience to guess the truth before the final scene, just as there are in *About Elly*. Let me give you an example: Mozhdeh (Hedieh Tehrani) is suspicious of her husband, Morteza, and questions how Simin (Pantea Bahram) knows that they have a flight the next day at four o'clock in the morning. Rouhi then decides to lie. She tells Mozhdeh that a courier tried to deliver the tickets, but, as the buzzer to their apartment was broken, he left them with their neighbor, Simin, who then handed them to her. She does that in an attempt to restore peace to the family. We actually included a detailed scene of Rouhi entering the building so the audience would know that she was lying, but they still believe her somehow, despite seeing everything from the very beginning. The writing and directing in *Tambourine*, however, is partly intended to mislead and surprise the audience.

SG: You once told me that the idea for *About Elly* first entered your mind after seeing an image of someone standing on a beach looking out to sea as he waited for a body to wash ashore. You then said that you had always wanted to make a story out of your group trips with friends. . . .

AF: My friends and I have been traveling together as a group for many years now—you actually know a few of them yourself. Most of them are friends from my university days. Some of them are now parents. I enjoyed our trips together. During a trip to America, someone once asked me where the story of *About Elly* originated. I explained that I'd read a story by Jafar Modarres-Sadeghi about a group of students who gather behind a university literature building and watch a game of table tennis between two of their friends. There was an energy and a certain tone to the author's descriptions that captivated me. Someone else then told me, "But in Germany I heard you say that you'd seen a man standing on a beach and staring at the sea, and that was what sparked the idea for the film."

I explained that there can be many different flashes of inspiration that help to shape a story; they're various components of what makes the final work. I couldn't say which of them was more influential. What is important, however, is that it all starts with a story and then you begin to focus on themes. Some people start with just an idea, or a subject, or a theory, and then they try to find a story that fits their idea. I work the other way around! I find a story and then, as it continues to take shape, I think about its potential content and gradually enrich those ideas. In its earliest form, the story itself may be less of a priority and more of a tool to support an idea. Jean-Paul Sartre, for example, was a great philosopher but not a great playwright because that was his writing process: he wrote to support his own theories.

SG: Was the main storyline in *Fireworks Wednesday* also inspired, like *About Elly*, by a personal experience of yours?

AF: *Fireworks Wednesday* evolved in the same way: I just happened to come across a cleaning service that sent maids to clean people's homes.

SG: So, not a live-in housekeeper like in the old days, but rather a maid with no connection to the family who enters a new property for a few days at a time.

AF: I went to Farahzad, northwest Tehran, one day and spotted the company there. What you said is exactly what stood out to me: that abrupt and untimely entry into the private space of others for a brief period of time.

SG: That central idea is actually the only thing that your four films have in common: strangers entering the private lives of others, getting to know them for a brief period of time, and then going back to where they started, albeit as different people compared to who they once were. After a dispute with his fiancée, the young man in *Dancing in the Dust* enters the life of an elderly man and then returns to where he belongs; the young prison inmate in *Beautiful City*, accompanied by his friend's sister, is given a chance to seek the forgiveness of his victim's parents, and then he returns to prison; Rouhi, the housemaid in *Fireworks Wednesday*, enters the lives of another family for a day and then returns to her husband after her work is done; and the group of friends in *About Elly* go on holiday together and become entangled in each other's lives. The difference with *About Elly* is that, as well as spending time together and judging one another, what keeps the friends entertained is their curiosity about the newcomer in their midst—unlike your previous films, it is a group of people who enter the private life of someone else.

AF: That certainly seems to be the case. Those who enter the story and then leave are not the same people they were at the beginning. I always like to introduce the story and then lead into the main incident. I don't like to begin the story after something has already happened and deal with the consequences of something that occurred before the plot even began. The story of About Elly, for example, could have started after Elly had drowned, or Fireworks Wednesday could have told the story of another day in the family's lives. I follow the days when those key events actually occur and something is discovered; and our protagonist is also at the heart of those events.

SG: Looking at your work from an aesthetic viewpoint, or even a commercial one, I get the impression that you very deliberately place either yourself or your audience in the position of a character that has entered the private lives of others as an onlooker.

AF: The beauty of that technique is that I'm not forced to narrate an event in heavy-handed ways from the writer's perspective. The audience enters the house or the group just as the protagonist does, and they get to see everything as it gradually unfolds before their eyes.

SG: And the audience makes judgments at the same time as the film's characters.

AF: Yes, because the audience and the characters move through the story together.

SG: And your "observer" characters are presented without any distinctive characteristics and shown as rather impressionable.

AF: Every character has many different facets, but we sometimes draw on one of those particular facets and accentuate it. It all depends on the situation that they're placed in. I hate film scripts and plays that have the names of characters and their attributes listed on the first page. For example: "Abbas, construction worker, 25 years old, gripped by suspicion!"

It can be hard to distinguish the basic, prominent differences between characters during the first half of the film, but when circumstances change, they all reveal their individual hidden traits.

SG: Would you agree that your "observer" characters are quite straightforward people that don't have very multifaceted personalities?

AF: They actually reveal themselves little by little, and they're not often very complex individuals.

SG: Unlike Fireworks Wednesday, the "observer" character in About Elly is not the stranger who enters the group but arguably the group itself. In Fireworks Wednesday, Morteza, Mozhdeh, and Simin are not interested in who Rouhi is or where she came from. Elly, on the other hand, is the one who attracts the most attention and scrutiny from the other characters. Rouhi is a different person at the end of Fireworks Wednesday, and all of the characters in About Elly are different people after Elly's death.

AF: Hence, the audience follows that group of characters rather than viewing people and events from the perspective of Elly or the "outside observer."

SG: Absolutely. And this idea of the stranger entering a group of friends has also been explored time and time again in Bahram Beyzaie's[4] plays and films, and it seems to be a good vehicle for telling a story.

AF: It creates a lot of potential in and of itself. American Westerns often revolve around the same idea.

SG: I want to ask you about the sea—the most influential character in *About Elly*—but I don't know what to ask. Directors often use the sea or the shore as the romantic backdrop for a pivotal moment in the relationship between two characters in their films. But the sea in *About Elly* is something very different. The way the film is framed both aurally and visually by the sound of the waves and the deep blue hue of the sea is very similar to what we see in the TV series *Lost*. But after Elly's death, the sea, once so tranquil, suddenly turns into a terrible nightmare. You had some experience working in the desert for *Dancing in the Dust*, but that was not used to the same effect. My question is, why the sea? Why couldn't they be in a forest or by a river?

AF: When you first look at the sea, you don't think about anything other than its positive aspects. But as soon as you're told that somebody drowned and died there an hour earlier, you no longer look at the sea in the same way. This film has the same effect. The sea has no metaphorical significance in the film. I went to the beach one day during filming and just stared at the sea. I thought to myself, "There's nothing more beautiful than this—it's like a small piece of heaven." Later that day, a few members of the crew came very close to drowning and we were all shaken by their narrow escape. I went back to the shore and realized that this little piece of heaven could actually be the most terrifying place in the world. The sea always has those two opposing sides to it.

SG: . . . Like the characters.

AF: In the sense that, like the sea, they always carry their conflicting traits around with them. One particular aspect of their personality might stand out in one instance, but other aspects can surface in different situations. If they'd gone to the mountains and one of them had fallen, or they'd visited a forest and one of them had become lost, would it have had the same effect? I think, in nature, it is the sea that has the greatest capacity for both good and evil.

SG: I think *About Elly* is a film that becomes even more intriguing on the second and third viewing. When watching it for the first time, many viewers don't realize that there are signs beyond the characters' outward behavior that become more apparent later on. In other words, although nothing drastic is happening, every tiny detail of the characters' actions has been carefully considered.

AF: That was one of my concerns while making *About Elly*. If you only watch the first half of the film, you don't really see anything of significance happen; it's a compilation of people behaving in a way that is both normal and familiar to us. Having seen my previous films and written some critical things about them, you may have watched the first few scenes of About Elly and thought to yourself, "Why is everything so simple and mundane?" But as the film continues, all of those details from the first half start to become more important. Like a storage box that you can rummage through and pull something new out of, those details are all little hints and signs that take on new meaning later on. Take the scene where Shohreh (Merila Zarei) claps and cheers, for example: it doesn't seem to mean anything at the time, but that's one of the things we look back on later in the film. That's what I mean by "signs": when you reach a fork in the road, you go back and look at the signs in order to figure out which path to take. My intention was to make sure that their behavior remained completely normal throughout the film and hit all the right notes.

SG: Many of the film's events are repeated at least twice. . . .

AF: Now we're getting into the good stuff! I like to boast that no action only ever happens once throughout About Elly. If the villa's broken wall is ever mentioned, then that is certainly a prelude to some part later in the film where it will be brought up again. It seems obvious that something might be more shocking if it isn't foreshadowed, but I dislike that approach because the audience is only taken aback in the moment and then it starts to feel random and out of the blue. We use various signs to foreshadow Elly's death, and clever viewers will certainly be able to see it coming, but it doesn't matter if those viewers are less surprised when it actually happens—it's more important that the impact of her death stays with them, rather than trying to give them a quick scare. During the sequence where they play charades, Naazi, played by Rana Azadivar, pretends to dream about losing a tooth, which is usually interpreted to mean death. That scene then cuts to a shot of the child that is always playing by the beach, which plants a feeling of trepidation in the minds of the audience.

SG: They're the details that make the film interesting to watch over and over again. Sepideh, played by Golshifteh Farahani, lies to the old local woman, either as a joke or as a way of manipulating her, and tells her that a newly wedded couple have joined them on their holiday. That lie ends up having disastrous consequences, but the thing is, you can easily take for granted that she is lying when you watch the film for the first time because lies are so intertwined with the daily lives of those characters.

We've talked about actions that are repeated throughout the film. When Amir (Mani Haghighi) first enters the villa, for example, he asks where the bathroom is and heads straight for it. Sepideh also jokes that if he uses the bathroom, they'll have to keep the villa. But that same character goes to the bathroom again, both at the end of the film and during the climax of the film's events.

AF: Sepideh also makes her most important decision in front of the bathroom mirror at the end of the film—in the same bathroom that she joked about.
These are all the subtle tools of storytelling. Storytelling is not just a simple case of
"Once upon a time. . . ." What matters in drama and storytelling is how much information you choose to reveal at any given time. The film's introduction is not
just an amusing setup and lead-in for the actual story; there are traces of the
film's conclusion hidden in its introduction as well—you just have to look for
them. It goes back to the logic of crosswords; everything is connected and intertwined. When you find the answer to one question or riddle, it helps you to solve
several other questions. That's why *About Elly* has a much longer setup than my
previous films. Based on Syd Field's rules of screenwriting, I could have inserted
the first catastrophe, i.e., Elly's disappearance, about twenty minutes into the film.
But I waited an extra fifteen minutes to do that because I think that the details in
the introduction serve a major role within the story. All of those details reveal their
true function after Elly's disappearance and death.

SG: Did you try to add things during the writing and directing process that
you hoped would keep viewers entertained when watching the film for a second
or third time?

AF: I think some viewers may decide to rewatch *About Elly* because they
were too caught up on an emotional level the first time around and they want
to examine how and why certain events unfolded throughout the film.

SG: A lot of people also appreciate and pay more attention to the first thirty-
five minutes of the film on their second viewing, knowing Elly's fate.

AF: You can sometimes fill in a crossword without knowing the answers to all
of the questions. Once you've solved some of the columns, you can automatically
figure out the answers to other questions—that's when you go back and review the
empty boxes. None of the suspense or the twists matters when you watch *About
Elly* for a second time, but there is something beyond those plot devices that keeps
you engaged. If it weren't for those hidden ingredients, audiences who understood
everything on their first viewing would have no desire to watch it again. I cannot
stress enough that it is the strength of the story that makes a film entertaining.
If the story is strong and engaging, it distracts the audience from certain details
of the film. Stories like that affect the audience on an emotional and sentimental
level, but that emotional impact gradually leads to more thought and reflection.

SG: Because the audience is so captivated while watching the film, they
can't think?

AF: In a good way, of course.

SG: What's essential is that the film isn't weighed down by some overpowering
idea that inflates the significance of certain scenes. The details that you and I are

discussing do more than just convey an overall message; they serve the story first and foremost. Like you said, every action in the film is repeated. You could also argue that all of those actions and pieces of dialogue are essential to the story. There isn't a single piece of dialogue or development in the film that makes the audience think, "I wouldn't have said that" or "I wouldn't have done that if I were on holiday in the north of Iran."

AF: Imagine if they'd traveled to the north of Iran and Elly hadn't drowned, and they'd all enjoyed a wonderful holiday together—would their behavior in the first half of the film seem unusual or out of place?

SG: No. When they first stop for a break on their way to the Caspian Sea, for example, Elly leaves the group and walks back to the car. Later on, while everyone is laughing and dancing in the villa, she goes outside. While they're eating dinner, Elly leaves to get some salt and takes her time before returning. When they're playing volleyball, Elly suddenly claims that she's tired and has to go. Even in the original film poster, which shows the group watching one of the children during a game of charades, everyone is seated around a large sofa while Elly is sitting on a separate armchair. All of these things seem to me like they're laying the groundwork for Elly's death. But you said something that intrigued me: "Imagine if Elly hadn't drowned." Even in that scenario, her isolation from the group would have been justified; she was a stranger, after all.

AF: You mentioned the volleyball scene as an example. I don't know if you remember this, but after Elly stops playing, the ball bounces toward her and she gently hits it back onto the court. When Sepideh finds herself in the same situation, however, she kicks the ball in the air and out of court. That is the essence of the conflict between Sepideh's character and the rest of the group throughout the story.

SG: She actually does something similar prior to that when she removes the charcoal from a hookah that the men had been smoking—it feels like she's ruining their game there, too.

AF: That is why we as the audience are not taken aback when Sepideh tells the truth about Elly at the end of the story, because we know that Sepideh isn't a character who plays by the rules. That is another example of an action repeated twice.

SG: A lot of information is also repeated. Before finding out what Elly does for a living, for example, we see her escort Morvarid (Sepideh's daughter) to the bathroom. When some of the other characters tell her not to trouble herself, she replies, "I'm used to it." Afterward, we learn that she is Morvarid's kindergarten teacher.

AF: Do you remember when Amir tells Sepideh that they'd found Elly's cell phone in Sepideh's bag and asks her what it was doing there? Sepideh replies, "I spotted it by the porch last night when I was coming inside." How is Sepideh able to respond so quickly with such a lie under those circumstances? If you go back to the first half of the film, Sepideh at one point asks Amir where the key fob is, and he tells her that it's on the porch, next to his cell phone. It's as if that sentence had already been formulated subconsciously in her brain, because the word "porch" was still in the back of her mind.

SG: After hitting Sepideh, Amir seems shocked at himself for raising a hand against his wife, despite always having a short temper and trying to control her since the very start of the film. The way Amir behaves before hitting Sepideh is exactly the same as his behavior during the sequence where he finds out that Sepideh had lied about reserving the villa.

AF: Amir is one of those characters who likes to be reserved and keep a tight lid on his emotions. During the film's opening sequence in the tunnel, everyone except for Amir sticks their head out of the car window and yells. When he is asked his opinion of Elly, he just says that she's a nice girl, while everyone else talks in detail about her personality. That emotional restraint suddenly gives way to the violent outburst that we see in the scene you mentioned.

SG: You could say it's actually the characters that unwittingly reveal themselves in the second half of the film. The way Shohreh defends her child goes way beyond what you'd expect from any mother, and Peyman's harsh treatment of his child after he misbehaves is equally surprising. When Shohreh asks Peyman to make breakfast for the children a few minutes later, he refuses and tells her that the children can go a day without breakfast. While there's no reason for Peyman's outburst, it does seem a strange time, among all the commotion, for Shohreh to start thinking about the children's breakfast. Elly's death almost seems like the perfect excuse for all of these hidden personality traits and grudges to finally reveal themselves. Naazi's extreme state of shock after Elly's death explains why she'd been so passive until that point and only responded, "Whatever my husband says" when asked for her opinion. Most significant of all, the way Amir and Ahmad interact with one another also suggests that they have an unsettled history, which the film refrains from ever addressing properly.

AF: This is the type of film that tries to avoid saying too much. Sometimes, we can spark a great story in the minds of the audience with just one line of dialogue. When Amir and Ahmad get into an argument, Amir tells Ahmad, "You of all people need to keep your mouth shut right now!"

That one sentence is enough to make us start speculating about the troubled past that Amir, Ahmad, and Sepideh all seem to share.

SG: And you don't want to elaborate on it to any degree beyond implication.

AF: That's the whole point. Those are the things that make the movie fun to watch again—because the viewer can look for signs of other stories. That's how the world within the film becomes more expansive.

SG: That is precisely what separates *About Elly* from *Fireworks Wednesday*. When Amir berates Sepideh for trying to help Ahmad, he asks her, "What are you? His sister? His mother?"

There's also a moment when Ahmad and Sepideh are alone together in the car, and he reminds her that Amir will take it the wrong way if she accompanies him: "You know what he's like. . . ."

Those details are presented much more overtly in *Fireworks Wednesday*, and you deal with a similar relationship in that film by announcing it to the audience in no uncertain terms. There are just as many clues in *About Elly* to substantiate that relationship as there are to disprove it, but that back-and-forth dynamic is fascinating.

AF: The more I reveal about backstories that aren't mentioned in the script, the more I restrict the audience's imagination. Useful and concise information broadens the audience's scope for creative speculation.

SG: Watching *About Elly* and hearing some of your thoughts on it has really confirmed to me just how clever and often shrewd you were when crafting this film. You mentioned somewhere that Saber Abar was the only actor that you'd already decided on before making the film. With that in mind, Abar's state of bewilderment after Shirin's sudden departure in *Tambourine* almost seems like practice for *About Elly*. Furthermore, Ahmad and Sepideh's relationship bears many similarities to the relationship between Ali (Bahram Radan) and Mina (Taraneh Alidoosti) in *Canaan*. And the story of the neighbors' trip to the north of Iran in *Tambourine* is also an idea that is expanded upon in *About Elly*.

AF: I don't really know. Those things must have influenced one another because all three films are basically cut from the same cloth, although I should say that I only collaborated on the script for *Canaan*. I was always very careful about revealing just the right amount of information to the audience while writing the script for *About Elly*—too little or too much information could have altered the dynamics of the story. That's one of the things that distinguishes this film from *Fireworks Wednesday* and *Beautiful City*. In order to confirm that Rouhi was aware of Simin and Morteza's affair at the end of *Fireworks Wednesday*, for example, I showed Morteza using the same lighter in front of Rouhi that she'd noticed in Simin's apartment. Furthermore, I also focused on Rouhi as she recognized the scent of the perfume that she'd tried in Simin's apartment earlier that day. So, I drew attention to two different clues there. Thinking about it now, though, one would have probably sufficed.

SG: Apart from two very important shots, there are no moments in *About Elly* that go unseen by another character. In other words, every scene in the film, other than those two scenes, is witnessed by another character. The first is a shot of Elly after Ahmad leaves her alone in the car to go to the shop and she talks to her mother on the phone. The second is a shot of Alireza driving back home at the end of the film. I regard those two similarly framed shots as a sign of the connection between Elly and Alireza, despite all the obstacles that fate threw in their way. The irony of that scene where Elly is alone is that even Sepideh, who is supposed to know everything and repeatedly lies and withholds the truth throughout the film, has no idea that Elly had told her mother she was on a trip with her co-workers and had asked her to feign ignorance if anyone asked where she was. That information is revealed at just the right moment after Elly's death to make Sepideh lose all of her trust in Elly and tell the final lie to Alireza.

AF: How many times have you watched the film?

SG: Twice.

AF: So, you got it! Those two shots also convey the fact that Elly and Alireza are both outsiders. I was always eager to find out why Elly wanted to leave Alireza. I even asked the actors to improvise a few scenes in character together in order to uncover the reason for their irreconcilable differences. I learned one thing as a result of those improvised performances: they drifted apart because they were too passionate about one another. Alireza is a hopeless romantic whose love for Elly torments him and takes away his freedom.

SG: The reason for the breakdown of their relationship can be inferred from Elly's decision to join the group on holiday. Being the child's kindergarten teacher is obviously not a good excuse for going on the trip. Her death, like in Hitchcock's films, could also be the result of a sin that she has committed; she lies to her mother about being on holiday with her co-workers and is also unfaithful to Alireza.

AF: So, she's not innocent.

SG: She's not innocent, but you could also consider Sepideh culpable for her role in the story if you assume that she was once close to Ahmad but ultimately left him and married Amir instead. The fact that Amir is much older and drives a more expensive car than the others certainly steers our thoughts in that direction. What we see in the film is Sepideh's plan to make up for her past mistakes by setting up Ahmad with Elly. On the other hand, she also seems to be using Elly unwittingly to fantasize about a scenario in her own life where she leaves Alireza and rekindles her relationship with Ahmad. So, if you add up Sepideh's reasons for not telling the rest of the group about Elly's engagement, her desire to justify whatever she did in the past is just as important to her as Elly's reputation.

AF: That may have been completely unintentional on Sepideh's part. We're asking ourselves why Sepideh devotes so much time and energy into looking after Ahmad, but, at the same time, why does she keep insisting that Elly spend time with them during the holiday? I find your analysis of the film fascinating, but I didn't really give any thought to the parallel between Elly and Sepideh while writing the script.

SG: I've often seen *About Elly* described as an accurate portrayal of the Iranian middle class, but I don't agree with that description. First, the characters' socio-economic background does not influence their personalities or their behavior and, second, people always try to fit in with others on group holidays regardless of their social status. The most notable aspect of their behavior is not their social status but their temperaments, their customs, and their beliefs. Shohreh, for example, is portrayed as a character with attitudes typical of Iran's more traditional working class throughout various situations in the film. She sometimes acts like a gossiper and a schemer; we see her stirring up trouble from the very beginning, but that act is completely unraveled in the second half of the film.

AF: That's why Shohreh is closer to Alireza than anyone else and understands him so well. When Alireza wants to pray, Shohreh uses a subtle gesture to point him toward Mecca. My concern was whether those nuances would actually be noticed by the audience. That's the behavior of a housewife. There are many other occasions when that point is alluded to: when they're all waiting for the boat to reach the shore and no one knows whether or not Elly has been found, for example, we see Shohreh reciting a prayer under her breath.

SG: Shohreh is also the one who intervenes and lashes out at Amir when he starts hitting Sepideh. I thought to myself that she must have experienced something similar many times before in her own life.

AF: Shohreh is forthright. She's not like other traditional housewives who are quiet, reserved, and never interfere. She doesn't fit the stereotype of a traditional woman.

SG: In fact, it's those modest, traditional women who really fight back when they have to. When Shohreh feels that her child is being mistreated, it really provokes her.

AF: On the other hand, Shohreh is also the type of person who is very quick to judge others. She remarks on how "calm and reserved" Alireza seems after watching him walk toward the rocks by the sea, but she doesn't notice the anger boiling up inside him—again, judgment based on very limited knowledge.

SG: The same can be said of her clapping and cheering.

AF: Shohreh got married and had children rather quickly compared to her university classmates. She doesn't work for a living and has become a stay-at-home mom despite the fact that she has a law degree. You get the impression that she never fulfilled her dreams and has now lost her way.

SG: And she has aged prematurely as a result. She also seems to look at the other women with jealous eyes—from her disapproving comments to the snide remark she makes to Ahmad and Elly when she sees them alone together: "Watch yourselves!"

She basically takes issue with anyone who doesn't speak to her child nicely. She has a lot in common with Amir, who is several years older than the rest of the group and doesn't really fit in with them. It also seems like Amir's relationship with Sepideh lacks affection.

AF: It's completely obvious that there's no love in their lives.

SG: The whole reason Sepideh drags them all on holiday and puts herself in charge is to provide some relief and an escape from the monotony of her daily life. Golshifteh Farahani doesn't really seem like a good choice for the role of Sepideh at first, but her excellent performance quickly puts those doubts to rest.

AF: It's obvious from the way her hair is dyed that she has become detached and indifferent to a lot of things, and she couldn't care any less about what others think of her clothing or appearance. She's always thinking of others and likes to keep everyone together, but in the end we find out she's really the loneliest person of them all. Even I find Sepideh's personality very strange.

SG: Let's go back to some of the film's more pleasant details. The only slogan-like piece of dialogue that we hear in the film comes from Ahmad when he says, "A bitter end is better than endless bitterness."

I noticed a few small details when watching the film for the second time. When Ahmad is asked why he separated from his wife, which is actually a very funny question to ask, he doesn't just quote the German proverb for the sake of sharing its wisdom—he's trying to shut the conversation down before it goes any further. On the other hand, Ahmad's words are an accurate representation of the plight of the characters at the end of the film, who must endure the endless bitterness of Elly's death.

AF: All of the connotations and emotional resonance of that German phrase could have changed the whole tone of the film, so we tried to downplay its significance by doing something different when Ahmad first recites it. To begin with, Ahmad quotes the phrase in German. When Elly asks him what it means, he repeats it in German and tries to make her repeat it before finally explaining what it means. The incomplete story that Ahmad tells Elly before quoting the phrase is also important: "We woke up one morning and washed our hands and our faces, and. . . ."

I thought that Elly had very little time to get to know Ahmad. She was also looking for an excuse to leave Alireza. In that regard, you get a good idea about Elly's reasons for asking Ahmad about his divorce. At the same time, Elly is trying to determine whether Ahmad would actually be a good match for her or not. After asking him about his divorce, Elly is actually wrestling with another thought in the back of her mind. "Why did you split up? Because I also want to leave my fiancé and I don't know how to go about doing it."

After hearing the German proverb, Elly remarks, "That's so true." She seems to have made up her mind about resolving her endless bitterness with a bitter end, and leaving Alireza based on that same logic. I completely agree with you that the proverb reflects the plight of the characters at the end of the film—they told Alireza something that they'll never be able to erase from their memories. Elly is not around to be able to defend herself and tell Alireza that they lied to him.

SG: Those characters then have to pay the price for their lies when Alireza leaves it with them to inform Elly's family of her death at the end of the film. The final shot of their car stuck in the sand is also very symbolic.

AF: I thought a lot about Alireza's character and how to avoid having him come across like a bad guy. Those who read the script were surprised that I'd chosen Saber Abar for the role of Alireza[5]; they all thought that I should choose an actor who would strike fear into the audience when he appeared on-screen.

SG: Both his anger and his restraint are excellent.

AF: And his silence.

SG: The scene where he is sitting in the car with Sepideh and suddenly becomes agitated, and then gets out of the car and starts fighting with another driver, is really a prelude to his subsequent encounter with the rest of the characters.

AF: Yes. Alireza enters the villa and takes five minutes to think about things before going to the bathroom and then looking for a suitable place to pray. But the judgments about him begin immediately. One of them comments on how reserved and nice he is—just like the judgments made about Elly. Peyman claims that Elly's behavior was "all for show," and Shohreh says that she feels ashamed for having cheered for Elly and Ahmad and then declares in front of everyone, "I don't have the heart to lie to [Alireza]." They completely forget that Alireza had lied to them just a few minutes earlier about being Elly's brother.

SG: Then they take another vote on whether or not they should lie to Alireza.

AF: Throughout that scene, I was trying to pose the question: is the majority always right? Could the opinion of one outstanding person in the minority actually be wiser than the majority? That's where all moral standards start to fall by the wayside. In the end, despite all of the lies that she had told until that point, Sepideh wants to tell Alireza the truth, but the rest of the group decides that hiding the truth would be the best course of action.

SG: Is the charity box that we see at the very beginning of the film the same one that Amir refers to at one point?

AF: Yes. It's another one of those things that is referenced twice throughout the course of the film.

Notes

1. Translated for—and appearing as the first interview in—this volume.
2. Usually the differences between spoken and written Persian are considerably significant.
3. The 2008 film, written by Farhadi and directed by his wife, Parisa Bakhtavar.
4. Iranian stage and screen writer-director and a key figure in Iranian New Wave cinema, now living in self-exile and teaching at Stanford University.
5. Abar is mostly known for playing calm, gentle characters.

Bitter Truth, Sweet Expediency, and Denied Redemption

Massoud Mehrabi / 2011

From *Film Monthly* (Tehran), Vol. 29, No. 424, March 2011. Translated by Philip Grant.

My interview with Asghar Farhadi took place after his joyous return from the Berlin Film Festival, where his film *A Separation* (2011) won the Golden Bear. Our conversation explores in detail how the film took shape, Farhadi's methods and techniques, and his use of dramatic storytelling to craft this jewel of a film.

—Massoud Mehrabi

Massoud Mehrabi: Before we talk about the film itself, let's talk about what was happening offstage, some of which might be described as out of your control, as it would be for any Iranian filmmaker in your place.

Asghar Farhadi: I had anticipated that there would be offscreen stuff going on, more so than when *About Elly* was screened at the same festival. Because of what has been happening this year,[1] I was prepared beforehand for people to talk more about the issues of the day in Iran than about the film. At the first screening at the festival, though, something happened that focused attention on the film itself. The press reviews that came out the following morning meant that there was more talk about the film than about other issues.[2] At various festivals there has been a curiosity about Iranian society that has meant that we have had to answer questions about that as well as about the film. I've had to prepare myself to respond to those questions in a helpful way, without casting a shadow over the film, so that people don't see it from a noncinematic point of view as just something made under particular conditions in a different society. I believe as a filmmaker that, whatever problems I may have, I don't have the right to impose this on the audience just because of those problems. It was me who chose this profession; no one made me become a filmmaker. For the same reason, I don't like the audience to know about my mishaps and problems before seeing the film.

In fact the film helped in the sense that these issues didn't take up as much time and energy as I had expected, and we talked much more about the film itself. Even so, there wasn't a single journalist who, alongside all their other questions, didn't ask a question about the state of Iran and of filmmaking there.

MM: These questions offscreen have been around for more than two decades now, going back to when Iranian cinema started appearing on the international festival scene. Those days were even more eventful; people watched the films in astonishment and their first question would be, "You mean to say cinema exists in Iran too?" And after that the political questions would begin, the kind that rained down on filmmakers caught in an impasse, about the Iran-Iraq War or whether cinema was religiously forbidden. The mood has changed significantly since then, however, and these days Iranian cinema has managed to find its own particular audience. Which features of your film have provoked curiosity in critics and audiences?

AF: Not only in Berlin, but at other festivals too, there are two types of people who watch Iranian films. One is the kind of person who regards Iranian cinema as if it were encyclopedic information about a society from which, otherwise, not a great deal of information is forthcoming. This group of people likes to get their information from cinema and see it as a means of acquiring everything they need. Information about the culture, politics, and people of Iran. And then there's an audience that in recent years has learned to separate these two categories; in other words, they know to get that information elsewhere, if that's what they want, and not to belittle film by turning it into a tool for that purpose. Fortunately in Berlin most of the audience for A Separation came from this second group. When they saw the film they treated it as a work of cinema. Even so, there are places in the film where they had no choice but to seek answers to their curiosity about Iranian society. One such question: if your society is in such and such a state—since that is how it seems from the outside—then how were you able to make your film and get it released? This is one of the hardest questions they ask. You can't tell them in a short reply how you did what you did. In my responses I always tell them that the situation there is so complicated and multifaceted that pretty much anything can happen. That means that despite all the problems, it is possible to work.

A second group of questions was about the characters, especially the female ones. Female Iranian characters generate a lot of curiosity in them. On the one hand, they hear that limitations on women's activities in society exist; on the other, in the film they see how active women are, how strong their presence is, and, in fact, that they are the ones who get the film's motor going. Their question, then, was whether this is the reality of your society or rather what you hope it might be. My answer was that this is the reality of a part of our society, that women, perhaps because of the inequalities imposed on them—not just in recent years but throughout history— are for that very reason more active in society than men. The second point is that, dramatically speaking, women are better at starting the motor of the story.

MM: At first glance, if we compare *About Elly* and *A Separation*, it seems like the first has a more universal theme, and perhaps non-Iranian critics and audiences might find it harder to relate to the latter. Because its themes and issues are Iranian and therefore the product of our social conditions. Yet reactions were the opposite of what might have been expected, and they were able to relate more to this film than the earlier one. Were the questions you got concerning *About Elly* different only in relation to the role of women, or were there opinions and assumptions about Eastern culture in them too?

AF: I had also imagined that non-Persian-speaking audiences might not relate to *A Separation* as fully as they did to *About Elly*. Non-Persian speakers won't get certain parts and aspects of *A Separation*, and for that reason I wasn't too hopeful that it would impact them much. Maybe because I'd had the experience of *About Elly*, I thought I knew from which angle they would relate to an Iranian film. But things turned out the opposite way, and it was right away at that first screening. I asked many of those who saw or wrote reviews of the film what they thought, and most of them said that what attracted them about *A Separation* was one thing, namely the attention to details. They said they came to believe in the world of the film through its details, and even though those details were specific to Iranian society, when each of those little pieces was laid out beside one another, they saw the bigger picture of the film as a whole.

Foreign audiences were certainly quicker to relate to and understand *About Elly*, and after the screenings they would stand outside the cinema and talk to me about it. Whereas after viewing *A Separation*, they preferred not to speak about it that day. Most conversations were deferred until the following day, and the reviews came out a little later. I was totally aware of the difference. The night *About Elly* came out, I was deep in conversation about it until the middle of the night. Conversely, when *A Separation* came to an end, I saw the audience on its feet applauding for ten minutes, but afterward they preferred to go to a quiet corner, perhaps in keeping with the film's mood and ambience. This difference in the reception of the two films was palpable. It seems that it was easier for them to understand *About Elly*, but not because that film has non-Iranian components, more because for them getting beneath the outer layers of *A Separation* required more time.

MM: You've won a number of prizes at different festivals for *A Separation*: the Berlinale's Golden Bear—also the two Silver Bears for the actors—is a very important prize. Will these prizes mess with your mind, or make your work harder?

AF: The further away I get in time from winning these prizes, the less intense my happiness is. I hadn't expected to win the Golden Bear, and I actually thought we'd get the two prizes for the actors. In Berlin it was unprecedented for anyone to win more than two prizes. As it happens, I was completely prepared not to win anything. I was happy when I got the prize. But I was conscious of the fact that if I got stuck in that moment then I would find it hard to make my next film and that I shouldn't let it cast a shadow over me.

I believe that festivals and prizes are more useful for the films than for the filmmakers. That's because it helps them get better known and find more audiences across the world. But getting prizes doesn't lead filmmakers to make better films. The reason is that festivals, despite all their good features, suffer from a major defect: they bring the cinematic tastes of filmmakers closer together. That is to say, they provide filmmakers with a definition of good and bad in cinema, which they then try to follow. After a while they see that their films are quite similar, because they are unconsciously following a single model. And for the same reason it shouldn't be forgotten that the prize is for the film, not the filmmaker. They give it for the best film, not the best filmmaker. When we confuse these two ideas, the filmmaker's task becomes more difficult. You can never say to a filmmaker, "You are the best," any more than you can say to a driver, "You are the best driver," because all that needs to happen is for them to have a minor accident and then that's all over. This job is a difficult one and someone like me needs to be aware that this prize isn't the prize for the best filmmaker, because if I imagine that I've won the best filmmaker's prize then I won't need to make any more films.

MM: Let's keep looking at the previous question, but from a different angle. Wherever someone travels in the world, the world gets smaller for them. Do these prizes motivate you, or is it like traveling, and they make your motivations smaller and smaller?

AF: When you hold these prizes in your hand, they're no longer as big as they were before you'd held them. When you come close to this kind of success, because you've won them, other things grow in significance instead. You search for other motivations to carry out your next project. To be honest, at the moment I'm so close to what has happened that I can't see it properly and figure out what my own relationship to it is—whether this prize will be a motivation for me or a tool, a cane I can use to go up the next step more easily. I constantly tell myself that it's just a tool so I can jump forward and start the next stage. It's very easy to say, but in practice you have to be careful, because experience has shown that for all the joy and confidence prizes give to filmmakers, they can just as easily be banana skins that make filmmakers fall flat on their faces in their next projects.

MM: Experience has indeed shown that getting a prize tends to cause people to fall flat on their face more often than not. For example, if we look at the filmmakers who've won the big prizes over the last five decades at Berlin, Venice,

Cannes, and in general the other major festivals, most of their follow-up works haven't been as good as the films they won the prizes for.

AF: In reality filmmakers—not always but often—start competing with themselves after this happens to them. That is to say, they try to surpass themselves so that they can repeat their previous success. After *About Elly* and the prize I won in Berlin, the method I adopted, maybe unconsciously, was to think that it would be a mistake—if not impossible—to imagine I could duplicate that success on the world stage with my next film. I should make a more locally rooted film and depict that Iranian atmosphere I know so well, so that the film might forge a stronger relationship with domestic audiences than the previous one had done. This method actually helped bring this about. I mean, when I showed the script for *A Separation* to some of my friends, they all unanimously said that, compared to my previous work, this film couldn't be successful outside Iran. I remember that I had a foreign producer for another film, and they were worried that the reputation I'd acquired outside Iran for *About Elly* would be damaged by this script, and the project we were working on outside Iran would be affected. That's how great the concerns were. But I thought I shouldn't take that path, I mean to compete with myself, and I was fortunate that, while I didn't think these things would happen for me, they did.

MM: *A Separation* is an excellent screenplay, full of complicated details. It could be said that it encapsulates your earlier scripts, with characters that could all be assigned parts in those works. You've probably already been asked where you found the main idea for the film. What was the source of the first spark?

AF: From several different places. From a thematic point of view, it's a continuation and expanded version of the theme of my earlier stories; I mean that some of the themes in *About Elly* and *Fireworks Wednesday* take on greater significance in this film, becoming deeper and acquiring new facets. I start with the story and then I find the theme in the story, rather than having a theme that I then find a story for. If you ask where the story for this film came from, I have to answer that it came from several different places. It was partly a product of my personal experiences, particularly Nader's relationship with his father, who has Alzheimer's. I had someone close to me who had Alzheimer's, and I was haunted by that. I had a number of images of this person in my mind. There was nothing to tie these images together, but gradually a story emerged to link the different images, like the image of Nader washing his father in the bath. Before the story existed, I had this image in my mind. It was one of those images that wouldn't let me go, as if it kept showing itself so that it could be used somewhere.

Something else that drew me to this story was that every morning for years I used to take my daughter to school and then in the afternoon bring her home. I always thought it would be novel to depict my relationship with her and the conversations we had in the car cinematically: a father's relationship with his adolescent daughter. It was one of those things where I was constantly looking for an opportunity to put it in a film. These sparks came from different places and landed next to one another and led me to finding a story that could fit all the different pieces of the puzzle together, pieces that originally had nothing to do with one another. I believe that all of the themes in the world are hidden in any one story. Depending upon the concerns of the writer, the process of writing the story makes those themes they are most concerned with become clearer and more prominent, whether consciously or unconsciously. For that reason most of the things I've written, when it comes to their themes, are continuations of one another, and in each new film I've tried my best to expand upon them.

MM: The problem with most films in Iranian cinema is their endings. It looks like people find a good subject, then say, "Let's go and make it," and then—God is great—when we get to the end part we'll figure it out. This is a defect that applies to many of our prominent filmmakers. But your films have good endings. Do you figure out what the ending will be as you're writing the script, or do you build your story around it from day one?

AF: For me, writing has a number of stages. First, I think that the most ordered part of filmmaking is the writing part. I mean that you can't be disorganized when you're writing, because what you're actually doing is arranging a geometrical structure, and you need everything to be organized, including your writing method. Spontaneity and intuition are part of writing, but that doesn't mean you should be disorganized when writing and allow yourself to write just when the feeling comes to you. To start the process, I have scattered notes, I write down individual ideas or images on a piece of paper. This turns into a big pile of notes that have nothing to do with one another and sometimes even contradict one another. These include anything from characters' appearances to the locations, scenes, and images that are in my mind. They're not ruled over by any logical relations or cause-effect relationships. After this stage, I sketch out the structure of the story. I started writing this way after collaborating on the script for *Fireworks Wednesday* with Mani Haghighi. It's very easy to do. I draw a line on a piece of paper. I divide it into different parts: beginning, middle, and end. Then these sections are subdivided into smaller parts. In reality what I'm doing is finding a place for the pillars of the structure I want to build. In any story there are two really important pillars, the pillar of the beginning and the pillar of the end. Or as a friend says, they are like two nails between which you hang a clothesline. If either one of these nails is loose, then when you hang out your clothes they fall to the ground. That's why if I don't have the ending at this stage, then I won't start writing or working on the details. The reason for that is obvious: you arrange all the details so that they lead up to the ending. If that's not what you have in mind, you don't know what the path to the ending will be or what path the story will take. In my opinion, writing a screenplay without an ending is much harder than first determining the ending, then writing. For that very reason, in all my work I make sure to find the ending when I'm working on the structure. Now, it's possible that while I'm writing, the way I execute the plans or the form of the building, and even the ending, might change or get moved around, but at every stage I know what my path is and what my destination is. It's possible that in the middle of the story I might decide that the ending's no good, so I'll find another one, but you can't move without knowing where your endpoint is.

MM: Given what you've just said, it sounds like you really prefer the model and rules for screenwriting set out by Syd Field. That is, plot points, confrontation, climax and reversal, the arc of development, and dividing the storyline into the first thirty minutes, the second sixty minutes, and the final thirty and so on. After all these years of filmmaking and all the experience you've acquired, why are you still so interested in this great master and his rules? And to what extent do you change the rules and the grammar to make them your own?

AF: Because I don't have a better model, I follow this model completely, but I do change certain things when appropriate for the story. The first point to mention is that these rules are not an end in themselves. They are tools that can help us more easily do what we want, namely make an absorbing film. What does that mean? It means a film that from its opening convinces the viewer to sit down and watch the whole thing. And in reality the model Syd Field gives us helps bring this about, and nothing else. This means that Syd Field's rules don't provide us with a better theme, don't tell us how to do that or what the theme should be; they only tell us how to make a more engrossing film. They simply help us to get to our destination more easily. The rules can be changed to some extent, but the general validity of these rules has passed so many tests in the history of cinema. It's impossible or at least very difficult to make a film that tells a story and is full of suspense without following this model. And contrary to what many think, the Syd Field model isn't just a dry, formulaic structure; rather, it comes along with you and opens up a path for you. It's impossible to say exactly in what minute of the script which event should take place—normally it says between x and y minutes. The second point is that Syd Field didn't invent these rules. These rules already existed, and he extracted them from many of the world's most successful films. He himself saw his work as the fruit of reading so many of the great screenplays.

As regards the second part of your question, according to Field's rules one ought not have such protracted openings as I have in mine. In *About Elly*, the inciting incident takes place at the thirty-fifth or fortieth minute, which makes it a very long introduction. In *A Separation*, if we consider that the old man being tied to the bed is the inciting incident and that the storyline changes at that point, then, again, we're dealing with a very long introduction. I mean to say, in these cases I haven't followed Syd Field's rules, but I justify them to myself by thinking that much of what takes up so much time in the introduction isn't really being deployed as an introduction. Rather, these are clues and details that will become meaningful in the closing stages of the film, so that, for instance, as the child is taking the trash bag downstairs in one scene, the bag splits open. This takes up a lot of time in the opening, and we might ask why that is so. But at the end of the story, when there is a reference to the bag splitting open, we realize that it was right for it to be in the opening. It yields returns elsewhere. That's why there are differences of structure in the introductions of my two most recent films—and to some extent *Fireworks Wednesday*—and the Syd Field model. My introductions are longer because I use them to establish clues. Then the audience has the luxury of being able to go back and watch the introduction again.

MM: Have you ever wanted to go to one of Syd Field's classes?

AF: I've never felt like going to a class, but I do want to hear the latest version of what he has to say, to find out what he thinks now and to find out what changes he's made to his theory. That appeals to me, and I'm following up on it. I'd like to know how he intends to adapt his rules to the kinds of narratives that have emerged in modern cinema. I think it's probable that new theories can be extracted from the more modern films that have been made in recent years. But let's not forget the fact that Syd Field's rules owe more to classical theater than they do to cinema. That is to say, the story arc that he speaks about in a screenplay is in large part taken from definitions that belong to classical theater. What he says about the rules isn't in fact much of a departure from what Aristotle says about drama. So, let me correct what I said. It seems that he has extracted these rules from a history of artistic performance rather than from cinema itself.

MM: I am guessing that you enjoy screenwriting more than you do filmmaking. I mean to say that the pleasure you get from being a creative writer is more than what you derive from putting it into action on set.

AF: Yes, definitely. When I write, at that very moment I know what I've done, whereas when I'm shooting I have to wait for a whole series of things to happen, and only then do I understand what I've done. I find it really hard to just sit around not knowing what will happen or what kind of film it will be, whereas at the writing stage I can read the script very quickly and figure out what's happened. At school we've all experienced having to solve equations with a number of unknowns. Aside from the intuitive part of writing, which comes from inside you in an unconscious way, it's the mathematical part of it that's attractive to me. You arrange a number of elements and ultimately you find the one you want. I'm not really one for hustle and bustle, so writing sits better with my character. I find solitude pleasant.

MM: How much do your screenplays change during shooting? Do the ideal scenes and feelings that you create freely during the writing process turn out the same as when you are filming, or do the films always have to catch up with the scripts?

AF: It's pretty rare for my scripts to undergo major changes on the set. There are changes to the details, of course. During preproduction and when I'm choosing actors, I make changes based on others' suggestions. On the set, however, I don't believe in accepting suggestions about the film's overall structure, because there you don't have the opportunity to consider how a suggested change might alter one of the pillars of the script and the rest of the film. You might get deceived by an attractive suggestion and then see that it's damaged the film. In any case, I don't take that risk. I might make a change to the details on set, but not a fundamental alteration to the overall structure. There have been scenes that were better in the script but when performed didn't turn out as well. There have also been scenes that didn't seem quite finished in the script, but when we shot them they turned out to be complete. During the shooting of *About Elly* and *A Separation*, if I encountered a scene that wasn't as good as what I'd had in mind in the screenplay, I repeated it. That's why in *A Separation* we have four or five sequences that we had finished shooting but then shot again.

MM: On this basis, then, you're saying that people working on the film, from the production and costume designers to the cinematographer and the actors, shouldn't interfere with the film.

AF: No, they can, just not when we're shooting. Shooting is when we perform, it's not when we make fundamental changes. I don't give myself the right to make fundamental changes to the script, either. But during preproduction, and when we're rehearsing with the actors, then it is possible for colleagues to make their suggestions, and I keep things open for that purpose. As soon as the day comes when the key is turned in the lock, though, no one has the right to create any doubts about the script. This may sound stern, but it yields good results.

MM: Before you start shooting, do you have a complete read-through of the script, or do you work with each of the actors separately on their parts?

AF: Rehearsal methods for these two films have been different from the more usual method. I'm not a great believer in read-throughs, and I don't rehearse the scenes as they are in the script, because I want it to stay fresh and for the actors to get a feel for the scene. Instead I sketch out scenes that don't appear in the film, and the actors work more on rehearsing those.

MM: For example?

AF: For example, in *A Separation* Nader and Simin's relationship is never a good one, but in rehearsal they practiced scenes from their good times together as actors. Or nowhere in the film do we see Ms. Ghahraii—played by Merila Zarei—getting involved in Nader and Simin's private life, but in rehearsal we sketched out scenes where she talked with Simin about personal matters and they performed studies of these. These studies don't exist in the film. In this way the characters got to know themselves and the people they were playing opposite better. Another part of the rehearsals was done out in the field and carried out depending on the character. For example, Babak Karimi, who played the role of the interrogator, spent a lot of time attending court and watching an interrogation we had found. Sareh Bayat practiced putting her chador on in public. We made her take the bus to the shrine of Shah Abdolazim[3]; she spent the whole day on the move and there was someone with her the whole time to make sure she rehearsed properly. I showed everyone a documentary several times, a documentary about shoes, so that Shahab Hosseini could see it and familiarize himself with shoemaking. When you're just talking about it, it seems like it can't have much of an effect, but in practice it has a huge effect and the actors get very close to their roles. Then we start on the part of the rehearsals that is completely about technique, practicing voices and posture, something we did in a theater space and according to the rules of theater, at night on a theater stage, rehearsing expression and posture.

MM: On what basis did you select the characters' names? Nader, Simin, Termeh, Razieh, Hojjat, Somayeh. . . . Were they taken from people around you, or were they based on how the audience would imagine such people, or types, in Iranian society?

AF: More from my own personal life. About the time my daughter was born, I thought that her name might be Termeh, but it didn't happen, so I wanted the character to be called Termeh instead. The character of the old man, whose name we never actually hear in the film, is called Morteza in the script, which was the name of someone close to me who passed away. I often get inspiration from the names of people I know in my own life. But when it came to the film's title, I needed two names that would be in harmony with one another. The "a" of "Nader" and the "i" of "Simin" go well together.[4] No other names went well together like that. If, for example, I'd chosen "Sara" instead of "Simin," "Nader and Sara" wouldn't have had the same harmony. That's how these two names were chosen. Rather than helping the audience when they are watching, these names help me when I'm writing, so that I can imagine what the characters look like from afar. Constructing a model—and not always such a clear one—of the person I'm writing about really helps me to get to know the character.

MM: When you're writing a script, do you have particular actors in mind? If Shahab Hosseini or Leila Hatami are going to play in the film, do you write so that the parts are tailored to their physique and behavior—like Shahab's momentary flashes of anger? Or do you let yourself be free to write and tell yourself you'll choose later? How did you choose the actors for this film, for instance?

AF: It depends. Every film is different. For *Fireworks Wednesday* I knew whom I wanted for practically every character as I was writing it, except for Simin, the neighbor's wife. For *About Elly*, too, I knew most of the actors I wanted. For *A Separation*, I had some of the actors in mind before I wrote the script. For instance, I knew that Shahab Hosseini would play the role of the working-class man. At the time I hadn't yet found a name for the character. I knew that my daughter would play the role of Termeh. And I knew that Leila Hatami would play the role of Simin. But I didn't know who would play the parts of Nader, his father, and Razieh. There were people I had in mind, but they didn't happen. For Nader I was thinking of Babak Karimi, without ever having seen him up close. The reason was that I imagined that his own father, Nosrat Karimi,[5] could play Nader's father. I thought that if they were played by an actual father-son duo, the story would really come alive. Despite my best efforts, I couldn't get Nosrat Karimi for the part, which meant that Babak also didn't work out, but I straightaway thought of Peyman Maadi. I was halfway through writing when I realized he would play the role of Nader. One of the people I found very late in the process was Sareh Bayat. In fact, I found her early on, but the process of choosing her took a long time. We rehearsed for a very long time, on the condition that if she turned out not to be suitable for the part she wouldn't be upset. She accepted my terms, came to all the rehearsals highly motivated, and, in the end, out of the two candidates I had, she was the one who was chosen. But often it turns out that I know which actors I want when I'm still working on the outline of the film.

MM: How do you prepare the actors so they get into character and really enter into the depths of their personalities? You can develop the characters in your mind, and write instructions for them on paper, but actually getting them to that point where they are playing the parts is a complicated job. What kinds of tricks do you use? Would you share them with us?

AF: I don't accept the theory that a role is like clothes that you can tailor to the individual actor. In practice nobody is able to do this. Everybody is made up of multiple facets existing all at once. That means someone who is generous and free can be dependent and uptight at the same time. Someone who is hardhearted can also be very gracious at certain moments. This means that every person and every character has multiple facets. If you can find those personality traits that are common to both actor and role and rub them together, then the two become very close. For instance, an actor is to play a part in which anger is very prominent. You have to know an actor whom you can carefully observe to learn in which situations they get angry, and then try to harmonize the actor with the part. In *Fireworks Wednesday*, in *About Elly*, and in *A Separation*, I tried to make sure that the piece connecting the role and the actor were made of the same kind of material.

For example, in his personal life Peyman Maadi has multiple psychological, mental, and behavioral traits. After many years of friendship, the main impression that I have of him is of someone who is highly principled. That means there are clear lines in his personal life. And then I have a character called Nader in whom these characteristics are also prominent. In my conversations and rehearsals and studies with Peyman, I try to constantly emphasize these facets of his personality and in that manner bring him closer to the character. After a while, all the actors say that the part they're playing is themselves, because if they were put in a similar situation they would behave in the same way. They're not aware that because all their efforts come from a place where they resemble the character they're playing, they end up being closer to that character. When actor and character have come close in that way, the rest of the job isn't hard, we're 90 percent done. You just have to find a way to bring out those common characteristics, which is something you can do in rehearsals where you focus on technique. Most of the time the actors' voices are not prepared, which is not a problem at all. In every film they have to be ready to work toward the required voice.

Another part of the job is to know themselves and their character. The worst way of doing that is for the actors to constantly talk directly about the different facets of their character. If, however, you set up situations where the actors can discover themselves and get to know those different facets of the character, it becomes a mental habit. For instance, if the image Leila Hatami—and we, too—has of herself is a calm and flexible person, we can then try to bring out that side of her that sometimes behaves differently, not calmly. I make use of the actors' own personalities in order to bring them close to their characters.

MM: It sounds as if you dial up the actors' feelings for the role to a very high level, indeed, so you can get the performance you want. For example, in the behind-the-scenes footage I saw of Shahab Hosseini hitting his head in the courtroom, you worry that he hurt himself. Doesn't this give cause for concern? Because he'd gone so deeply into his role, there might've been trouble for you both.

AF: Yes, this danger does exist. Both in *About Elly* and the film you just referenced, *A Separation*, we found ourselves in this situation. You can't turn up the dial on an actor to exactly where you want it, keep it there, and control it. It can go higher than you intended, and the actor's distance from the role can get so small they forget they're acting. This is dangerous, but most of the time it helps. There's no problem if others imagine that I am merciless. What matters is that the roles are good ones and in the end the actors are satisfied with the work they've done. I watch out so that nothing bad happens to the actors, and fortunately, despite all the rumors, nothing bad happened to anyone either in *About Elly* or in this film. I don't think there's any solution, because we have to suppress the gap between the actor and the character, and the actor should feel that they are the character.

I'll give you an example so that we can see if in practice this is what happens or not. In *About Elly* I wanted to shoot the scenes in which Elly disappears. Elly had drowned in the sea and the rest of the actors were searching for her. I asked Taraneh Alidoosti, who had been with the group every day, not to join them from now on, to stay behind so that the others would really feel her absence. So, remember that she had been together with the rest of the group for some time, whether she was needed for a scene or not, but then from that day when she was supposed to be drowned onward, she stayed in the hotel and didn't come to set. Everyone felt her not being there. One afternoon when they had been looking for Elly in the sea—it took us fifteen days to film these scenes—everyone had been in the sea and was wet from head to toe. They were going back to the hotel when we ran into Taraneh Alidoosti, who had left the hotel to run some errands and was heading back there, too. Shahab Hosseini said, from the bottom of his heart, "Thank God she's alive!" He had believed in the scene so much that when he saw she was actually alive he was profoundly happy and relieved. I believe that if we arrange the actors' inner world, the exterior sorts itself out and we get good performances.

MM: This begs the question: don't you think this method could be considered manipulating the actors?

AF: As it happens, when you simply arrange the actor's exterior, and you ask them just to carry out the movements mechanically, you are using them like an adjustable wrench. Whereas if you get help from the actor's inner world and put them in the right environment, they do lots of things without even being asked. For instance, when Shahab Hosseini hit his head on the door, I hadn't asked him to do that, but that situation had been arranged in such a way that he just went and did that himself. I hadn't asked him to do that with so much force. But it happens that the actor is so involved and enjoying it so much that they are totally on board with what you want to do and sometimes they are even ahead of you when it comes to the performance. I happen to think that using this method shows how much importance you give actors, rather than choreographing their every move and then fixing the rest ourselves in the editing phase. That said, I do accept that the way I get a performance out of actors is a little unusual, but they themselves like this way more.

MM: I asked this because after working with you, all the actors move on to act in other films. If the actors have had the role imposed on them, it's possible that other films, or even the actors' lives, might be affected. Of course, there are ways to compensate for this. For example, when volleyball players come off the court, they don't take them to the locker room straightaway. They stretch for half an hour until they get free of the atmosphere and pressure of the game. What methods do you use to help actors get free of their characters?

AF: After we've finished shooting pretty much every sequence that drains the actors' energy, we take an unplanned break so that the actors can get away from that environment. And in both films we had fun activities throughout the project, things like celebrating whenever it was someone's birthday. It wasn't like we spent the entire time in an emotional and high-pressure environment. Even so, I tried to make sure that people's relationships with their characters weren't entirely severed when off set. For example, if an actor didn't have anything to do for four days, that didn't mean they could just go away and come back four days later. During those four days, even if they had nothing to do, I'd have them come back to the set under some pretense or other. After a while the actor began to enjoy this atmosphere and wasn't hurt by it. And after a film is finished an actor can't immediately go and work on another film. It takes a while to come slowly out of the role and the story and the general atmosphere of the film; for example, a little while ago I was talking with Shahab Hosseini and he said that some nights he still feels for Hojjat and worries about what will happen to him.

MM: So, in reality you trust the actors' professionalism to help them distinguish between your film and those of others. This confusion happens more in those films with nonprofessional or child or adolescent actors. There are notable examples where the character they play in the film remains with them forever and spoils the rest of their acting life.

AF: One of the reasons I didn't look to use nonprofessional actors was exactly that. Because when working with nonprofessionals I've seen how dangerous their expectations are after the film. My preferred method is to work with professional actors but get them to perform like nonprofessionals: I mean exactly like life. That's why I chose Peyman Maadi. He knows cinema, he's a trained, professional actor, but the substance of his performance style is "nonprofessional." Even Hamid Farrokhnejad, despite all his acting experience, still acts substantially like a nonprofessional. Mani Haghighi too. It's better that way than bringing in someone who doesn't know cinema. Because there's no hiding how much damage it does to nonprofessionals. In any case, since *Beautiful City*, I don't think I've used nonprofessionals. I've only brought in actors who are at least familiar with cinema.

MM: Actors, from professionals to extras, have different temperaments. How do you coordinate all those different temperaments on set?

AF: I think that if you have relations based on respect, even with extras, then they will do their work properly, never mind actors who have a thorough knowledge of cinema and who trust the director. In some of the scenes from this film we had 100, 150 extras in the corridors of the court. In order for them to work as well as possible and not be like clichéd extras who put their heads down and move around aimlessly in the background, we have to treat them like human beings, so that they know their job is important and will be seen. You won't believe how much the extras' emotional relationship with the group helped create good backgrounds for the court scenes, without making it seem as if we had orchestrated everything. They are very realistic. If you tell them their job is a valuable one, it makes a big impression on them. For professional actors, too, whatever their temperament, as long as they feel that they are being treated with respect and not like a tool, they do the job you ask of them.

Fortunately on this film we didn't have a problem with the actors on a single take. Everyone bent over backward to make things work. They made so much sacrifice that at some point it got me worried about their health. Relationships were completely mutual and respectful. As a director, the key to the whole affair is not to discriminate between people and to treat everyone with respect.

MM: After this film, is your relationship with your daughter—who gave a great performance—the same as it was before, or has it undergone changes?

AF: It has had an effect on my relationship with her. Part of that is a good thing, as I have changed the way I look at my daughter. Before I used to imagine she was a young girl who didn't yet understand many of the issues of the world, but as we were working together I realized that she understands many things I once assumed she didn't. I had to get to know her again so that she could play this part. Both of us reached a certain maturity when it came to our relationship. She got to know what sort of person I am outside of the house and beyond my being her father, and I got to know what her world is like. That was really great, because I found something I had been trying to get hold of for years. Inhibitions went out the window because we had to talk about the characters without any curtain between us. But a new one went up because she saw her father at work as a filmmaker. The part of it that might not be so good is that she went from seeing me as a father to seeing me as the filmmaking father. This is not such a pleasant prospect for me. During the first days of filming, she started calling me "Mr. Farhadi" although I hadn't asked her to, and I didn't find it at all pleasant. I preferred her to call me "dad," and I asked her not to call me Mr. Farhadi again. Overall this film had a positive impact on our relationship, but I will have to try my best to convert our relationship from one she has with a filmmaking father back to just one with a father.

MM: What did you see in Mahmoud Kalari that was special, that made you choose him as your cinematographer, even though you had a successful and fruitful relationship with the cinematographer for *About Elly*?

AF: In this film I needed a cinematographer who didn't pay much attention to the established rules of aesthetics. Given that requirement, the last person I should've chosen was Mahmoud Kalari, because he's famous for his perfect compositions and clean, carefully arranged lighting; he's known as a DP who gets splendid images. This method was completely at odds with what I wanted. But I thought that if someone like that got to do something he had done very little of until then, perhaps it would be attractive to him. What do you have to do to get someone like Mahmoud Kalari, who has been DP on sixty-one or sixty-two films, excited about his work, so that it is interesting for him, so he can do something new? If you just want him to do what he's done before, maybe it's not so attractive to him. It might be that what I want to do, to get him to set aside all the rules, would be exciting for him, a new challenge. That's why I spoke with him and without any flattery, much of this film's success is thanks to Mahmoud Kalari's efforts and his intuitive self-deprecation. He has two special characteristics. One is that he is a very sensitive person in a moral and spiritual sense, which gives quality to his work; if we accept that the cinematographer's role is to play opposite all the actors, then we need someone in whose behavior and state of mind the actors can see a reaction. This characteristic really helps the actors, and Mahmoud Kalari has just this sort of spirit. I saw how often he was moved by a scene, including that last scene where Sarina is standing in front of the judge. He was so affected emotionally that he could barely control the camera. This was a big privilege, that the actors could, at the very first stage, see the reactions of their first audience, namely Mahmoud Kalari. Second, he was self-deprecating enough not to turn up on set and wave around his resume of everything he's done in cinema. He brought all that experience with him, but he came to do something fresh and he did it well. Throughout the three months of shooting, the camera was on his shoulder for every shot. I really had my eyes open to see if this person would frown even once, but he came to the job with love. He is one of the dearest people I've worked with so far. Sometimes his relationship with a scene was even more profound than mine. His presence was so warm, that one of my motivations each morning for coming to the set was to see his face.

MM: Kalari started working with public photography and documentaries, and the structure of *A Separation* is rather like a documentary. Was this in the back of your mind?

AF: I had seen his photographs, especially those he took at the beginning of the Revolution. Even before I chose him, I had seen his photo collections and liked them. But what made me certain that I had made the right choice was that he has the courage to take on new things. He was one of the first people to work with a digital camera, which is to say he wasn't afraid of digital cameras and technologies and new narratives. In *The Pear Tree*,[6] his style of cinematography is very daring. In *Mainline*,[7] too. I needed someone daring, so that I could do that kind of cutting. He was completely on board and from the very early stages understood how the film's visual language needed to be. We found a common visual language, and we went ahead with a minimum of debate and discussion.

MM: It's important for the cinematographer not to be suddenly confronted with an already completed script and told, "This is it and nothing else." Did you keep Mahmoud Kalari updated as you were writing the screenplay?

AF: I talked to him once the fifteen-page draft was completed. I didn't actually give him the whole draft to read, but I told him everything that was in it. At every stage something got added to it. I informed him about every change and read the updated draft to him. At later stages, when we were working on the details, we were together. He was one of the most present people during preproduction. We watched a number of films together. What we were looking at most was the overall color of the film and how best to find a shared language when it came to framing. I mean, let's say he is holding the camera, how loose and free and flowing should it be? We had to find agreement on that level. By watching others' work we were able to more or less choose our own method, and we stayed loyal to this point of view until the end of our work; there were no strange alterations.

MM: Which documentaries did you watch, for example?

AF: For example, one thing we saw was *Divorce, Iranian Style*. Another was Michael Winterbottom's film set in Pakistan.[8] The style of its cinematography I found very attractive, although it wasn't on 35 mm. I liked its colors. We watched scenes from several other films before we went on set. When it came to blocking and script breakdown, it was clear what we had to do. In those first two or three days, it became pretty clear to us what kind of framing we needed.

MM: Which scene had the most takes, and why did you have to repeat it so many times?

AF: For the one where Shahab Hosseini is in the kitchen hitting himself, we had a lot of takes. But not so much that it meant the actor's feelings were hurt. In every take Shahab had to hit himself, and more than anything else it was the feeling we had to bring out. It was a difficult night, but everyone kept encouraging me to do the take again, and without saying they were upset about it. Of course, there were other scenes where we did multiple takes. But it's difficult for me to remember which ones now.

MM: Location plays a key role in your films. Do you find them when you're writing the script and make notes about them, or do you leave that for when you've finished writing?

AF: I try to find the principal locations during rewriting. Fortunately, I found the house early on. I was looking for a house with a lot of glass and glass walls.

This was exactly the house we were looking for, and finding it helped us avoid having to make even the tiniest changes in those sequences. I'd also visited the court before, so I knew what it looked like and what was inside it. Sometimes we got what I wanted, sometimes we had to build it ourselves. We couldn't get permission to film inside a real courtroom, so we had to build one. We built a replica of the family court, because when we initially gave the script to the judicial officials, the number of changes they demanded was so great, we would have had to give up on the film altogether. I preferred to build versions of all this in another location. The buildings we used for the exterior of the courtroom are actually schools we transformed for that purpose.

MM: Razieh and Hojjat's house was the total opposite of Nader and Simin's, with its tight spaces that have a strange effect on audiences. It didn't look like you built it yourselves.

AF: This is a real house—we didn't change it at all. From the beginning I gave the plans to the team. They looked at a large number of houses, and eventually this one was chosen. We had a problem when looking for the house, though, which meant we found it late. The placing of the kitchen, its distance from the bedroom and the window was very important. It was very hard to find a kitchen with such tight spaces. It was one of the last locations we found.

MM: The role and work of your production designer in this film is striking. Working with like-minded people bore fruit.

AF: The production designer[9] had the advantage of understanding what I was saying. I gave him the responsibility of finding these locations. All the locations have common features. Like the window and the glass wall, which were a model we had in mind when we went looking for different locations. But in this kind of film, the work of people like the production designer and the DP isn't so visible because it's not supposed to be. Nader's house in the film was an empty house; we moved its walls around, arranged things in it, decorated it . . . but in actual fact it wasn't lived in, it had been empty for years, and we built it ourselves. But the production designer had worked in such a way that none of that was obvious, so it would look like a house that had been lived in for years.

MM: The way glass keeps breaking in different locations, like Nader's house, Hojjat's house, the school, and especially in the last scene, is extraordinary. It shows how the characters and their world also break apart.

AF: This was a motif I had in mind. That's why we chose places where there would be a window or a glass wall between the camera and the subjects.

MM: The stairs in Nader and Simin's house are a location full of meaning, the center of the film's gravity. From the grotesque sequence where Simin comes back to find the piano stuck on the stairs and the workers haggling over the number of steps and how much they should be paid, to the symmetry of the place where Razieh falls (to which they later return to reconstruct the scene with Nader defending himself). Throughout the film the staircase functions as a kind of crossroads for the characters and the audience.

AF: The staircase is an important location because, if we consider the dispute to be the crux of the story, then that dispute is over the number of stairs. Nader states that if Razieh was thrown onto this step, then it can't have been me, whereas Razieh's husband states that she fell two steps higher up, so it could have been you. If we look at the matter in depth, then we see how trivial the basis of this dispute is. If they can prove he fell onto the first step, the matter turns out one way, but if it was two steps lower, then it turns out another way. From this point of view, those stairs are very interesting to me, too. This story is both funny and very painful. In the film as a whole, the motif of going up and down the stairs is also repeated a number of times. There are a number of shots where people are constantly going up and down. These shots could have taken place somewhere else, like the corridor of the house, but I wanted them to be on the stairs. And in the first scene, where we see the piano stopping Simin from getting past, the argument is about the number of floors, about a single floor. In that scene, too, Simin's character is such that she is willing to pay money so she can get past; she gives in. She thinks that realistically there is no way other than for her to pay if she wants to get past. But if Nader had been in that scene, there is no way he would have paid, because he would have considered himself in the right. In some ways this scene is a confrontation between two social classes, a hidden war between them.[10]

MM: How significant was the creative contribution of the film's editor, Hayedeh Safiyari?

AF: An awful lot. This is a dense, large film from the point of view of the number of situations and events that occur in it. If the editor hadn't been creative and had been deceived into leaving everything in the film, then it wouldn't have ended up with the ambiguity it has now. A second point is that we are shut up in closed spaces like the interrogation room for long periods of time, where all we see are people sitting opposite each other talking. These lengthy periods could have been hidden during editing. There were many cuts made when filming in this closed space. When the subjects are stable, it's very hard to cut from one subject to another. One part of the editor's creativity is to make it so that the first cut isn't apparent and it looks like everything has been taken in one shot; a second part is not to ruin the actors' performances and to find their best moments. Having worked with Hayedeh Safiyari on several films, we have come to share the same taste in acting and pacing, which I find very helpful.

MM: Sometimes adding or subtracting a few frames from a film turns its world upside down. Did you select where to cut, or Hayedeh Safiyari?

AF: She made the cuts and did that completely intuitively. By that I mean that it's her senses that tell her that a frame needs to be cut. It was very interesting that most of those places where I felt a cut needed to be made were cut. I sit by the editor for the entirety of the editing process; I don't take time off until after I've seen the edited film. During the sound editing process, too, I sit by the sound editor, right up to the end, because it's a real pleasure for me to do so. In my time working with Hayedeh Safiyari we've developed a shared taste, which is a real boon to me, because I can count on it when writing.

MM: Given all these tendencies of yours, has it never happened during the editing phase that you've expressed a regret that you hadn't shot such and such a scene or insert?

AF: No, but I have regretted the fact that a film can't be three hours instead of two. Because there were a number of really good sequences in this film that we didn't include because of time constraints; cutting them out was really difficult for me. I never get upset because of cutting out a sequence; it gives me pleasure because when a sequence is cut out, then I know that the film's pacing will improve. But in this film, cutting sequences out was very difficult, for both of us, and if we hadn't had to do it, we wouldn't have. We might include those sequences on the DVD. Some of the secondary actors in the film gave really great performances in those sequences, but we were forced to cut them.

MM: The fast pacing of your last two films has given your cinema a different personality when compared to your earlier works. Do you establish this pacing in the script or when you're editing?

AF: This takes place at every stage of the process, but the foundation is laid in the script. I mean that the basic rhythm that determines the temporal relationship of events with each other comes from the script. But the blocking on set, cutting, and the kind of movement in the scene also help determine a more external rhythm. You get to harmonize all these details while editing, so the final rhythm passes through the filter of editing.

MM: Some of my colleagues who saw the film at the festival are of the belief that you drip feed, so to speak, the audience details of what was to happen, just like in *About Elly*, and sometimes it seems like this kind of imparting of information causes the audience to get lost. Particularly because the fast pacing doesn't give the audience a moment to think and reflect.

AF: Mainly I don't provide information so I can maintain suspense and drama. In reality, a suspenseful structure stipulates to me that I shouldn't give the viewer all the information. Because if I do, then there won't be any drama. But it doesn't mean that this hurts the audience or is a kind of subterfuge. I try not to censor the information, but instead of presenting it directly I offer clues so the audience can obtain that information itself. For instance, in this film there is an accident scene that we don't see, only hear about. This is an important scene. If you see the film more than once, you see the clues telling us this accident has happened. The audience just has to trust itself and participate in making the film. In that scene the ground has been prepared for the accident to happen. You even hear the sound of brakes and of the accident scene, and in the next shot you see that Razieh is not well. And in the bus you see that she feels sick, her head is spinning, and she falls. If I really planned not to give the audience any information, why would I have included that scene? Instead of showing the accident, I included its consequences. All of this can lead the audience to realize that something has happened. *About Elly* was also like that. We didn't see the scene of Elly drowning, but we left clues about an event that had apparently happened and allowed the audience to imagine what the event had been. This is something I insist on. And from now on I will show the most important scenes by means of such clues and allow the audience to use their imagination, because otherwise showing the substance of the issue is straightforward. In my opinion, this is a more modern language and shows more respect to audiences. But this isn't today's taste and audiences aren't used to getting information in this way. It even gets called "drip feeding of information." In my opinion, it's only the material form of the information and the way it's presented that are different.

MM: I am in favor of this method of suspense, and I don't think that had you made what happens in that particular scene clear, the film would've been so solid and invulnerable. Did you actually film the accident scene?

AF: Yes. I cut two versions of the film, one with the accident scene and one without it. We showed the first version, the one with the accident, to an audience of seven or eight, one of whom was a critic, one a filmmaker, and the rest ordinary people who only knew cinema from watching movies and so didn't watch it like specialists. Not one of them liked watching the accident scene. In the second version, which Hayedeh Safiyari and I worked on a few days later, we took the accident scene out and added more clues about the accident. The same group came and this time the film was something totally different for them.

Some of these theories might sound attractive when you talk about them, but when you put them into practice that's no longer the case. Like the idea that it would have been possible for us not to see the dead body at the end of *About Elly*. We tried that and without good results. I really believe in testing the film with audiences once it's ready. I showed the film to a number of groups made up of totally different people and then used their feedback in the second round of editing. For them, being taken unawares at the end wasn't dependent on seeing the accident scene. When the woman came and said she had doubts, because of the accident that had happened, the audience was also taken unawares. But to say that it wasn't consistent with the language of the film is not quite it. Take the scene when we see Razieh falling from behind glass. That's why that door was a glass one, because I didn't want us to see the actual event. We shouldn't forget the more important point, which is that this film's plot is full of suspense; that is to say, it tries to create suspense. It's with this trick that we can create that suspense. So why does it seem so odd? Because we have few films with documentary-style plots that also have suspense in them. These two things seem like they don't go together. What's new that's happening in *About Elly* and even more so in this film is that you are creating suspense, but your language is totally the language of documentaries. It's a little odd. Because the suspense films or police thrillers we know of don't really have a documentary-style language. This is a new method and it will take time for people to adjust to it.

MM: In *A Separation*, people's lives are connected to one another like dominoes; a push on the first one reaches all the way to the last one. Perhaps we could interpret the film as an instance of the butterfly effect. That is, the structure and perspective and worldview are what make the film stand out, unlike *Fireworks Wednesday* or even, to some extent, *About Elly*. The audience for this film is one of the "legs" of the story, and it's not just that the audience can identify with one of the characters, but it's a part of the entire adventure.

AF: Yes. An important point in my opinion is that the relationship of the audience to the film is not made of the same stuff as it was with *Fireworks Wednesday* or *About Elly*. In those films, you decide whose side you want to take depending on your own frame of mind and concerns and on the basis of the principles you are loyal to. A lot of people take Sepideh's side in *About Elly*, a lot take the side of the group, and a lot take Elly's side. But in *A Separation* you can't pick sides so easily. Whichever side you find yourself on, you can imagine yourself being on the other side and understanding that person. You're not just a bystander: you're present inside the story and constantly have to define your position and whose side you're on. At the same time, though, you can't figure out quite where you stand. This is what requires a little energy. This is why the audiences for *A Separation* don't like to talk about the film straight after coming out of the cinema, because doubt still exists about whose side they should have taken, whom they should defend, and whom they should condemn.

MM: We could go further than that. The audience thinks that if something unpleasant happens in a corner of society, somewhere in which it has played no role and had no responsibility, tomorrow it might be pulled into it anyway, even before it's thought about taking sides. Take the teacher, who had nothing to do with Razieh's miscarriage. Hojjat nonetheless comes to the school and insults her in front of her colleagues in such a way that there's no doubt her life will be turned upside down thereafter.

AF: What makes it so troubling to watch is the feeling of responsibility we have for the smallest and most trivial actions. I'm of the belief that the turning points of life are not our really big and terrible actions and reactions. Our lives are made up of a series of daily details. Sometimes the most trivial actions can take us in directions we cannot believe at all, just like the dominoes you mentioned. This level of responsibility for the tiniest actions is frightening for the audience. I mean that people don't know what a great responsibility they have for the smallest actions. The actions of the people in the film are all small ones, but they come with massive consequences.

MM: The fundamental theme in all three of these films—*Fireworks Wednesday, About Elly, A Separation*—is the absence of sincerity, the cheapness of lies and subterfuge, and the disastrous consequences of lying. Setting aside value judgments, why is this theme such a concern for you intellectually?

AF: To be honest, I don't know myself where this comes from. This is also a question I ask myself, why along the path I have taken with my work these subjects have become so prominent. Part of it is certainly intuitive and unconscious. I don't want to make a film about morality, to go away and find a story that would be a container for that sort of content. Instead I find stories that have those themes in them. I have to go and look for why I'm drawn to these kinds of stories, why I find them. That said, what has been growing in me over the course of these films and has turned into a major concern for me is that fundamentally how I define morality is changing. I mean that I can't morally judge a certain action, one we might term a lie, and say that this is an immoral action, whereas that is a moral one. The reason is that when you see that a particular situation leads to someone telling a lie, and you understand and think that they had no alternative, or if you realize that if you were in their place, you'd do the same thing, then you can no longer dislike that person and declare what they did immoral. It seems that today with the conditions and complexities that humanity has to live with, that a part of these value judgments and definitions no longer has much use. This means that we don't dislike Termeh when she lies to the interrogator on her father's behalf. We don't dislike Nader when he lies—and it's a very big lie—about not being aware that Razieh was pregnant. We don't dislike Hojjat when he gets his wife to swear a false oath, even though his wife doubts that the miscarriage was Nader's fault. Yet what they are doing, ethically speaking, is immoral and we should dislike it. So why don't we dislike it? It seems like the definition of morality that has come into being in new conditions is not made according to traditional measures and criteria. Those understandings are no longer effective. This is something I've learned from these films and the feedback I've gotten.

MM: In *A Separation* you have a compassionate perspective on women. As you suggested, the women move the story along. Your perspective is one of forgiveness, compassion, and the pursuit of some kind of redress. Is this a way of achieving women's rights in a male-dominated society?

AF: In my opinion, women suffer more in this society than men do. At the same time I've tried my best not to impose my own judgments and point of view on my stories. That said, in certain places I've given myself away. But I do think that in a society where women suffer more, men suffer too in their own ways. I don't draw clear lines between the women and men in my stories. But I feel it's the characteristics of drama itself that make women the main agents of story events. In dramatic art across the world it is often women who take the lead. Perhaps it's the enigma of women that makes for stronger drama. Suppose that in *About Elly*, instead of Elly we had a male character. It is easier to imagine that enigmatic, vague character as a woman than a man. Maybe it's because we are men that we feel this way, but in my view the way that women are less understood gives a depth to the character that is always useful for dramatic purposes.

MM: The structure of the film is a complete circle. It begins with Nader and Simin in court and then ends in the same place. Yet between the first court scene and the last one, there is a whole world of events. It's as if Nader and Simin's marriage symbolizes all marriages in all times: Adam and Eve, the eating of the forbidden fruit, driven from paradise and punished.

AF: When it comes to the marriage relationship, experience is of no use. As a dear friend says, whenever a wife and husband start a life in common it's as if the odometer of the world is reset to zero and everything must be defined again from nothing. One thing that's clear about Nader and Simin's relationship is that throughout the film both of them try their best to explain and defend what they said in that first sequence. If we were to break up the film, taking out the first and last sequences and placing them alongside one another, they would make a complete short. My entire film works as an example, explaining what the characters claim in the first sequence. That's why I separated the first sequence from the rest of the film by placing the title of the film after it. All the events that follow explain and repeat what they've said in court. There they expressed in words what we see in practice afterward. On the surface it seems as if there is no quarrel between them. Both of them are respectable people inclined to dialogue. Unlike Razieh and Hojjat, who are much less likely to engage in dialogue about a problem, Nader and Simin converse and debate time and again in order to find solutions. They appear to be logical people, and it seems like they can live together. But the problem lies outside their family. They quarrel about a problem that comes into their life from outside. There are two approaches to living. One is the one Nader believes in, sticking to one's principles whatever the price. The other is the one Simin believes in, living realistically and giving way in order to move forward. It isn't possible to live a life in common and keep both approaches.

To go forward together, one of these approaches has to be selected. And this is what Termeh has to choose in the end. Termeh doesn't have to choose between her father and her mother, she has to choose between two approaches to life, and we don't know which one of these she will choose to be her future. The tragedy and sadness of this choice is that she might not like either one of them. This is where she has to go unprepared, with no method or guidance for her future life. This makes things harder.

MM: One reason for the lasting appeal of *About Elly* and *A Separation* is their indeterminate quality. The scene that has the greatest impact in the film is the one that takes place in Hojjat's house, where Nader tells Razieh to place her hand on the Quran and swear an oath. It moves along the fine—but also sharp and cutting—line between doubt and belief, and this jolts us, because of the double suffering that Razieh, the film's most downtrodden character, feels.

AF: When religious people find themselves in situations where they are caught between remaining loyal to their principles and being realists, they suffer more than anyone else. We could say that Razieh and Nader are made of similar stuff. Both of them try their best to stand firm when it comes to their principles, and both of them ultimately want to stay loyal to those principles despite the costs they have to pay. One of them is terrified of the consequences of not sticking to their beliefs, while the other is not; Nader isn't afraid of anything, and this is why Razieh's suffering is all the greater, because she does fear the consequences of not sticking to her beliefs. Throughout the film the image you see of Razieh is one of hesitation. When she wants to wash the old man, it looks like she does indeed want to, but her beliefs and principles tell her that this is not right. In the final scene she wants to help her husband and her family, but her beliefs don't allow her to. This suffering presents her with a massive and costly dilemma.

MM: From your first work in television right up to *A Separation*, all your work has a bitter flavor, very bitter. It's as if the characters can have no redemption or repose on this earth. Isn't it?

AF: It's not that I don't allow them to be redeemed. I'm not, as someone who places characters in different situations, imposing this bitterness on them by force, just as I'm not closing off a path to redemption for them. It is these situations, which are without any artifice or manipulation, that are entirely believable and realistic, that don't allow them redemption.

MM: But you write the stories. Are there no sweet and charming stories in this world?

AF: Yes, there are, but my mindset and character are such that bitter stories tend to seek me out. I'd love for it not to be this way. Because I suffer more from this bitterness than anyone else; when I write these stories and live with these characters for quite a while, it bothers me. I'd have loved to have found characters and stories so I could see what it feels like to enjoy their happiness. We have to look to the future. But I'm careful not to let this bitterness, as one of the components of my work, be imposed on the characters. Suppose I wanted to have this story end in a different way, for instance, by allowing Razieh to swear the oath and Nader to pay the money. Would the story have then been a happy one? No. In that case Razieh would have acted against her own beliefs and accepted money that had come from an illicit source. That wouldn't have been redemption. It would have made matters even more bitter. Razieh's redemption lies in her swearing that oath. What would have had more value than that? In the same way, the fact that Nader stood up for his principles gives me hope. I don't like my films to be an interpretation of myself; that's how my stories are.

MM: If you had to choose between bitter truth and sweet expediency, which would you choose for yourself?

AF: It depends on the situation. It's very difficult. I want the bitter truth to be spoken, but in practice I probably tend to opt for expediency.

MM: Do you think that one's personal judgment and conscience take precedence over collective judgment and conscience?

AF: Yes, the person takes precedence, it's more genuine.

MM: Do you believe that the artist is a social reformer?

AF: Not at all. I am a filmmaker who writes stories and at the end of them places a question mark in front of certain issues, to which I don't have definite answers myself. When I don't have definite answers myself, how can I describe myself as a social reformer? Fundamentally I feel like this way of looking at the artist is an old-fashioned one. It comes from literature, and it's mistaken.

MM: What's your opinion about the Wikileaks founder, Julian Assange, and his revelations?

AF: I agree with what he's done. More than anything else, today's world needs facts and truths to be publicized. Even though it comes with big costs and the world will be more bitter for it. Hiding things makes for peace and quiet, but these days so much is hidden that the real meaning of life escapes us. I agree completely. I follow the news on this and I'm happy this happened.

MM: In my view he would be a good subject and an interesting character for your next film. After *A Separation* it would probably be well received outside Iran. Are you managing to get *A Separation* released abroad?

AF: Just like *About Elly*, this film is doing well when it comes to foreign release. We are doing our best, with the help of the Memento distribution company, which is itself the international distributor for Dreamlab Films,[11] to get, if we can, a simultaneous release for the film inside and outside Iran. The public release will start in France, with seventy copies of the film. Then a day after its first screening it should be released in thirty-five other countries, and I think this number should go much higher. So the film's situation abroad is a good one. There's also been really wide publicity for it, so it sounds like everything's moving ahead well.

Notes

1. There was a series of political events in Iran, from the rigged election of June 2009 to the time *A Separation* was shown at the Berlinale, that brought Iran to the headlines again.

2. Iranian filmmakers often complain that the majority of questions asked of them at press conferences of international film festivals are about the political situation in Iran rather than the films they've made.

3. An important Shia Muslim shrine in Rey, a city now in the southern suburbs of Tehran.

4. In Persian, the film is called *Jodāyi Nāder az Simin*, which translates literally to *The Separation of Nader from Simin*.

5. Nosrat Karimi (1924–2019) was an Iranian actor, director, and artist. He directed a series of very controversial sex comedies before the Revolution but was unable to make any more films after 1979.

6. A 1998 drama shot in color and black-and-white, directed by Dariush Mehrjui.

7. Shot digitally as a monochrome film, this drug abuse drama was directed in 2006 by Rakhshan Banietemad and Mohsen Abdolvahab.

8. *In This World* (2002), which was also partly shot in Iran.

9. Keyvan Moghaddam, who also was art director on Farhadi's *Beautiful City* (2004) and *The Salesman* (2017).

10. In Persian there is one word for both a building's floor or level and a socioeconomic class: *tabaqeh*.

11. French distribution company specializing in Iranian films.

The Butterfly Effect: Asghar Farhadi and Ali Mosaffa in Conversation about *The Past*

Hossein Moazezinia / 2013

From *24 Monthly* (Tehran), Vol. 5, No. 15, July 2013. Translated by Philip Grant.

This joint interview with Farhadi and one of his leading actors in *The Past* (2013), Ali Mosaffa, was conducted in Paris, right after the Cannes premiere of the film. Mosaffa, also a film director, is married to Leila Hatami, the star of Farhadi's previous film, *A Separation*, and the couple enjoy relative popularity in Iran, owing to their regular appearance in independent films.

Hossein Moazezinia: In our previous conversation about *A Separation*, you said that everything began with you seeing an image in your mind of an old man being washed in the bath by his son. You were thinking about how the son might be feeling about this situation. Was this the case with *The Past*, whereby a little idea was the germ of everything?

Asghar Farhadi: It was a little different. The genesis of *The Past* goes back to just after *Fireworks Wednesday* to a seminar in Abu Dhabi, where they'd invited ten filmmakers from the Middle East and ten international producers, and each day one of the filmmakers would have a meeting with one of the producers. It was a sort of pitching forum. At the time I was busy editing *About Elly* and asked Peyman Maadi to come with me to the forum. Everyone was supposed to bring a synopsis with them. We didn't have one. In the time it took us to get to Abu Dhabi we wrote a one-page synopsis. And yet out of the ten synopses presented there, it was ours that attracted attention and found a producer. But because making a film outside Iran wasn't then a serious consideration for me, I didn't follow up and the synopsis remained just that. When *About Elly* came out, a foreign producer came to inquire about the synopsis. Peyman Maadi and I went to Berlin to work on it together. We were completing the synopsis when I suddenly realized my heart wasn't in it, and I went back to Iran to begin production on *A Separation*.

HM: You explained in our previous conversation that you had suddenly made a decision and gone back to Iran straightaway, starting preparations for *A Separation* practically that same day.

AF: Yes, as I said last time, after *A Separation* came out, the Memento distribution company read the synopsis I mentioned and insisted we start making it. So I got to work on it again, and this time I turned it into a more detailed treatment. They read the treatment and it was agreed that we'd sit down with Yasmina Reza[1] and turn it into a script. But there was a problem with the treatment that hadn't been solved and meant it wasn't credible. Then in the middle of one of our meetings with Yasmina Reza, we were sitting in a cafe in Paris busy working on the treatment when suddenly I said, "I have a two-line story; let me tell it to you." I started telling the story and got so detailed in telling it that by the time I'd finished I was convinced it should be my next project. I announced there and then that I didn't want to work on the old story. Memento found this rather strange after they'd made arrangements to produce that story. I'd even met with Tahar Rahim[2] and we'd spoken about the treatment.

HM: Was he going to play one of the parts in that story?

AF: Yes, I had chosen him for one of the roles. But in the end, I decided to work on the new story. My work with Yasmina Reza ended that very day, and I got to work on this story.

HM: How is it that these two stories got bound up together? What was the original story?

AF: The new story had nothing to do with the old one. The old story was about one night in the life of someone who, while traveling abroad, got stuck somewhere, but the one I went with was completely different.

HM: So where did this new story come from? What was the idea behind it?

AF: It came from the reminiscences of one of my friends. Several years after he'd separated from his non-Iranian spouse, he visited her country again, whereupon she suggested that since he was coming, they could go ahead and make their divorce official. They hadn't done it until then because the wife had wanted to pay lower taxes, but now she said that she'd sorted out the tax problem, so they could finally get officially separated. My friend went to stay with her for a few days in order to sort out the paperwork for their divorce. When I heard that, it struck me that this was an interesting scenario: two people who were far apart but with a common past, who then found themselves together for a few days, as if the flames had suddenly leapt up from beneath the embers again. That was how this story began.

HM: When did he tell you about all this?

AF: Ages ago, maybe even before filming *Fireworks Wednesday*.

HM: What did he do himself? What happened to him?

AF: Nothing. Everything went smoothly, there was no crisis, then he came back.

HM: When did this idea start to develop in your mind?

AF: After the meeting I told you about, it started to get serious. When *A Separation* had just come out in France I started to write some scattered notes about this story. During all my trips to promote *A Separation* in various countries, I was busy thinking about this story, in planes, airports, hotels.

HM: When you were in your meeting with Yasmina Reza, what happened that convinced you this was the story to pursue?

AF: It was so sudden that anyone who'd been present wouldn't have understood why I was telling it! Even I didn't think this story was very meaningful for me. It suddenly happened. I mean that when I'd finished telling it, I felt sure that everything was right and all its details were believable.

HM: So this means that you have a developed, detailed story that has already been set aside twice in favor of other stories and that has yet to be turned into a complete script?

AF: Yes, it's gotten to the verge of production twice since we made *About Elly* and yet hasn't been made. In that sense it's a good synopsis because twice now it's pointed me in the direction of other films! [Laughs]

HM: Do you think it will get finished one day, or won't it?

AF: I doubt it.

HM: The poor thing keeps getting filed away! It sounds like it was good just for the Abu Dhabi seminar.

AF: It's a good story, but it's not my kind of thing.

HM: Ever since this story and the production of this film got serious for you, and it was known you were working on it, everyone began to ask whether the great dramatist filmmaker, whose stories always had such a deeply social perspective, could produce work of the same quality in another country and with non-Iranian actors. Last year when we talked, you said that a lot of the ongoing consultations were about that, so that the gaze of the tourist wouldn't creep into the script. What did you do in the end to solve this problem? Some of the reviews that have come out in the last few days, after the screening at Cannes, claim that in comparison with *A Separation* and *About Elly* the social aspect of this film is less pronounced.

AF: We need to see if someone who has such an opinion is familiar with French culture, or whether they are not looking at it from afar like a tourist. As it happens, the reaction of the French audience, critics, and even filmmakers has been the same; for instance, yesterday I was talking about *The Past* with Michel Haznavicius.[3] They agree that for them, living here in France, there is less inclination to focus on that section of French society. That it's only when they talk about the problems of immigrants that they pay attention to these kinds of people. In the analyses of the film that I've heard, first they talk about the problem of the family and its role in the film, which is an important subject for them, but then they talk about the social dimension, the question of immigration in recent decades and the impact it's had on the social order of the city and the culture. They talk about how all of the characters, except for Ahmad, are French and yet don't have French roots. So Marie, played by Bérénice Bejo, whose roots are Argentine, has Argentinian things in her house. Samir, played by Tahar Rahim, has roots in Arab North Africa. Naïma is also Arab, while Lucie, the family's daughter, has Belgian roots. These are all elements of the story, but not in a loud or ostentatious way. Naturally, for those of us who live in Iran, the social aspects of *A Separation* are more palpable, whereas perhaps for the French the equivalent is *The Past*. Just like when American audiences saw *A Separation*, they didn't have as much access to the film's social dimensions, but the individual relationships within the family were clearer for them.

HM: So, setting aside both positive and negative assessments, I would like to know how you managed to avoid the tourist perspective and how you could identify the concerns of people living in that city and culture. Did you do any research in particular? Did you talk to anyone? Observe people within that society?

AF: Once the first treatment of the film had been completed, my family and I came to spend a little time in Paris so that we could experience life here. It was made possible for me to come and live here with no trouble at all. We only did fieldwork in areas that the film made necessary. In the areas of medicine and law, for instance. At first, I thought that I should look around and figure out what the difference would be if the story were to take place in Iran rather than France. I spent a while on this question. But after a while I saw that this approach was a mistake and it would be better if I tried to find the common elements.

HM: Why?

AF: Because discovering differences requires an awful long time, whereas it's easier to find common ground, the reason being that part of those common elements belong to you, you know them, and therefore you can go and look for the other half. After I'd been looking for those common elements for a while and found them, my concerns went away. I wrote the script without the burden of such concerns weighing on it. The first draft was ready and I gave it to a number of people to read: French people, from Jean-Claude Carrière to ordinary people. I expected they'd find loads of things that they'd tell me couldn't happen in Paris, that don't fit with the way people live here. But when we had a meeting with Jean-Claude Carrière, he'd only written two or three things on the script, one to do with the tone of one of the dialogues, and one or two suggestions about adding or deleting dialogue. I insisted he explain all the differences to me, but he quite confidently said that there wasn't a single moment in the script where someone might imagine it isn't taking place in Paris. There were other people who read the script: a female schoolteacher, a female doctor, a female filmmaker named Agnès Jaoui who makes more popular, commercial films, people whose opinion we wanted, a number of lawyers, even completely ordinary people, and finally Iranians who'd lived in France for years. We gave it to a lot of people to read. It was a very long process, but we managed to get a common evaluation of the film based on all these opinions. And then once we started filming, the actors themselves offered some corrections when it came to the behavior of the characters, things we might not have known about, and throughout rehearsals we kept going like that. For example, when Marie comes home, takes her shoes off, and throws them in a corner, I shouted "cut" and said, "This is part of our culture, but does anyone do this here?" Our script supervisor, who is from Paris, said that she did the same thing at home. So we shot the scene in that exact way. Perhaps these things seem unimportant, but as a whole that's how you save the film from the trap of the tourist gaze.

HM: What about if we look beyond these kinds of details? The example you gave was more about lifestyle and people's habits. My question was more about whether, for example, we can say that the characters we see in *The Past* are demonstrating "Frenchness" to us? That is to say, when we see their attitude to life, the place of the family and human relationships for them, can we be sure that we're seeing a French person's outlook?

AF: In my view, just as it's possible French people might have a deformed and superficial perspective on our life in Iran, we are also full of illusions about them. When it comes to notions such as love, hate, internal family relations, loyalty, and so on, we are in the grip of illusion. Particularly with regard to notions of ethics. When you come here and observe their life from up close, you see that although their lifestyle certainly differs from ours—for example, the way they express love or display disgust—the principle is absolutely the same. You see exactly the same sort of emotions from a mother with regard to her adolescent daughter as you would see in Tehran. Now I've been hearing from the French audience here that *The Past* is closer to the reality of their lives than many films made in France by French filmmakers. This has really made me happy.

HM: I am trying to figure out how you got here. Because the biggest threat your film faced was that you wouldn't hear anything like that, but that the French audiences would say that your film is far from the reality of our lives. What did you do to prevent this from happening? Have you gotten to a point where your general perspective on people's relationships today, in the modern world, is no longer confined to a particular geography?

AF: It's very simple. I looked for those common points I was talking about. Of course, this common ground doesn't exist between people living in one of the provinces of our country and those living in a French province, or very little. But the overall picture of the life of people of moderate means in Iran is actually, when it comes down to it, remarkably similar to that of people of similar social class in France. The way feelings are displayed is different. That's the key to the puzzle. I don't want to depict the matter as being so simple that I encourage other people to rush off and succumb to the temptation of thinking it's possible to make a film about any subject in any culture, not at all. If I went and made a film about something really local and specific to Paris, the film would just turn into a tourist flick. Those kinds of subjects are complicated; they have very deep cultural and social roots. But now I've made a film about a subject whose roots I can locate in my culture too. In any case, in developing the story I have tried to prevent any blemishes of this type appearing. When we were scouting for locations, we went to see a lot of different houses, which came with the advantage that we could see how people lived. Unlike in our culture, here when you go into someone's home, they don't try to hide their life from you. You can see everything just as it is. It was during this hunt for the right location that I realized that the impression we have that people's emotions are limited here, that their personal relations are cold, is not true; it's rather the way they are displayed is different. Here, too, just like in Iran, you see people who hold everything within them and others who put it all on display.

Ali Mosaffa: The big problem we have is that the image we have of Europeans or Americans is one that has been made for us in films.

AF: In films and the media.

AM: Yes, and it's already work enough that we don't let ourselves be fooled by this image. I mean, the image of a culture of "foreigners" that has formed in our minds, whereby we think they are always cold in their reactions and don't say something or other the way we do, whereas they think it's rude if we speak in such a way in front of them—it's just not true in either case. Perhaps our differences lie in the fact that in our culture we have a deeper and more fundamental form of the same reaction they have, which means that it's enough for us to go and look at our own roots. Then you see that they have the same reaction to a given situation as we do, but perhaps the way in which their behavior takes shape tricks us into imagining that the foundations are entirely different.

HM: So you have both encountered this problem, the oft-repeated presumption that "we Easterners are warmer and are much more in touch with our emotions than Westerners," and believe this isn't right?

AF: The information I have about a general category called "the West" isn't complete enough for me to give a definite "yes" or "no" answer. And these days

I don't know whether, when we talk about "the West," we mean a particular geographical zone or whether we are talking about whatever lies beyond the borders of Iran, or whether we are just referring to a lifestyle that is different from our own.

HM: Let's say "Europe" instead, so that the zone we're talking about is clear.

AF: Okay, the Europeans. So how can we claim that in general Europeans are colder than Asians? This is a very big area, and no one can claim total control over it. I can only say that I have seen examples that contradict this presumption. Of course, I've seen coldness in relationships, too. I'm not saying I've never seen it. I lived in Berlin for a while. So, at first sight, that is a very cold city. One winter night, I came back home around midnight. An old woman lived alone the floor below us. She was over seventy and only spoke German. We had no kind of relationship beyond saying hello to one another in the elevator. But that night, even though it was so late, she came and knocked on our door and said, "It's my birthday tonight. I was waiting for you to come back so I could invite you to my place!" My daughter knew a little bit of German. We went to her place so we could celebrate her seventy-something birthday. That night she behaved with us and conveyed feelings to us that made us imagine we were spending the night with one of our closest family members! Well, wouldn't you say that something similar could also happen in Tehran? And afterward we had a number of similar experiences. I think we need to distance ourselves from this stereotypical gaze that the media have constructed about our cultural differences. Not to say that no such differences exist. But we would be wrong to assume that we are the warm, emotional ones while the other side is strictly detached and cold.

HM: What you say is quite right. But you know what I'm after? Look, for example in *A Separation*, though we are caught up in the story, the narrative, the characters, and the knots that are untied one by one, at the same time we don't forget that the filmmaker has, consciously or not, reconstructed an image at once symbolic and profound of our life in society today; although he is occupied with moving the story forward in accordance with the rules of the drama, at the same time he sets before our eyes an interpretation of our most burning issues and concerns. What I would like to know is whether it is possible, on the basis of a temporary stay in Paris, one or two years living alongside its people, to make a film that can explain the issues the French have to the same extent?

AF: You should ask a French person. I tried to make sure that there was no obstacle in the way of French viewers relating to the film, so, for example, in the opening credits no one's name appears because I didn't want the audience to think that the maker of the film wasn't French. I tried to make sure there was nothing in the way, so that the audience could enter into the world of the film without any prejudices. Let's suppose a French director had made *The Past*. Then you'd have to ask people in Iran whether what they see in the film speaks to their concerns or not. These days the "family" is the most important such issue for people. How the family should be defined is a concern for them. On the other hand, not knowing what to do with the "past" is also a concern; for example, is it best to let the modern world rush on ahead, so that the past does not imprison us, or to delve into the past in hopes that it will enrich the present? This is one of the issues of the day here. But we'd have to ask a French person whether this film has ultimately been able to express these issues in such a way that they feel spoken to.

HM: Now things are clearer. The "family" and how it should be defined might be a good subject for discussion.

AF: Here one of the fiercest social reactions, something that makes people come out into the streets and demonstrate, is the issue of the family. The question of how to define the family is a tense and burning one here, which has recently been the subject of much debate and division. I don't mean to say that it was because I was influenced by this state of affairs that I decided to write this story. No, I went along the same path that had led me to the germ of my other works in the past, but this time the germ happened to be close to the ongoing crisis here about the definition of the family.

AM: I don't know if this was planned and part of the design, but during the production several times people came up to us to say that this is exactly the issue kids living in such families have these days. I mean kids who don't have a house of their own, kids who one night go to their mother's, even though she is now living with a new husband, and then the next night go to their father's, although he's gone and married another woman. This is a daily issue here. A woman came up to me after seeing the film and told me that she has seen a number of Iranians in recent years who have a French spouse, and the way you've portrayed this echoes their experiences. She asked me how long Mr. Farhadi had lived here to be able to notice all these details. She wanted to figure out how long he had lived here.

AF: It's true that it is extremely difficult to make a film in a culture that you haven't grown up or lived in. Actually, because everyone said it wasn't possible, I was really motivated to see if there was a feasible way of doing it or not. For me it was the same level of challenge that I had before *Beautiful City*, when I decided to make a film that would be as attractive to a general audience as to cinephiles. Everyone said it wasn't possible. With this new film, too, I realized that people often believed that the decision I'd made would have no consequence and would inevitably fail, and the film would turn into a tourist flick. It's too early to determine the verdict, but based on the reviews and the number of people who've seen the film, it seems like we don't have this problem.

HM: You like to take on difficult challenges!

AF: I try to find a way to make difficult situations easy. It's definitely impossible for a filmmaker to go and make a film about any old subject outside their own culture, but I'm telling a story. In all cultures there is a need to hear stories. When I'm telling a story, my work is easy. When I'm telling a story about a family, it's even easier. The family is a common experience and concern for all people of the world.

HM: Definitely. The family can be a common concern for us and for French people, but you can't deny the differences are real. For example, in *The Past* we see a character like Marie whose two daughters belong to neither of the two men she's currently involved with—they come from her previous life. Now she has a past with Ahmad and she's busy dealing with it and its consequences, while at the same time she's building a future for herself with another man. It appears as if her identity has been sliced up among all these men who have come and gone in her life. She has had a really complicated life. There's no way we could say these concerns would be the concerns of an Iranian. This can't happen here.

AF: That's right, family reconfiguration of this sort is far more common in Europe than in Iran, just as I said that lifestyles are very different. But for a woman to be of two minds about her past, for her to fall in love with a man she's lived with before and with whom she has memories, and for her to react to him or to behave in such a way because she wants to take revenge on him—these are all common human feelings. This is what I mean about having things in common. It's not as if the emotions this mother has toward her daughters are miles apart from the emotions a mother in Iran might have. Otherwise, of course, the differences in lifestyle are many. If that wasn't the case, then I could've made this film in Iran.

HM: Both of you have been living here in France a while now. In your opinion, how much have the definitions of the family and relationships between women and men changed? For instance, in Iran the majority of people still believe in having traditional relationships between women and men, with recognized and legal marriages, and society cannot accept people who live together in one house without having gone through the necessary steps to make their situation legal. Do you get the feeling that today, in Paris, people have accepted these kinds of changes? For instance, what kinds of reactions do they have to homosexuality?

AF: This is a subset of those concerns I was talking about, those having to do with the definition of the family. There is a very serious debate here about whether a woman and a man should have to take legal steps in order to live together. This is a question, because many young people in this society no longer believe that they must go down the legal path in order to live together. I can't speak for all of French society, only those parts of it I've experienced. My suspicion is that economic issues have had a big impact on the changing form and definition of the family.

AM: We should take the economic situation very seriously. In Iran, too, the conditions are such that many are no longer able to keep their grandmother living with them, because their house is small and income limited. Now, something that once seemed really harsh to us might become necessary and normal, so that we'll have fewer qualms about sending our grandmother off to live in a home.

HM: What about religion? Do they still have a religious sensitivity toward marriage?

AF: Based on the examples I've seen, I can say that a part of society, in reaction to this growing phenomenon I've been describing and because of their traditional and religious beliefs, places a lot of value on those legal and bureaucratic procedures. The situation here in this society is still a challenging one. Society is divided on this issue, and people debate with one another about it often. When it comes to the question of homosexuality, this division has broken the bounds of normal and respectful debate; there is open conflict.

HM: Did those examples you encountered and the way these people were living have a meaningful effect on the film's plot?

AF: A lot. When you go to live somewhere with the intention of observing things you were already looking at pretty closely, you observe the city in another way, you look at your neighbors in another way, so being here for two years has had a big effect on me. I got to know a lot of people. The production crew, about seventy people, was itself a sort of minisociety, and they were constantly debating these questions off set. We talked about all the issues you see in the film.

HM: So then how did the concerns you always deal with in your films make their way into this new one? Subterfuge, people lying, events getting ever more complicated? People who don't like your films say things like, "Farhadi always starts off with little things like this because he wants to say that Iranians are liars or like to sneak around in secret." If we follow this line of thinking, then we could say that the French are also like this! So it would seem this is one of your main concerns when it comes to humanity in general. Are these themes always on your mind, taking shape in your characters when you come to write, or do you decide at a specific point that the characters of this new story should have these specific characteristics?

AF: I never select a theme for my stories before I've found the story itself. I never ask myself what the issue of the day is or go and look for it in society. At least I don't like to make a decision first of all about what I want to say and then go and look for a relevant story. I find a story to tell and then I try to define the story properly. Every story in the world contains every theme in the world, so all you need to do once you've written the story is bring out the theme you have in mind, putting up certain signposts and creating patterns here and there. Along the way you discover other issues and concerns germane to the surrounding moment and culture.

In this case, I wrote the story, then afterward I discovered that confession and apology have a particular quality in this culture. Confessing in order to be forgiven is a part of their culture. They have to express the sin they've committed very precisely. That means they have to refer to their past and, however difficult it may be, describe what the fault is they've committed so that they can be forgiven. I realized that this is one of my constant concerns and related to a theme I have in mind, namely that when we apologize, we are referring to the past. So it was enough that I insert the signs of this behavior into the script. You'll see that apologies frequently recur in this story, with every character apologizing at least once. This is a cultural characteristic of people here. I didn't arrive here with the idea that I would make a film about "confession" and how we're all forced to return to the past and confess things so that our faults may be forgiven and resolved. As the story emerged, I saw that this was one aspect of it that I should emphasize. So with the understanding I had acquired of French culture, I tried to make this element more prominent, although not so much that it would stick out.

HM: So it's probably happened before that when you've finished writing the story, you see that some of its themes are weak and others strong, and you decide to make one of those weaker themes more prominent, or the other way around.

AF: Yes, this has happened. Sometimes I see that themes have found their way into the story that weren't really intended or my concern. It might be the case that if I were to strengthen them then the film would be more exciting, but I can't build a sincere relationship with them. And that's why I'd made them less prominent in the first place. As far as the theme of lies and subterfuge goes, the day I decide to retire from filmmaking, if I ask myself what I've done in cinema that makes me happy, and if I'm being honest, I'll say that it's all the attention I've paid to lying and subterfuge. In my opinion, it wouldn't be enough even if every film made in Iran were about that subject, because it's not just our issue—in France, too, it's an important one.

HM: Have you really run into examples of this?

AF: Here?

HM: Yes, in Paris.

AF: Yes.

AM: Of course there is a difference, because here they've gotten used to confessing a little after they've lied and then to apologizing for it. We haven't acquired this habit yet. We Iranians are surprised when here someone says to their spouse that they are not attracted to them anymore and they want to go and live with someone else. We comment that this is highly immoral, when they are at least admitting what their situation is.

AF: What I get from what Ali is saying isn't that no one hides what they're doing here in France, that no one is two-faced, because this does exist. Here, for example, taxi drivers fiddle with the odometer on their cars, there is double-dealing and subterfuge in family relations. . . .

AM: But when their hand is revealed, they accept their mistakes and apologize.

AF: The point is exactly that, that people don't resist. It's easy for them to apologize openly and directly. Allow me to explain why I insisted that the Iranian audience see this film with subtitles that I myself approved, with a precise translation. It was because I wanted them to see the directness of Marie and the other French characters contrasted with the indirectness of the character of Ahmad. In one place Marie says to Ahmad, "Either don't speak, or if you do speak, speak clearly." She can see how Ahmad's indirect way of speaking is harmful. This is a cultural difference between us and them. When we say, "cultural difference," we think that two people from two different planets have come face-to-face with one another, but, no, these differences are details like this one, and yet in my opinion these differences are very important.

AM: I would like to ask a question to do with our earlier discussion of the treatment.

HM: By all means!

AM: Is the reverse model of filmmaking you mentioned—I mean, going from the theme to the story—do you think it should be totally rejected or is it just extremely difficult? Are you worried it won't give good results, or do you think it's mistaken? Do you mean that you would find it completely wrong for someone to come along and say that they are going to make a film about lying?

HM: What a great question!

AF: Well, look, in my opinion, it's very hard indeed to take something that is an endpoint, some place where the story will end up once you've written it, and make it a theme from the outset. It means that everything you write will come up smelling of that theme. It will end up as a heavy and difficult film. The film will of its own accord finish up far from the plausible level of ordinary life. This type of screenwriting produces unrealistic results. How many works of this kind turn out very well but with an unrealistic perspective? Something like the play *Hamlet.* It's a masterpiece, but the entire time you're aware that you are following a story that has a central, unifying theme—because everything that happens in it was selected in order to have the theme of hesitation and doubt sink into the depths of the audience's soul.

AM: So what about Kieślowski, who comes along and makes a film on the basis of the Ten Commandments? He must have gone out and found stories that have themes of the kind he wants to express.

AF: I said this about realistic films, not about any film. As far as I know, Kieślowski began with one or two stories and then went and finished the rest of them. An American producer suggested to me, now that I've made *The Past*, that I should go and make *The Present* and *The Future*, too! But I can't say *The Present* to myself and then go off and find a suitable story. This seems rather stupid to me. I'm not saying it's impossible, but I can't limit myself to one predetermined theme when I'm writing. Listen, Ali, you know that in the stories we tell our kids, there is the story of Mr. Wolf who hides behind the door and says, "It's me; it's me, your mother." There is lying in it. There is subterfuge. There is ignorance. . . . But it depends on how you tell it to them, what language you use, which parts you emphasize.

HM: Now that you've kicked off this fascinating discussion, tell us how you write your scripts. Is your own method different?

AM: When you were speaking about whether it is possible to write a story differently, I was actually thinking it must be very hard. When writing, I've thought myself that if someone were forced to write in this way, it could only be in service to a particular theme. And this would be obvious and annoying for the audience. Forcing symmetry and symbols into the story annoys the audience.

HM: This is a fascinating but also complicated discussion, so we should arrange to meet up another day and explore it in all its details. Because in our own country there are many who do write scripts based on that model we've been saying is impossible or ill-advised, and indeed a number of those who have become famous in world cinema owe their fame to exactly this method of reverse-engineered writing—starting with the theme and ending with the story. Of course, there is a subtle difference that exists within this method we've been talking about; there is a kind of cinema we might call ideological, with many examples from the classical age of film up to the 1970s, when filmmakers considered themselves duty-bound to express a sort of manifesto by way of cinema.

AF: If, when you start writing, you don't bind yourself to expressing a particular theme, the circle opens wider for you, but when you have a manifesto and you want to make a film that disseminates an absolute theory, you end up becoming so limited that. . . . For instance, you've begun writing a script in which you want to denounce contemporary capitalism from a left-wing perspective. Like an absolute creator, you shape all the people in the story and everything they do in such a way as to confirm your worldview, because you want to compel the audience to accept your opinion. This is in fundamental contradiction to the kind of cinema I believe in.

HM: So my follow-up question is why then do themes like lying and subterfuge always crop up so prominently in your stories, if only unconsciously or circumstantially? While putting up the signposts in your final story more prominently, do you ever consider why you choose these themes? When a film critic sits down and considers the whole body of a director's work, they try to find reasons for the prominence of certain themes. Truffaut tells us that the theme of fear in Hitchcock's films is so prominent because he had spent several hours locked up in a police cell when he was a child. This is to say, we want to peek into the personal life of the filmmaker, so that the deeper reasons behind these themes may be revealed.

AF: I started to take this seriously when I got to know drama. I came to understand that drama was valuable and also the result of a puzzle. A MacGuffin. In other words, you hide a part of the truth and you lead the audience, as if they were detectives, to discover what's been hidden. The desire to write dramatically inadvertently propelled me to give full rein to the theme of subterfuge in my stories. Eventually it was the films I'd made themselves that taught me that this was a sensitive subject, one that society needed to discuss and debate, and so it was something I could work with. After *Fireworks Wednesday* I realized that the subject of subterfuge, and the subjects of judgment and lying—and it is of course a subset of those rather than a principal theme—that these had all become more prominent in my work. A common mistake that is always made with these kinds of subjects is to separate form and content. Sometimes it's the form that tells you what kind of content you have at your disposal.

HM: That said, I think that the question common to all of your last four films is actually "What is the truth?" The characters in the stories you write are constantly trying their best to cover up the truth or to take it apart, while we as the audience are doing our best to find a little window for ourselves to look past their efforts, so we can figure out what the truth is. This was very striking in *The Past*.

AF: Yes, this was more obvious in *The Past* than in my previous films. I read in a book somewhere that you should never trust any historian, because historians are always trying to find a main reason for anything that's happened, whereas for every event that's ever taken place there are a multitude of reasons for their occurrence. This means that in this life we cannot talk definitively about truth. And I don't mean to start debating the merits of relativism! I want to say that even a really simple event can be fluid in character. It can be reflected in different ways across time and place and in people's inner worlds. In *The Past* we accompany each of the characters in order to find a part of the truth. In the classic narrative form, when the answer to the puzzle has been provided, we discover which person or group of people was responsible for which event or crime, and we know exactly where we are.

HM: By the way, *The Last Step*[4] has that tone!

AF: Yes, *The Last Step* does indeed work like that.

HM: Very good, so let's continue with our earlier discussion. Your initial idea started to develop, and the story began with the entrance of Ahmad into Marie's life. Ahmad arrives so that they may complete the legal steps necessary to conclude their divorce. Did you originally intend to gradually ease him out of the story and have the film end with other characters?

AF: I had had this experience in my earlier projects. It's a satisfactory method that leaves my options open. For me to get into the atmosphere of a story I always need to accompany someone or something. In *Fireworks Wednesday*, I enter an unfamiliar environment in the company of a working-class girl. I could never have imagined the film beginning inside the apartment with the girl ringing the doorbell and going in. I wanted myself to go into the house like a stranger. In *The Past*, the house of *Fireworks Wednesday* has turned into a big, foreign city. I needed a city's help to gently ease us into this life. When I feel that both the audience and I have become acquainted with the atmosphere and the characters, then I didn't see the need for us to stay with that character till the final moments.

HM: Weren't you worried that cutting out the character of Ahmad from the final thirty minutes would upset the audience?

AF: It's not thirty minutes; it's much less. Maybe a few scenes. Only for as long as Samir is absent at the beginning. They're not removed; they're just absent. You feel Ahmad's presence everywhere; you don't see his image but people talk about him, and his influence on what's taking place is felt. In that final sequence where she sees Ahmad in the house, the audience has become prepared to bid him farewell.

HM: Weren't you afraid that at that moment when they're bidding him goodbye, the audience might feel the film is coming to an end?

AF: I'm not worried about the audience making this kind of prediction. I don't think there's anything wrong with getting the audience to understand the film is coming to an end. I avoid having films end unexpectedly, at least with this kind of narrative that follows an arc, reaches a climax, and then comes gently down to Earth. Same thing happens in *About Elly*: when they see the dead body, the audience understands the film is reaching its end and then, after a few scenes by way of conclusion, they're ready to get up and go.

AM: What you said about the character of Ahmad and how he leaves the film at a certain point—in my opinion, the structure of the story is such that the characters are constantly passing things between themselves, and after a certain point it is Samir who has to carry on with everything. It's as if the character who's at the center of events is Samir's wife, who's in a coma and who draws everything in her direction. As if the entire film is what the person who's fallen into a coma desires, as if she is giving shape to events, so that Ahmad will come and a set of events will take place that eventually brings Samir to that point and to the final sequence. That was my take, that the characters are passing things between themselves until we eventually get to Samir's wife.

AF: When we say that something happened in the past, and now we want to evaluate what the contribution of each person to that event was, we have to follow different characters who have a variety of relationships, close and distant, to the way in which that event was shaped. Someone has committed suicide in a dry cleaner's: perhaps she really did kill herself, or perhaps the person working there caused her to kill herself, maybe her husband because of his relationship with another woman. It's like that theory of the butterfly effect: if in one corner of the world it flaps its wings, can it set in motion a chain of interconnected events that builds in impact with each link. We often think that, because we are far from certain events, we are simply observers, with no impact on them. But if we look carefully, we see that there are rings linking us to each and every event.

HM: And so this is why you reached the conclusion that the film shouldn't have a single hero or protagonist? Because it would be incorrect to say that *The Past* revolves round a central figure.

AF: From that perspective, its structure is like *About Elly* and *A Separation*. This form of narrative is very attractive to me. In fact, one of the reasons I set the earlier story aside was that it had a single hero. Everyone else was subordinate to that character, and everything they did was in reaction to it. I wasn't able to go and look at events from different angles. When you have a number of characters, you have the ability to look at the situation from a number of angles. It creates a sort of balance in the story. Every hero gives you a certain angle and dimension. I insist on this narrative form and try to foster it. In this film I tried to implement everything I'd learned and experienced in my previous work.

HM: Did you finish the script and then start production, or did the actors you cast have an influence on it?

AF: The script hardly changed at all. It was written with all the details in it, and it was very thorough. After several rewrites and corrections suggested by my advisers, the script was complete. It was really attractive to look at, too, because one page was in Persian and opposite there was a page in French, and the typeset was such that each French sentence was opposite its Persian equivalent.

HM: What impact did your advisers have on the script?

AF: Nothing that could be counted as a major change. Their role was more to give me confidence that this story could credibly take place in France. After the first edit, we showed the film at a number of private screenings to ordinary people. The first thing I asked them was whether they found the story believable. So what the advisers did was tell us how to get to the point where it was believable.

HM: That said, in your films a part of what makes them believable is down to choices made by the actors and the way they've been directed.

AF: In this film a number of the minor parts are played by actors who have those roles in real life. For instance, the family court judge is actually a family court judge in real life. The female lawyer is really a lawyer.

HM: When you were casting, was Tahar Rahim the first actor you chose?

AF: Yes, because we had already been talking to him for the earlier story. When we set that story aside, I still felt that Tahar would be the right person for the part of Samir. So, yes, Tahar was the first person to be cast.

HM: And then you went and spoke to Marion Cotillard about the role of Marie?

AF: Yes, when the treatment had been written and was complete, I thought of Marion Cotillard. The initial agreement was made. But then when we sat down together a few times and I outlined my working conditions. . . .

HM: Had she read the script before meeting with you?

AF: Yes, she'd read it and she liked it a lot. But she had imagined that it would be like French or American films, where the actors turn up on set once filming starts. So when she heard that she would have to start rehearsals three months before the start of filming, given that she was busy with her newborn baby and also shooting a film in America that would be shown at Cannes. . . .

HM: *The Immigrant*, directed by James Gray. . . .

AF: Yes. She said that because of her situation she could only work with us on condition that we postpone filming. That was impossible for us, because it would start to get cold and we wouldn't be able to shoot. So we had to look at our other options.

HM: Did you negotiate seriously with anyone else, or did you go straight to Bérénice Bejo at that point?

AF: We thought about pretty much every French actress who was the right age for the character, and we met with some of them or looked at their work. In the end we had three options: Sophie Marceau, with whom we met a few times; Charlotte Gainsbourg, whom we also spoke to; and Bérénice Bejo. I knew Bérénice a little because we had met when she was traveling for *The Artist* and I for *A Separation*, but I'd never actually thought about working with her. I gave her the script to read. Everything went so smoothly that after a few conversations I chose her.

HM: How did you choose Ali Mosaffa?

AF: We wanted an Iranian actor who. . . .

HM: So from the beginning you wanted an Iranian actor.

AF: For me, definitely. A few times my producer worried that we wouldn't find an Iranian actor, and so maybe we should bring someone from South America, because he thought there were similarities between our culture and South America! He had even thought of Gael Garcia Bernal. But I needed to get into this story with someone from Iran, so that I wouldn't end up making a film completely unrelated to what I'd done in the past. The character was familiar to me, because I had a character of the same type and with the same name in *About Elly*. This Iranian actor also needed to know French or be able to learn it quickly, and at the same time have an acting style I liked.

HM: And so Ali Mosaffa checked off all these boxes?

AF: I didn't initially know that Ali could speak French. I once asked him by way of an intermediary, and with his usual modesty he said he didn't, that he couldn't speak French! But then completely accidentally I learned from Leila Hatami that Ali could speak French. We set up a meeting and . . . let him tell the rest!

AM: For the first few sessions I memorized the lines and then performed them over the phone for Masoumeh Lahiji, who was here in Paris. They were filming in the office. . . .

HM: This was an audition then?

AM: Yes, I mean that the aim was to see whether I could act out the conversations in French with an actor opposite me or not. The first text I learned was very confusing, because it was from a script for a gangster film. Two people were speaking a really rough-and-ready colloquial French and I thought to myself, "Oh no! I really can't speak French with this tone." I was scared!

HM: So why did you give him this text?

AF: I wanted the test to be as hard as possible.

HM: You were certain that his acting style was the kind you liked?

AF: Yes, in my opinion the character of Ahmad shouldn't talk much—one of those people who at first glance seems to have a lot of unsaid words hidden behind their quiet gaze. In my first two films, *Dancing in the Dust* and *Beautiful City*, I made Faramarz Gharibian play this kind of character, and then Shahab Hosseini in *About Elly*. So here, too, I wanted an actor who could play this kind of character, a character who is mysterious and whom we want to know more about. Ali has these qualities in the way he looks and acts.

HM: After you'd been cast, the first challenge was acting in a language that wasn't your mother tongue, wasn't it?

AM: Yes, to begin with that was the only challenge. But as we progressed, it turned into a secondary issue. I was lucky to be able to take an intense course here in Paris before we started filming. Living in this environment and continuing to practice meant that it got easier for me, because at first my French wasn't at the level where I could comfortably have a conversation. I'd decided to try to learn French properly several times, but every time I'd not pursued it further. When you do that with a language, it becomes like a chronic ailment, something you can never overcome. But the strange thing is that just a month before we started speaking, I had gone and bought a CD and was working on it.

HM: Didn't Leila Hatami warn you beforehand that working with Asghar Farhadi is hard?

AM: The experience I've had with those directors who can get a sensitive performance out of an actor is that they all try, up to a point, to influence the actor's inner state, so that they can intervene there and take control. Naturally this kind of method comes with a certain psychological pressure. It's never going to be effortless or breezy. Those films where the actor just turns up and does their job and then leaves, and the director has no involvement with them, well, that's another sort of film. But this kind of film can't take shape without this method. I mean that the relationship between the director and the actor has to reach a level where maybe some people are bothered by the intensity, even to the point of creating tension. But the kind of film we're talking about can only be made using this method. It's not possible otherwise.

HM: Perhaps we could say that you don't make merely technical demands of your actors?

AF: It's different depending on what stage we've reached. It's one thing during rehearsal, another thing altogether during the shoot. Every scene is different. It's possible that for a particular shot you don't give any instructions to the actor and don't let their performance get too lively, because it's possible the actor wants to use up too much energy for that shot when you don't need that energy. It's possible their energy comes out in regard to other elements, like the image and the sound. It's possible you do four takes and the actor thinks they've performed really well. But perhaps from my point of view too well, too ostentatiously, because I don't want it to be so striking. So perhaps we'll repeat it many times until I've got the performance I want. I suppose that my explaining nothing on set, just saying that it was good but now let's do another take, could get annoying to some people. But if the actor accepts that the whole point of this method is for them to play the character in the way it should be played, then they accept the method—unless the actor is a show-off or overly insecure or something. Happily there was nothing of the sort during this production. This was the least tense film I've worked on and, in fact, the calmest period of my professional life.

HM: Do you feel like explaining the secrets of rehearsal now, or should we turn to a different subject?

AF: Well, look, it's not that complicated. You have a character and an actor. At the end of the day, the two of them have to come together. On one side you have a body with multiple faces. On the other another such body. The two of them have to turn around so that ultimately one face of each of them is touching the other. When this happens, the actor feels they've found a way of entering into the character. The sort of explanation you might give to the actor along the lines of "This character you're playing is very generous or romantic" is of no use whatsoever. You have to use the actor's own character so that, somehow, they become molded into the character they're playing. And you shouldn't explain this openly to the actor. You have to do things so that this comes about of its own accord.

AM: It's just like what we do with kids. I remember Khosrow Shakibai[5] saying that if you want to act well you have to be a child. He used to say that your relationship with the director should be like a child with an adult. And the point here is that you cannot behave in the same way with every child. The same is true of actors. For example, one actor might like to have things explained, and if stuff isn't explained then they won't do their job. It might turn out that you explain things incorrectly but still manage to guide the actor to the result you want. But there might be another actor who benefits from having nothing explained.

AF: During the rehearsal period you gradually establish yourself in the inner world of every actor. Not because of the things you say, because every one of us lies behind so many masks that nothing can be understood by speaking. But after a while you manage to get something out of a person's inner world. More than helping the actors, these rehearsals help me. I understand what kind of a person I'll be building this character with. I put more energy into rehearsals than the actors do. For instance, in rehearsal I realized that Tahar Rahim has the energy of six people! His body cannot be contained in one place. Before a shot where he needs to be calm, he has to go and somehow let out all this energy. Sometimes I saw him going off set and punching things so that he could get all this energy out of his system. Do you remember?

AM: He is explosive!

AF: It's impossible to describe the energy he has. So when you want to give this person a complex and introverted role, you can't allow him to behave like that. And if you constantly tell the actor directly to reduce their energy levels, eventually they completely lose their sensitivity to the word. Instead, you keep rehearsing and each time you tell them it was good until gradually they reach the desired level.

AM: It's exactly how you'd treat a kid! And that's what people might not like in actors, exactly that. Maybe they don't like treating an actor like a kid. I mean it!

AF: Using exactly that strategy, I would get to, say, the ninth take and I would see that Tahar's energy level was now where I wanted it. Is what I'm saying clear?

HM: Yes, totally. When you were saying that it is just this aspect of acting that annoys people, did you mean treating people in this sort of way?

AM: Yes, well, people often don't like that once they've reached a certain age [laughing]!

AF: Or being tricked [laughing]!

AM: And for you to say quite consciously that we should go and put ourselves in this position again!

AF: But there's something really lovely about it, too: you enter the world of children's games. You distance yourself from the complex world outside and go back to the world of childhood. I remember that once I asked Bérénice and Ali and the two children to go to an amusement park and, like a family, to go on the rides from morning to night and eat lunch together. The day after, you could see in everything they did—even the way they looked at one another—that their relationship had changed. They'd become closer. When something like that hasn't taken place between the actors, of course you can give them technical instructions on set, tell them to lift an arm up, tilt their head to one side, let tears well up in their eyes, and then take the shot and finish it, but the audience can sense that this isn't realistic.

I'll give you an interesting example. Toward the end of filming, we had a shot where Bérénice was standing alone in the kitchen holding her cell phone, hesitating over whether to call or not. Bear in mind that in her real life, this is someone who lives with a director and who has acted in another style and, whether she wants to or not, compares these two styles in her head. I asked her to start thinking about a story I was going to tell so that she would be able to show us her hesitation in that moment. We made a few takes and I said one of them was good, and then we moved on to the next shot; the next shot was more important and I worried we wouldn't have time to do it. That day she said to me how interesting it was that this was the first time she hadn't done what I wanted her to do, and yet I had still approved of the result! I mean that I had just realized that while she was acting she was thinking about something else, and not what I had told her. When I heard this I started to doubt my method a little. I told myself that it is possible for something to happen internally but for the audience on the outside to be fooled and not realize that they are witnessing a different feeling. I thought that I was being oversensitive. Then when we came to the end of the production, and the whole film had been edited, one day the editor said to us, "I have a problem with one of the shots and I'd like to cut it." I asked which one. I saw that she was referring to exactly that shot, saying that she didn't find the feeling in it believable. It was really strange. I realized that what I had used to think about the audience sensing the inner state of the actor was in fact true. In *About Elly* we never say anything about the pasts of Ahmad and Sepideh. Nothing, not a word. So many people who saw the film thought that these two must have had a romantic relationship in the past. The reason for it was that during rehearsals we had rehearsed the two of them getting to know one another and their past friendship, and this remained in the way they looked at one another. Maybe what I'm saying seems rather abstract, but in cinema these things really do happen.

HM: Wonderful. This part of our discussion is complete. I still have a pile of questions to ask about the details of the film, but you must be tired. Let's leave them for another time. By way of a final question, why don't you just tell us about the conditions the film was made in? For the first time both of you were involved in a completely non-Iranian production. How was it? Was it very organized?

AM: For the first time I felt I was being supported by someone called "the producer." The French have rules that initially feel very strange to us, and we made fun of some of them. We made fun of taking the day off on Saturdays and Sundays. We would tell them to let us do our job!

HM: What else?

AM: In our cinema we have a sort of spirit of sacrifice, which isn't the case at all here. Or at least you see it less. I'm still not sure if that spirit of sacrifice is necessarily a good thing. Perhaps it sometimes damages what you're trying to do, but in Iran you feel that if you say to your team, "Come on, everyone, let's keep going until morning," everyone will throw themselves into it heart and soul. Instead, here people just go and do their paperwork.

HM: So if someone messes up what they're doing, no one else comes to help them?

AM: Yes, yes, they do.

AF: Actually, team spirit is very strong here.

AM: Off set, everyone does what they need to do and they do a very thorough job. Everyone respects everyone else. You really feel the equality in the team. The sometimes horrible stuff that goes on off set in Iran, which has a lot to do with the class system, doesn't exist in France at all. The extras are treated in exactly the same way as the actors, everyone is treated the same and has the same possibilities. Of course, I'm sure there are other ways of doing things in France, too, so for the moment we're just describing the experience we had with this film. The producer and the production team pay careful attention to all sorts of factors that, however small or detailed they might appear, nonetheless have a big impact on the quality of the work.

HM: Were you free to do what you liked? Could you shoot on as many days as you wanted? Were there no restrictions?

AF: There were none. Ideal conditions. I'll avoid passing judgment on which is better or worse. Because in Iran I always worked according to my own methods. And here I didn't necessarily work according to French methods. So I can't talk about the differences in film production between Iran and France. I can only say what the differences are between how I work in Iran and how I work here. In my opinion, there have been two distinguishing characteristics: one is that in Iran there is a sort of passion that exists that is often necessary for artistic creation. This is to say, too much order can be damaging.

HM: You mean something like the spirit of sacrifice Ali was talking about.

AF: Yes, but there is a fine line between passion and agitation, and if we manage to keep that, then passion is very valuable. The second point is that in Iran we are more creative. I don't want to exaggerate, but in practice I've seen that Iranians are more creative.

HM: What do you mean by that? Can you give an example?

AF: I mean that in Iran an assistant director, a production assistant, a gaffer will solve problems more quickly.

AM: Here it seems that they'll only think within the framework that has been set out for them. On no account will they step outside that framework.

AF: I also want to say that when it comes to anything that's outside Iran, we have a sort of inferiority complex. If it's true that we are quick to say how wonderful we are, then surely that's as good a sign as any of our inferiority complex. Then again, if we look at the quality of films that are made around the world and compare them with Iranian ones, it's obvious that Iranian films are better; just because there's a whole bunch of unfamiliar names appearing in their credits, we imagine that we must have fallen behind them.

Where they are better than us, in my opinion, is in their organization. It's really extraordinary, the organization they have, and it doesn't come from cinema itself but from the industry more generally. Their professional regulations have their source in their factory regulations. This way of organizing things was new for the Iranians in our group. To begin with, I kept insisting to the producer that two days off from filming would make me lose touch with the film. As it happened, the professional rules wouldn't allow us to work any other way. But after a while I realized that even if they had told me to work on the two days off, I wouldn't have wanted to! There are many benefits to it. It meant the team could rest before they got really tired and tensions started creeping in. And then afterward everything was fresh. So organization of this kind is important here, and then another point is the division of labor. Here four people would do something that in Iran a single individual would carry out. That's why people don't get tired. Over here the crew is much bigger. There were ten or fifteen trucks with trailers following us around just so that everyone could have their own personal space, their own dedicated container. Of course, when you make a film here on eight million euros, but in Iran on two hundred thousand euros, these differences will exist. Everyone is careful to make sure no one gets hurt, no one's spirits drop. In any case, the experience of working on this film has been very valuable for me, and I think the Iranians who worked on it can transfer part of our experiences back to Iran.

AM: Yes, you get really excited when you think about which part of these experiences we can put to good use on our own films.

Notes

1. Award-winning French playwright and screenwriter.

2. French actor who would eventually play Samir in *The Past*.

3. French director, screenwriter, and producer best known for his award-winning film *The Artist* (2011).

4. Ali Mosaffa's second feature film, independently produced in Iran and released in 2012.

5. Iranian actor (1944–2008) best known for starring in Dariush Mehrjui's *Hamoun* (1990).

An Interview with Asghar Farhadi about *The Salesman*: This Hidden Hell

Massoud Mehrabi / 2016

From *Film Monthly* (Tehran), Vol. 34, No. 514, September 2016. Translated by Shahab Vaezzadeh.

Massoud Mehrabi: You have traversed many long paths in recent years, and most of those paths have elevated you to the pinnacle of cinema. But you've also had to step over some thorny debris during that journey and to keep an eye out for rocks being hurled at you from the wayside. Given how sensitive the cultural climate is nowadays and the unique position that you've attained, I have to ask: how hard is it to be Asghar Farhadi in Iran, and what kind of challenges does it pose?

Asghar Farhadi: There are two sides to it. On the one hand, the popularity of my work creates certain expectations, which I, in turn, feel motivated to match. That's the positive side. But there's another side that can be quite toxic and that some people can use as an excuse to focus on irrelevant gossip. I have always tried to distance myself from those trivial distractions and make sure that my films are not negatively impacted. I think those types of stories and gossip columns are becoming more popular, but they have absolutely nothing to do with cinema and are just circulated around the release date of a new film.

The best solution I've found is to just stay away from that side of things and keep myself occupied with other projects outside of Iran. I'm very fortunate to have so many people who connect with my films and are not influenced by those misleading headlines—I really do appreciate their support. But I'm well aware that some people are just negative and can't accept that support. They become more and more outraged with every film that I make and feel they have to express that outrage however they can. I know what my purpose is and I just try to enjoy my life and work as a filmmaker, but those people only take joy in being angry.

MM: Some figures in the media were offended after not being invited to a private screening you held. That's what the cultural climate is like now: even when you reach out and try to involve a few critics in your latest project, it just results in both your character and your film being disparaged. How much does it hurt your personal life, being so prominent and constantly under the spotlight in Iranian cinema? You are invited to all kinds of film and non-film-related events and you're always expected to happily accept those invitations. Do you think these issues will ever wear you down so much that you'll just decide to pack it in one day and call it quits?

AF: Nothing could ever permanently drive me away. No matter how hard it gets, I could never stay away for too long. In the words of Ahmad Shamlou,[1] "My light burns in this house."

But people do expect me to participate in every non-film-related event and other projects not directly related to film, which my schedule simply doesn't permit. I try to attend what I can with the little free time I have, but I really can't accept every offer. I am invited to theater productions and private screenings at least three or four times a week—how could I possibly attend them all? Perhaps I should use this opportunity to make something clear for the first time: I have a personal life and I'm the father of two children; if I were to accept every invitation kindly sent to me, I wouldn't be able to make any films.

MM: Doing so, in fact, could hinder your creativity and would be detrimental to Iranian cinema as a whole. If you were to make a poor film as a result, those same people would be the first to call you out and demand to know why you made such a poor film and why it wasn't as successful as your greatest work.

AF: I always turn my mobile phone off and sometimes even change my number whenever I start writing. But that can spark a lot of questions for some people. The truth is, I cannot write if I leave my phone on. Reza Mirkarimi[2] once asked me, "How do you manage to keep writing and working with so many other obligations?" I told him, "The only way is to turn your phone off and avoid all contact with the outside world while you're writing."

I hired a PR professional to answer some of my calls, but that has upset and offended a few people, including some who actually know me personally. So, what options am I left with? Take yesterday, for example, when someone came to my office and asked to see me. He was a taxi driver with a master's degree in acting and he demanded to talk to me. I was busy making plans for my film screening at the time and asked him to wait until next week so I could arrange a meeting with him. If I'd turned him away, he would have held a grudge against me forever, but if I'd let him in, I would have had to sacrifice my writing time, and time is precisely what I'm short of. Of course, it's very kind of people to invite me to concerts, theater productions, private screenings, charity events, etc., but I'm only human and have only twenty-four hours in the day, just like everyone else.

MM: You have your phone turned off while you're working, but when you turn it back on, you're faced with all of these questions and issues that impede your concentration and creativity when you get back to work.

AF: It's a great honor and very gratifying to see such kindness from colleagues, friends, and so many others, but I just don't have enough time in the day for all of them, and that can unfortunately cause offense to some. I really don't know how to respond to some requests or what advice to give to people who are trying to become actors, for example. I used to tell them to go to university or study at reputable academies, but now those same people are contacting me saying, "We followed your advice and went to university for a few years—now what?"

The only thing I can suggest is auditioning as a nonprofessional actor—assuming we require any—when I start work on a new film every two or three years. I'm certainly not complaining, anyway. I'm very happy to have all of these connections. It's just another part of life. That's why I'm still here, and I have no intention of stepping down despite all of the gossip, bitterness, and jealousy. But I must stress that I'm only human; I only have twenty-four hours in the day like everyone else, and I usually try to spend that time working on my next project. It is difficult to manage, but I try to keep things moving while causing as little damage and offense as possible.

MM: Have you ever felt so pressured by all of those requests that you just tried to get away from it all?

AF: I sometimes turn my phone off and stay with my parents, who live in a small town, when the pressure gets to be too much—that's the most peaceful place in the world for me.

MM: Let's move on to your film, which was screened early this morning during an incredible premiere event. *The Salesman* is a film centered on morality that shows that judgment and morality are still the greatest concerns on your mind. What common features did you find between your writing and the Arthur Miller play that served as the film's foundation?

AF: What fascinated me about the play, and what I became fixed on using myself, was the focus that Miller placed on the relationships between people within a family unit. The play has four main characters: Willy Loman, his wife, Linda, and their two sons. While the play centers on a family drama, that drama actually gives you a complete understanding of what the spirit and atmosphere were like outside the four walls of their home during that period of American history. That is the play's greatest quality and what really captured my interest; there is a strong social aspect to it.

When we talk about family relationships, it also raises a kind of moral debate. It's impossible to make a clear or straightforward judgment about Willy Loman, but he has obviously made mistakes in his life and his son is grappling with one particular mistake throughout the play that is unforgivable. Willy is having an affair with a prostitute when his son arrives at the hotel room and discovers his father's infidelity. Arthur Miller's play enters a moral debate, in that respect, as to whether that mistake justifies the son's degrading treatment of his father. Willy Loman is so tormented and humiliated by his son that he ultimately decides to commit suicide. Of course, one of his reasons for committing suicide is also financial. The theme of the play is obviously political at its core when you take Miller's own beliefs into account, but its exploration of relationship dynamics within a family and the moral debate it raises is very similar to what I have tried to do throughout my career.

MM: What connections and direct comparisons can be made between post-World War Two American society in the late 1950s and Iranian society today?

AF: *Death of a Salesman* is actually about the dawn of capitalism in America. Even Linda remarks during her final dialogue, "We're free. . . . We're free," as she sits by Willy Loman's body. I believe that line is spoken with contempt. Miller is criticizing the expansion of the capitalist system in America, and the play is based on that ideology. The social conditions during that time in American history were different than the social conditions in Iran today. Iran is a unique country, and the ruling class has an ideological foundation, but we do have one thing in common: we are changing just as quickly.

From the changing face of society and the physical appearance of our cities to the quality of human relationships, the relationships between people in Iran's urban society today are very different than those of twenty or thirty years ago. Our lives are changing at a rapid pace and we are racing frantically toward that change, but that does not necessarily mean we are stepping into modernity; we are similar to post-World War Two American society in that respect. Even at the beginning of the play, Miller devotes much of the introduction to describing the appearance of the city: the fact that the old houses are dilapidated and the lower working classes are being crushed as the capitalist system expands and takes over. It may not be happening across the entire country, but we are witnessing this superficial change in parts of our urban society. Tehran's appearance is changing rapidly: old houses are being knocked down and towers are being raised to the heavens, but beneath the surface nothing is really changing. I feel there are some similarities between our two societies in regard to how quickly they are changing, but the most significant connection between *Death of a Salesman* and my film is the characters. The elderly salesman who invades the couple's home and their privacy is a counterpart to the salesman in *Death of a Salesman*, and Ahoo is a counterpart to the prostitute whom Willy Loman sleeps with in the hotel. Emad is tracking down a man in real life whom he plays onstage every day.

MM: Is the crumbling building depicted at the beginning of the film actually symbolic of this change or a metaphor for the inevitable downfall that lies ahead?

AF: It is not symbolic. The building's near collapse is, first and foremost, part of the plot that gets the story's engine started and moves us along to the next building. It has implications that can be examined, but it shouldn't be described as "symbolic." As the writer and director, I was not using that sequence to convey a hidden message in the film. Throughout the film, you can sense that not only have cracks appeared on the walls of one building, but they are spreading through the relationships, too. It's an omen for what will transpire between the characters later on.

Ever since *Fireworks Wednesday*, the home environment in my films has been a reflection of the different moods and restlessness that exist within people. You can even observe it in *The Past*, which takes place outside of Iran, e.g., painting the walls in the house a different color.

MM: But the apartment block is seemingly unrepairable and will have to be demolished like the building next door, so that the foundations can be redone and a new structure can be built in its place.

AF: That's not how I feel and it's not really how I look at things. But I agree with the main point that cracks are emerging and not being addressed. Things are changing so quickly that we don't have time to stop and think. I don't really know if the house needs to be knocked down and rebuilt, or if it should just be repaired. I don't know what kind of harmony needs to be achieved between cultural, social, and religious issues before they can synchronize with the speed at which we're changing and we are truly able to evolve.

MM: Your latest film is similar to *Fireworks Wednesday*, *About Elly*, *A Separation*, and *The Past*, in that it depicts the tense and deteriorating world of two couples. It is, in my opinion, an extension of the tragic fall of Adam and Eve. In other words, where there is life, there is pain and suffering. It's like there is a hell on earth, and we can observe it through these couples who somehow evoke the bewilderment and torment of Adam and Eve and their perpetual atonement for "original sin."

AF: Family dynamics, especially the relationship between a husband and wife, are like an ocean that I can always dive into and discover something new in. The relationship between a husband and wife is one of the oldest and most profound in human history, but it always spawns new problems—for every husband and wife that have ever existed, there are just as many problems. In fact, those problems are even more complex nowadays because humans have become more complex and multifaceted. People now have a wider vocabulary with which to communicate with one another, but, ironically, the more they speak, the more they misunderstand each other. These days, we have the power of speech and communication, and that is obviously very valuable, but every conversation leads to a new challenge.

My films deliberately try to place couples in dire situations, which they must overcome and find a way out of. Their relationships reach a point of crisis due to the situation that they are confronted with. They don't usually have to deal with that crisis from the very beginning of the film, but they become more entangled in it as the story progresses. In *Fireworks Wednesday*, for example, the couple probably had a very normal and comfortable life before the woman moved in next door and the husband began an affair with her. All of their problems begin when they are faced with this new set of circumstances. In *About Elly*, tensions arise and all of the trouble starts after Elly drowns in the sea. In *The Past*, it starts when the husband takes a short trip to Iran but doesn't return until four years later. The couple in *The Salesman* were living a normal life until they were forced to move to an apartment previously occupied by a prostitute. At that point, they inadvertently become entangled in a new set of circumstances, which puts pressure on their relationship and reveals a different side to them that neither one had seen before.

MM: As in your previous works, the female characters in your latest release are mistreated and you seem to be more on their side. These women endure the pain and suffering inflicted upon them by the outside world and receive much deeper wounds than the men. The temptation of the forbidden fruit is, however, placed at their feet!

AF: A lot of men who watch the film seem to share that opinion, but many female viewers believe that the opposite is true. Women accuse me of favoring male characters and treating female characters as just a nuisance. The female characters in my films are substantially more forgiving and responsible, however. Because of their willingness to accept more responsibility, they are usually the ones who are blamed and put in harm's way when something goes wrong and they fail to live up to that responsibility. When those characters are able to turn the other cheek and endure hardship more easily than the male characters, it gives audiences the impression that I am actually taking their side. And there's a lot of truth to that; women are the superior characters in my films. Throughout the majority of my films, the female characters always try to look ahead. They are the ones responsible for bringing children into the world, so they are more forbearing and invested in the future. Male characters, on the other hand, mostly look over their shoulders and brood over past events. That may be because men used to work a lot more on the land and they prefer stability to change and progress. Selflessness and being responsible are two traits that are possessed by most female characters in my films. They are also forgiving of those who have harmed them. The female protagonist in *Fireworks Wednesday* forgives and continues to live with her husband under the same roof, albeit while sleeping in a separate room. In *About Elly*, Sepideh takes responsibility for managing the whole trip and everybody abuses her emotionally when a tragic accident occurs. Even though she doesn't agree with the group's opinion at the end of the film, Sepideh accepts their decision and is forced against her better judgment to tell Elly's fiancé the lie that had been agreed on by the group. At the end of *The Past*, Marie wants to put everything that had happened with her Iranian ex-husband behind her and move forward with the new man in her life because she is pregnant with his child and thinking about the life that she is carrying. It's the same kind of situation in *The Salesman*: we expect the female character to have a strong reaction because she was the victim of the attack, but she slowly seems to let go of her anger instead. While she does not forgive her male attacker, she is able to control herself.

MM: The name "Emad" literally means "pillar" or "support"; and "Rana" means "delicate" or "fragile," along with its other definition "elegant woman." Were these character names deliberately chosen to have symbolic meaning?

AF: No, they were not. I usually try to avoid anything that might steer me toward symbolism. Those names were chosen at random. I always use the names of people that I know in real life for my characters. In fact, Nader and Emad are the names of two brothers who are both good friends of mine in real life. Some viewers might not see it that way, however, and they may find other layers of meaning in those names. Film gives you those possibilities and freedoms, and it is not my job as a filmmaker to dictate which interpretations should be applied to my films.

I give audiences the freedom to find motifs in my films and engage in analytical debates, but I insist on using the term "clue"—not "symbol." When we use the word "clue," we're talking about piecing things together in order to shed light on a certain topic. With symbols, however, every example has its own independent meaning. When clues are pieced together, they can guide us toward the correct address, where we can confront the deeper questions that the film is trying to convey. The same thing happened with *A Separation* when the names of its two main characters, Nader and Simin, were also interpreted to signify something else. It is true, however, that Rana looks to her husband as a pillar of support throughout the events of *The Salesman*. Their relationship is very healthy and loving at the beginning of the film, but Emad becomes less and less of a pillar of support to his wife throughout the film as he tries to quench his own personal anger. His anger stems from both the fact that his wife was hurt and all of the pressure was placed on him indirectly and unknowingly by those around him, which he doesn't have the strength to ignore.

MM: Rana is not a particularly active character compared to other female characters in your previous films, like Sepideh in *About Elly*. Rana's passivity and dependence on others become apparent from one of the film's earliest scenes, where Emad calls out for her to hurry up as the building is falling apart and then lays some slippers by her feet on the stairway. She seems to remain silent and to refrain from taking any effective or drastic action throughout the film in order to protect her husband and their reputation.

AF: Both of those characters are transformed as the story progresses. Emad seems a very affable and considerate person at first: in the midst of all the chaos, we see him go back to help his next-door neighbor carry her disabled son out of the building. Rana is the one who seems more concerned about herself and her husband's welfare. But as we get further into the story, the two characters switch places and Rana becomes the one more concerned about others; she tries to protect the reputation of the man who hurt her, even though she has not forgiven him. Emad had a very forgiving nature in the beginning, but later on he only thinks about himself. Rana is actually very proactive at the start of the film. When they move into the new apartment, Rana is the one who helps Babak so that they can gain access to the previous tenant's bedroom. She also contacts the previous tenant and convinces her to collect her belongings from the apartment. After the assault, however, she becomes apprehensive about acting impulsively and being in the company of others. She even tries to sneak quietly up the stairs so that the man next door doesn't notice her. At one point, she has to walk offstage prematurely during a performance. She also avoids contact with others in case they react melodramatically to the news that she was assaulted.

Rana is a very active and spirited person at the beginning of the film and her gradual transformation can even be observed in the color of the clothes she wears, which begin to alternate between different shades of gray. Emad is kind and friendly toward others at the beginning of the film; even when he is dealing with the stress of moving house, he jokes around with the kids in his class and is good-humored when some of them ask inappropriate questions. Even when someone behaves or speaks inappropriately, he is open-minded enough to grant them that right. Under the weight of outside pressure, however, his character turns into someone that even he doesn't recognize.

MM: You are right about Emad. His character starts out from a place of stability, tranquility, amity, and kindness but ends up somewhere extremely turbulent. That character arc is much shorter for Rana, however.

AF: That may be because the incident involving Rana occurs at the start of the film, and that ordeal turns her into a reclusive person. Before that incident, she had been fixing up the new apartment and also had an active role at the theater. After the incident, however, she cannot perform properly onstage no matter how hard she tries. She seems to withdraw from society and tries to seek refuge in a child instead. I think her character's sense of isolation truly reaches its peak when she asks to take the child home at the end of the day so that she won't be alone.

MM: The act of cleaning objects and surroundings has an interesting rhythm in the film and seems to be either a futile or never-ending struggle that is repeated several times, yet practically nothing ever gets clean.

AF: In *The Past*, the theme of cleaning begins with the windshield wiper and continues with characters removing stains from clothing. Likewise, the repainting of the house and the stripping of old paints serve the same function throughout the film. In *The Salesman*, the two acts of sweeping the theater stage and cleaning the new apartment are juxtaposed, while the start of Emad and Rana's life at the new apartment also coincides with the first night of their performance. There seems to be an element of symmetry between what happens on the theater stage and what happens at the new apartment. They start everything anew but are struck by tragedy before they can take one step forward.

MM: Did your decision to use the Moluk Zarrabi[3] song "Ey Gol,'" also known as "Rana," come to you while writing the script or immediately after choosing the name "Rana"?

AF: I really like that song. Some people incorrectly claimed that it was sung by Qamar-ol-Moluk Vaziri, but Moluk Zarrabi was the actual performer of the song. What I really like about it is the fact that it is a love song that uses an unromantic word.

MM: It is a very beautiful song and aptly describes Rana during her ordeal.

AF: I think it's a charming and beautiful song regardless of the film. I always listen to it in my car. There is one particular word used in the lyrics to address the singer's lover, which I had never encountered being used in the context of a love song: "tyrant." I'd never realized that there was another dimension to the word "tyrant" that related to love. I truly connect with the message of the song every time I hear that word being sung.

After naming the character "Rana," I decided to use some music to accompany the scene in the apartment where she tries to forget about her ordeal and enjoy a night in. I'd listened to a lot of different songs, when it suddenly occurred to me that it would be quite romantic if Emad always played a song called "Rana" for his wife. So, that's the song I used and I'm really happy with how it turned out. Unfortunately, there were a lot of inaccurate reports that came out later based on the misconception that the song was actually performed by Qamar-ol-Moluk. Anyone who had any clue about music could have refuted that idea because there is only one version of the song, and the name of the singer is actually announced during the recording.

MM: That scene is like the film's center of gravity, in some way. The pacing of the film is quite slow until that point, but from there everything starts to accelerate and gain a sense of urgency.

AF: That is where one of the film's main plot twists occurs. Perhaps if that money hadn't been used to buy the food that night, they could have dealt with the matter differently, but that incident made it much harder to move on and forget about what had happened. The story moves in a different direction from that point onward. Emad, who himself is suffering due to an invasion of his privacy, decides for the first time to invade the privacy of the previous tenant. He listens to the messages on her answering machine and reads her letters. That's the point where he slowly begins to turn into someone else.

MM: Emad and Rana's profession is artistic and intellectual, and the attacker is traced back to a bakery. . . .

AF: His son-in-law works at the bakery and he sells clothes on the street at night. He is actually an Iranian version of Willy Loman; he even closely resembles Arthur Miller's physical description of the character. If Willy Loman were Iranian, that is exactly how I would picture him: a salesman who sets up shop on the street at night, like Willy Loman going from place to place peddling a particular brand of socks. He too is a vendor, and, incidentally, the first translation of the play was published under the title *Death of a Peddler*.

MM: In any case, Emad's search begins at the bakery, which calls to mind the story of Adam and Eve eating the wheat and committing the first sin in paradise. You could have chosen any other occupation for the attacker and his family. Food for the body is made in the bakery, but Emad and Rana, who are both artists, make food for the soul—it's an interesting juxtaposition.

AF: None of that happened consciously, but, now that I think about it, I can see how those details may have some psychological connection. I admire those who bake and sell bread. Historically, our culture has always regarded bakers as warm and kindhearted people. Their delivery drivers always catch my eye when I see them dropping bread off behind shops and cafes in the morning. That sight was actually one of my inspirations for the story of *The Salesman*. When Emad first enters the bakery, you look suspiciously at all of the people working there, but that prejudice is swept aside as soon as you see them baking bread. You assume that whoever is capable of invading someone else's home should have a much more sinister job and you should automatically feel repulsed by them. Instead, you feel a sense of warmth and friendliness as soon as you enter the bakery. You feel like the attacker is someone you know and rub shoulders with. You can't even guess which one of those people could be the assailant.

MM: But there is another symbolic aspect to that scene. There is an element of eroticism when Emad first enters the bakery and we see one of the trainee bakers rolling balls of dough.

AF: Perhaps. But I try not to make such conscious decisions when I work. I didn't choose a bakery for any of those specific reasons while writing the script. There must be some subconscious connections, but I prefer not to be actively aware of them—it gives the audience the chance to build that world up in their own minds.

MM: Filmmakers like you prefer to reach a point where their symbolism takes shape without having to consciously think about it.

AF: I think if the story is told properly, then all of those things will also develop properly, that is, if all of the social and moral layers are stacked in the right place. The only rule is that you don't try to force anything onto the story. I shouldn't ever choose a specific occupation in order to make someone seem scary, or vice versa. I always feel like the story already exists; I'm not the one creating it; I'm simply making my way toward the story and trying to uncover it.

MM: Beds are another example of a recurring motif that appears in the film. In fact, the film actually opens with a shot of a bed and mattress.

AF: That was something I did give some thought to. The film's opening shot shows a lamp lighting up a bed. That can be considered a motif or "clue" because it is repeated several times and, when those recurring images are pieced together, it reveals one of the film's main themes to the audience.

MM: Was that the only motif that you used deliberately?

AF: There are more, but please don't make me open that box!

MM: Is it a bed of sin? Does all sin originate from the bed?

AF: Well, the film certainly addresses issues of sex and sexuality: what happens in the taxi, for example; when someone enters the bathroom while a woman is taking a shower due to a misunderstanding; when sexual images are found on a schoolboy's mobile phone; when we see the bed, etc. All of those things help to create a specific atmosphere in the film, which provides the audience with a set of coordinates where the film can be viewed from a different angle. When all of those details are pieced together, they are like a new set of coordinates for the audience.

MM: Doesn't personal analysis and interpretation dictate what different people may infer from the film?

AF: What films and filmmakers actually try to do is just present those motifs and let the audience decide how to interpret them—they're not dictating anything. You may infer something completely different than my original intention and arrive at a separate conclusion. It doesn't matter. Once you start to think and expand on the story being told on-screen you are no longer just a spectator; you have become an active filmmaker.

MM: That is definitely true. In any case, you deliver those motifs to audiences and critics very well. The bed is both a place of birth and a place of sin. You moved the scene of the crime to the bathroom, however. The place where everything is supposed to be cleaned and washed away actually becomes the source of contamination.

Your stories usually revolve around middle-class characters. Do you hold a special view of the middle class?

AF: The most significant and crucial class in modern society is, in my opinion, the middle class. Of course, the stratification of social classes in our society is quite different than that of other societies. When we talk about the bourgeoisie in France, for example, there's a whole bourgeois culture attached to it. But our upper class doesn't have a bourgeois culture because those shifts in social order happened very quickly—almost overnight—and people from the lower classes became part of the wealthy elite quite suddenly. The stratification of Iranian society is based more on wealth and economic divisions than culture. Fortunately, the largest class in Iranian society is the middle class. As someone who lives in Iranian society, I am much closer and more familiar with the middle class here, and I find the people who belong to that class to be more real.

Whenever I focus on the middle class, I don't merely view them from an economic perspective. When you approach a story from the perspective of the lower class, the economic foreground overshadows your work and may prevent other themes from being recognized and appreciated. I worked on stories and situations from the lives of the lower class in *Beautiful City* and *Dancing in the Dust*, but since then I've always felt more comfortable writing about the middle class because I understand them more. I feel like when I focus on middle-class environments, a larger part of the audience is able to relate to the characters and the story is more tangible to them. I am not trying to criticize the middle class by centering my films on them. Some have taken the rather superficial view that I am insulting and ridiculing the middle class. On the contrary, my focus on the middle class actually demonstrates their importance and my belief in the power of their influence as a social class.

MM: Looking back on the history of Iranian cinema, most dramatic films released during the 1950s and even the 1960s were based on the ongoing struggle between the lower and upper classes, and many other films were set against that backdrop. We even see a contrast between the cities and villages, emphasizing the accumulation of corruption in the cities and the purity of the villages. More recently, however, the middle class has dominated Iranian cinema of the 2010s—particularly in your work.

AF: Iranian literature had been following a similar trend prior to that, as most writers of the time were more concerned about justice than freedom. And when they talked about "justice," they were more interested in economic justice. That trend led writers to focus more on the contrast between society's wealthy and poor strata, rather than trying to seek justice through their work. Sometime later, a concept known as "freedom" gradually emerged and took precedence over justice. That may explain why the depiction of the middle class became more popular, as freedom is a much greater concern for the middle class than justice. That's not to say that justice is not a concern, but freedom is what the middle class strive for more than anything else.

MM: Judgment and justice are very prominent subjects in *The Salesman.*

AF: Yes, but economic justice is not raised as an issue.

MM: Indeed. Unlike Arthur Miller, who mostly focuses on the issue of economic justice in his play, you use *The Salesman* to examine justice in a different way. The narrative structure of *The Salesman* is similar to that of a crime film, and Emad is essentially playing the part of an interrogator or a detective.

AF: Even the light hanging from the ceiling during the kitchen scene is reminiscent of an interrogation room.

MM: What really makes the film stand out with its fast, internal rhythm is the theme of revenge. Emad's desire for revenge gradually becomes stronger and more intense, but it is ultimately futile and only prolongs his pain. Do you believe in revenge and retribution? How does justice fit in this film?

AF: That is a very important point, and one that will surely arouse debate and many outlandish comments and suppositions based on that viewpoint. The question is, what should Emad do in that situation? His privacy has been invaded both spiritually and psychologically, after all, and his life has been thrown into turmoil through no fault of his own. What is he supposed to do at that point? In an ideal world, he would hand over the perpetrator—the one responsible for invading his personal privacy—to face the full force of the law. The story unfolds in such a way that he cannot turn to the law, however: honor and reputation are blocking his way. Emad himself repeatedly insists that they report the crime, and that is the best stance that someone in such a predicament could take. But there are certain obstacles in the way, and when others hear about their plight, they all express their disapproval about Emad involving the police. They feel, in this instance, that there is no legal punishment to fit the crime.

Emad tells Rana several times that they should report the crime rather than try to remove all of the evidence that was left behind. Emad takes a just and fair stance: he believes that the law should decide the man's punishment, removed from anger and emotion. He is led down a new path, however, after being pressured by others—most significantly, his own wife—not to involve the police. Emad may not have been able to endure the potentially long and drawn-out legal process, so he decides to take the law into his own hands and does the same thing that caused him so much anguish: he invades the privacy of the apartment's previous tenant; he invades the privacy of one of his students by looking through his phone; he betrays the trust of his coactor by slandering him onstage. Emad's transformation into someone else essentially begins when he decides not to involve the police, and he makes that decision based on reasons that we as the audience completely understand. In the end, the option of reporting the crime and trusting the law is taken off the table. That is an important point in the film that is sometimes overlooked.

Certain comments were made by critics before the film's release because they had read a plot summary and assumed that Emad pursues his path of revenge from the very beginning. Emad tries several times to act reasonably and rationally; he even manages to control his anger against the man responsible, perhaps because of his advanced age. In fact, it may be the old man himself who causes Emad to lose control and lock him in the apartment. Emad tries to discuss things with him at first; it is the old man who instigates the violence. He only becomes aggressive after the old man himself turns violent. I don't think that Emad is a cruel or sadistic person at heart.

MM: In some way, the film is a testament to the absence—or shortage, at least—of law and order in society.

AF: We have certain customs and beliefs in our society relating to honor, and they can sometimes make us feel that our honor or social reputation may be tarnished if we involve the police in such personal matters.

MM: . . . Especially given the fact that everyone at the theater very quickly hears about what happened to Rana.

AF: The first thing that Rana says to Emad on the rooftop is, "Does anyone else know about it?" and later, "Which one of the neighbors helped me out of the bathroom?"

Those things are obviously important to her, but they inadvertently stop Emad in his tracks and allow others to lead him down the wrong path. He even tells Rana that what happened was not their fault, so they should either report the crime or just put it behind them. They decide to put it behind them, and Emad proceeds to wipe the blood stains from the stairs. He knows that the break-in was a misunderstanding. But their neighbors take pity on Emad, painting an exaggerated picture of the incident and unintentionally stoking the anger inside him. He is an unfortunate product of the environment being shaped around him.

MM: When discussing the film *Gheisar*,[4] the late critic Houshang Kavousi used to say that Gheisar should have gone to the police instead of trying to seek revenge. With the society that we're now living in and the many apartment blocks where neighbors don't even know one another, one might argue that—realistically—the neighbors in *The Salesman* would have immediately taken a step back after finding the injured Rana and contacted the police, or possibly called for an ambulance in order to avoid getting caught up in any legal issues.

AF: But in this case, it seems the neighbors take Rana straight to the hospital themselves and even refrain from informing the police in order to protect Emad and Rana's reputation and to sweep the unfortunate incident under the rug. They act out of sympathy, but their actions only make things worse. The question is, why don't the neighbors inform the police? They seem to think that it might be immoral to tell others about what happened, and it would therefore be kinder to keep it under wraps. It is that compassion that leads to catastrophe; they believe that Rana was actually raped.

MM: The scene where Emad and his students watch *The Cow* is more than just a simple homage to its director, Dariush Mehrjui. In fact, that same sense of disaffection and metamorphosis can be observed in the disruptive and immature behavior of the students in class, which itself is more unsettling than the alarm bells that it sets ringing about the next generation. What is your view of the generation depicted in that classroom? From a pessimistic point of view, one might surmise that there will be no salvation for them in the future.

AF: It is actually the total opposite. I used to teach the same class, and I filmed those scenes in the same classroom that I taught in twenty years ago. My students back then were unruly and they would misbehave. I always used to wonder what they were going to do when they got older. I was genuinely worried about their future. Interestingly enough, many of them are now productive members of society and first-rate professionals in the film world. In fact, the set designer on *The Salesman* was one of my students in that class.

Once I'd decided that Emad would be an art school teacher, I began looking through a school book for a lesson that wouldn't seem banal and clichéd. I stumbled upon Gholam-Hossein Sa'edi's story *The Cow* by complete accident in a high school literature book. It was like opening a treasure chest. I was delighted because it made me realize that I could alleviate the stale and clichéd atmosphere of the classroom by having the students watch a film. But that scene where the students are unruly and disruptive is one of the turning points for Emad as a character; it is the first time that he demonstrates a lack of understanding and leniency toward others. Their behavior is normal for kids that age and that kind of reaction is to be expected when a teacher falls asleep in class. The point I'm trying to make is, why doesn't Emad let them off? How come he was so well disposed to their jokes and willing to humor them during previous scenes? What happened to make him go from laughing and joking around with his students to lashing out at them? The point you were making about the metamorphosis of the students actually happens to Emad. Perhaps that is where Emad decides to act on his earlier remark that the whole city needs to be leveled and rebuilt from the ground up, and he tries to rectify his surroundings. His first step is to invade the privacy of one of his students, which is something that we as an audience struggle to agree with. I think my view of that generation of young adults is actually a realistic one.

MM: When Emad is asked by one of his students how a man turns into a cow, he replies, "Gradually."

AF: That is exactly what happens gradually to Emad. The teacher who has always been a role model falls into the same predicament; the man playing the role of a salesman onstage, who seems so eager to present a charming and pleasant salesman to his audience. In actuality, Emad behaves very differently when he comes face-to-face with a real salesman. When he first realizes that the elderly salesman is in fact the man who invaded the privacy of his home, you immediately expect him to intimidate and strangle the man, but perhaps in that moment he thinks to himself, "This is the same character that I'm playing onstage. Isn't it strange that I am standing face-to-face with a real-life version of my own character?"

MM: Your previous films have all been rather open-ended. *The Salesman*, however, seems to end completely unambiguously and doesn't appear to have an open ending in the conventional sense of the term. Nevertheless, it is an extremely disturbing ending that says a lot about the innate cruelty that every human possesses. The endings of *About Elly* and *A Separation* leave you with a much narrower realm of possibility, but *The Salesman* makes you wonder, "Now what? Who was right and who was wrong? Should I try to pass my own judgment or not?"

Your previous films have always invited us to form our own opinions, but here we have no idea what is right and what is wrong. It's a very perplexing, open ending, which leaves the audience feeling bemused—what is one supposed to think?

AF: My previous films do have definitive endings as well: Elly's body is eventually found by the end of *About Elly*; Simin and Nader's divorce is finalized in court at the end of *A Separation*. Those stories do not have open endings; they have open conclusions. Elly's body is pulled out of the water at the end of *About Elly*, but the ultimate fate of the rest of the group is unclear. Likewise, *A Separation* provides an ending for Simin and Nader but leaves the future of their daughter unknown. As far as storytelling is concerned, *The Salesman* has an open conclusion because we don't know what will become of Emad and Rana's relationship as the screen fades out on the two of them getting into costume and preparing to go back onstage. We don't even know if the old man survived after being subjected to Emad's mistreatment of him. The circumstances at the end of *The Salesman* are much more severe than in previous films, but that doesn't cause bemusement for the audience. It may provoke the viewer to think about things that were previously too painful to think about; they reach a point where they have no choice but to reflect on things. I think we often turn a blind eye to incidents like these, but this story makes us feel like we have to think about these issues. The tone and atmosphere of the film pull you in that direction, and I think that in turn challenges you mentally.

MM: We can assume, because of her intelligence, that Simin and Nader's daughter in *A Separation* has a bright future ahead of her. The ending of *The Salesman*, however, just feels like the end of the world. Emad and Rana's old apartment block is falling apart and no longer inhabitable, and their lives— marred by grief and misfortune—cannot be repaired.

AF: Actually, watching the film makes you reflect on your own life. The film's emotional and psychological impact makes you realize that the feeling of anger that overwhelms you in such instances can actually lead to disaster and misfortune for others. I think the film is more unsettling than it is bitter or disheartening. When we get sick and go to the doctor, he can try to avoid worrying us by hiding our illness from us. That might make us happy and remark on what a good doctor he is, but in reality, we have no idea what is going on inside us. At some point, however, the doctor will have to inform us that we won't survive unless we start taking preventative measures. The doctor's words and tone of voice may worry us, but in the end it won't deter us from seeking treatment.

These types of stories are actually very reassuring because they give the audience hope and the motivation to reflect on things and to find solutions. Even ordinary people who aren't interested in finding motifs or analyzing the film on that level can watch the film and appreciate the potentially dire consequences of invading a family's privacy. The film can, at the very least, make some people take a step back and reset their moral compass.

MM: In addition to being a warning against invading the privacy of others, which is a major problem in our society, the film also suggests how best to seek justice.

AF: That depends on the viewer's perspective. I think the film is more of a recommendation to remain calm and collected. In the past, they used to tell you to recite a few prayers whenever you lost your temper. That could often prove effective even if you weren't religious, because taking the time to say a few prayers would allow you to calm down and make better decisions.

In more literal and basic terms, what you're trying to say is that we should treat others fairly. But what does it mean to treat others fairly? Would it have been fairer of Emad to open the door and let the old man go? Is the film telling us to let bygones be bygones and turn a blind eye to everything in such circumstances? Wherever you go in the world, people react when they are hurt. The film isn't urging you to forgive and forget for no good reason; the point is that you are not entitled to assume the roles of judge, jury, and executioner. Even according to Islamic jurisprudence, you would be sentenced to death for killing someone who had committed a similar crime. Even if you believe that Emad was weak and should have been more ruthless, an Islamic court would have considered his actions illegal, and he would have been punished accordingly. Islamic jurisprudence also states that you have no right to execute the sentence yourself. We must leave the administration of justice and management of such situations to the law, except in special circumstances. Why Emad decides to take the matter into his own hands and doesn't leave it to the law to resolve is another big topic for debate that can be contemplated and discussed by the viewer afterward.

MM: In any case, *The Salesman* is transformative and its greatest strength is that it continues to absorb its audience long after it has finished. I think that its effect on viewers is exactly what you talked about; they become calmer and pay more attention to their behavior.

The camera in *The Salesman* is the film's narrator. I was very surprised during one scene to see the camera enter Ahoo's bedroom before the characters themselves are able to. When they break down the door and enter the room, the camera is already positioned inside the room. I don't recall anything like that ever happening in any of your previous films.

AF: The camera sometimes enters certain environments before the characters do, and that first began with *The Past*.

MM: But here the door to the room is actually closed.

AF: That's true. But that also happens in several places throughout *The Past*; the camera moves and functions as if it were an independent character. The camera only acts like that in relation to Ahoo. We removed Ahoo as an on-screen character, but elements of her life are still present. The camera itself even seems to say that, in the interest of equity and impartial judgment, more of this character should be shown despite her physical absence—let's not just brush her aside. The drawings left on the wall by Ahoo's child; the messages left on her answering machine; her clothes and her shoes; her belongings cluttering up the room; and—most importantly—her reflection in the female actress playing the role of the prostitute onstage who is always accompanied by her child: they are all symbols of a character who doesn't actually appear in the film. The camera indirectly reveals that side of the story to the audience, however, and allows you to understand and learn more about the character. It was the first time that I'd used such a narrative device in one of my films.

MM: The film features a particular shot where the camera switches location to an adjacent building and uses a wide shot to show the roof of Emad and Rana's apartment block. What is the camera trying to say there?

AF: I don't think the audience is paying too much attention to the position of the camera there. That shot is somewhat of an interpretation of Arthur Miller's description of the Loman house and its surrounding area at the beginning of *Death of a Salesman*. The scene reveals a resemblance between the apartment block and the description given by Miller at the start of the play. It is the film's most open shot. It is also placed at the end of a sequence in which many judgments and assumptions are made about the previous female tenant, and I thought that by showing the mass of buildings that seems to encircle their small apartment, it would reinforce the feeling that the apartment and its inhabitants are being judged and scrutinized by others.

MM: Prior to the film's release, some were already noting similarities between Rana and the character of Leila in Bahram Beyzaie's unmade screenplay *The Facts about Idris's Daughter, Leila,* even though that screenplay actually contains traces of Roman Polanski's *The Tenant.* What is your opinion on the matter?

AF: I like all of Mr. Beyzaie's plays, but they have never had any direct influence on my writing. In any case, prostitution is a subject that is frequently depicted in film; I don't understand what the similarities are between my film and Mr. Beyzaie's play.

MM: The similarities lie in the fact that there is a room where a prostitute once lived, and when Leila enters the room, she experiences a feeling of dissociation and gradually begins to transform into the woman who once occupied the house.

AF: I was not aware of that connection, and the last time I read that play was back in 1991, when I was a student.

MM: Those kinds of similarities can be found in many different plays and screenplays.

AF: Even this year at the Cannes Film Festival, there was a French film released on the same day that we screened *The Salesman,* about someone invading a woman's privacy. I never actually saw the film, but I heard that the woman subsequently tries to find out who was responsible.

MM: You worked with one of your favorite cinematographers, Hossein Jafarian, on *Fireworks Wednesday* and *About Elly.* You then worked with Mahmoud Kalari on your next two films before bringing Mr. Jafarian back to collaborate on *The Salesman.* Is it the film's theme, structure, and set design that necessitated a change of cinematographer?

AF: They are two of my dearest friends in life, and I am always in close contact with them. I really wanted to work with Hossein again after *The Past* because we're very close and his involvement goes far beyond just cinematography. He's a wonderful partner to have on set for both the mental and emotional support that he brings. On the other hand, the emotion and passion that Mahmoud has for my work always makes the prospect of collaborating with him very appealing. I try to strike a balance between the two of them, and I'll certainly be working with both of them again in the future.

MM: The set design of *Death of a Salesman* is considered both innovative and avant-garde in the world of theater, with its use of metal scaffolding. Given your interest in theater, do you think you'll ever bring *Death of a Salesman* to the stage yourself?

AF: The cast and crew kept insisting during filming that we put on a performance of the play. With a few changes to the decor, it would have been great to have performed *Death of a Salesman* at least once with that group of actors. It's just a shame that I'm about to start work on my next project. Ideally, we would have begun rehearsing and performing *Death of a Salesman* after *The Salesman* had been released.

MM: . . . Or perhaps even in tandem with the release of *The Salesman*.

AF: Well, we couldn't have done both at the same time because the rehearsals would have taken too long. It's a pity that we couldn't make it happen, because everyone who saw *The Salesman* could have gone to see the play afterward, and that would have shed new light on the film for them.

MM: Do you think that you'll be able to make that idea a reality someday?

AF: I will work in theater again, but I'm not sure if I'll ever direct a stage production of *Death of a Salesman*. I'd much prefer to work on the production of a play that I'd written myself, if the opportunity ever presents itself.

MM: I've always believed that if you were to direct a play, you would either choose one of Ibsen's works, which focus heavily on the contrast between society and the individual, or one of Miller's works, which challenge society.

AF: Or even one of Harold Pinter's plays. I've always learned from the works of those three figures, not to mention Eugène Ionesco as well. It's such a shame that we have to read Ibsen's work in translation; a big part of his art is his language, and the same can be said of Pinter. Of all the playwrights from outside of Iran, I personally find that there is less of a cultural barrier with Arthur Miller and his works. In fact, he makes me think of Gholam-Hossein Sa'edi's[5] work, as they share very similar thoughts and beliefs.

So many great works have been produced over the years, based on plays by Ibsen and Miller; it would be tough to enter that domain, and we'd have to try to bring something new to the text.

MM: You mentioned how greatly you admire Pinter, and you're obviously aware of the black humor prominent in his works. Do you deliberately avoid black humor in your work?

AF: There is some humor in the scenes involving the students, but it's not dark humor. The film has already been accused of being dark and bitter as it is; there would be a riot if I were to start including dark humor too. In any case, there were never any moments in the story when I felt that I could have included some dark humor without it standing out. There is humor in some places, but it's not dark humor.

MM: Shahab Hosseini's performance is somewhat reminiscent of *A Separation* in a few brief moments, but it is a stunning performance nevertheless. How did you craft the film's slow- and then fast-paced internal rhythm, and how did you plan it out? Because it couldn't have been an easy task.

AF: Shahab actually plays three different roles throughout the film: one is the role of the salesman in the stage production; another is the Emad we see at the beginning of the story, who is a kind, friendly, and laid-back teacher; and lastly is the person he becomes, whose behavior shocks and dismays us. Shahab's immense talent as an actor plays an important part in the fact that both Iranian and non-Iranian audiences alike are able to relate to his character. Shahab's greatest attribute is that he is very intelligent with his performances; he understands what impact his actions will have on the audience. We were able to communicate easily with one another because we'd already worked together on *About Elly* and *A Separation*. Rather than just focusing on getting him into the logical mindset of the character, we also have to guide Shahab into the film's emotional space, because he is a very emotional and emotion-driven person. Once we establish the film's emotional space, he is able to find his place in the story.

MM: How do you create that space for him?

AF: There are various techniques. I kept reassuring Shahab that he had complete authority and creative freedom to the point where he became very protective of his role and stubborn about every aspect of Emad's behavior. His character may ultimately choose the wrong path, but Shahab believes strongly in his role. As we saw during the press conference at the Cannes Film Festival, both Shahab and Taraneh Alidoosti were very protective of their roles in the film and they defended them fiercely. What you can do is take each actor to one side during filming and talk to them in a way that indirectly makes them feel like they must be a defense lawyer for their individual role. If you talk to Taraneh, Shahab, or even Farid Sajjadi Hosseini, they can defend their characters for hours, and it's impossible to convince them that any of their actions were ever indefensible.

MM: Do you worry that this role of an intruder and a sinner might stick with Farid Sajjadi Hosseini for a long time?

AF: I think that actors can gradually distance themselves from their roles once they get back to real life. On the other hand, Farid is a very multidimensional person. He spent time constructing a nuanced personality for the character; he used to say that he'd actually gone to the apartment that night to help Ahoo move her things. Being so multidimensional is what ultimately helped Farid to view his character from more than just one angle. In any case, Farid is a very experienced and worldly person, so he won't have a problem distancing himself from the role.

MM: I always pay close attention to small details in the costume and set design while watching your films, knowing how much importance you place on every detail. There is a lot of writing on the whiteboard in the classroom, for example, that you can't help but read when you see it in the background. One particular sentence that caught my eye contained the words "Education in Germany." Did Emad write that or was it the teacher using the board before him?

AF: Emad wrote it. It was actually part of a lesson in the high school literature book that I had. But I can't remember what the full sentence was or what the lesson was about now.

MM: So, you copied it from that book?

AF: We selected a few bullet points and wrote them on the whiteboard, the same way a teacher would list headers and key points for each lesson.

MM: Were all of the pictures hung up on the walls of the apartment also carefully considered? Besides the photographs, there are also two classical European paintings visible for the audience.

AF: One of the photographs was taken by a friend of mine who is a professional photographer. I really liked it, so it appears more prominently throughout the film than any other picture. There is also a poster on the bedroom wall of Ingmar Bergman's film *Skammen*.[6] That film also depicts a husband and wife who experience the atrocities of war, and the husband loses his self-identity and turns into a completely different person as a result. I tried my best not to make the pictures stand out too much to the audience, but Emad and Rana are both cultured people, so I was also trying to decorate the apartment based on their tastes. I'd asked either Shahab or Taraneh—I can't recall whom exactly—to choose some paintings and photographs that were more consistent with their understanding of the characters, so their choices also influenced the arrangement of the pictures in the apartment.

MM: Please tell us about Hayedeh Safiyari's role in the making of the film. She has worked with you as the editor on all of your films and also played a big part in shaping their style and structure.

AF: I've been very fortunate to have worked with people like Ms. Safiyari over the years. We usually try to agree on the rhythm of the film without going too far into the finer details and then proceed based on that initial framework.

MM: Do you come to that agreement while writing the script?

AF: No, during production. Of course, I always show her the script while I'm in the process of writing it and ask for her opinion.

MM: Do you also share the script with the cinematographer?

AF: Yes. I should also mention Mr. Yadolah Najafi, the film's sound recordist who sadly passed away. Not only did he contribute to the sound recording, I also consulted with him many times during the writing process and incorporated his ideas. He knew a lot about Miller, and we had many deep discussions together. The fact that Ms. Safiyari and I have worked together for so many years has allowed us to develop a shared perspective on editing, and we've become so close that sometimes we can find where to cut, remove, and switch different shots around without ever saying a word—all it takes is a glance.

MM: How much of the film's tone and hue are formed during editing?

AF: It's impossible to differentiate. A large part of the film is defined by the story and its execution. Films are characterized by the dynamism that exists in every scene and behind every performance: the mise-en-scène, the decoupage, and various other factors. All of those things are like an assortment of disorganized materials, and the film won't have any hint of dynamics or tone if they're not arranged properly. As I've worked with Ms. Safiyari so many times before, I don't really know if I write in a way that suits her editing, or if she edits to suit my writing. Since I know that she will be editing the film, I have a good idea of where each cut will be made, so I write the scene accordingly. Our years of collaboration have given us a shared perspective that is invaluable. Her involvement is extremely influential and beneficial to me.

MM: Will your next film revolve around the same themes again? Themes like justice and morality....

AF: Yes. My work will always deal with issues surrounding judgment not only in theme; sometimes it is the drama that gives rise to judgment. There is actually a part of the story that is not seen, and characters therefore try to guess what has happened, which leads to judgments being made. Those judgments are made by the viewer in relation to the characters and events as well as by the characters in relation to one another. That theme will be present in my next film.

MM: Will you be using another couple as the focus of the drama?

AF: Yes, and again I'll be focusing on the relationship dynamics within a family unit.

MM: Your view of the world is rather apprehensive, and, with all of the violence and brutality that exist in the world today, things seem even bleaker than ever.

AF: That's not how I see things. It may not be apparent in my general attitude, but I am optimistic about the future despite what is being said and how things may seem. In this world so full of violence, the impression of violence is actually much greater than the violence itself. One person might be beheaded in Iraq, for example, but the news coverage is so blown out of proportion that it makes us feel like thousands of people have been killed. There was a time when killings and slaughter were rife in the Middle East. There was a time when millions were killed in Europe. The world today is much more peaceful. There were no news reports back then, so things only seemed more peaceful. I think that people nowadays live with more understanding. As life has become more complicated, however, people face more dilemmas and have to deal with more complicated situations. But today's world is much better than yesterday's.

MM: I can actually trace that sense of bleakness through your films. *Fireworks Wednesday* centers on a man cheating on his wife, but in *The Salesman* it feels like everyone commits an act of betrayal. The traitor could be Babak or the intruder's son-in-law, or anyone else. . . .

AF: That's not my interpretation. The hardships that the characters endure in *A Separation*, and the anguish that flows into their lives, all stem from the fact that they are honorable people and don't consider lying for even a second. Some have said that the film's characters constantly lie to one another, but it's actually quite the opposite. There probably would have been many more lies if the events of the film had happened in real life. I placed so much emphasis on the backlash whenever anyone in the film told a lie that it always carried a lot of weight and made it seem like everyone was lying. Like in *The Salesman*, when Emad slaps the old man. . . .

MM: How many takes was that brutal, violent slap recorded in?

AF: Just two, I think . . . thankfully.

MM: Shahab was so deeply immersed in the scene that the slap seemed completely real, and that was all that was needed.

AF: Just look at how disturbing one slap can be and how much it can upset you. To me, the film shows that even that level of violence is unacceptable. Those characters are generally quite honorable, but they have become embroiled in this situation and are tormenting themselves over the things they've done wrong. One person tells a lie, but they suffer a great deal because of it. The world in those films is actually a much more accountable one.

MM: Having said that, I don't think that the slap is a form of revenge; it is a painful reaction to being humiliated.

AF: Do you think that Emad should have just let him go and that the story should have ended there? That was the least that Emad himself thought he could do. I'm not trying to justify what Emad did; I don't believe that people have any right to take the law into their own hands, even to that extent. You should leave it to the law to decide. But in those circumstances, where Emad couldn't turn to the police, I can understand why he chose violence.

MM: When the little boy stays at Rana and Emad's apartment, he uses the same crayons to draw on the walls that the previous tenant's child had used—there's an interesting parallel being drawn there.

AF: The camera even focuses on the boy's face as we hear the voice of Ahoo's child on the answering machine—it creates an intentional juxtaposition between the two mothers and their children. The role that Sanam plays onstage also bears an analogy to Ahoo's actual life.

MM: Do you have anything else to say that you were hoping to be asked about?

AF: The most important thing to me is that people's personal privacy is respected, in addition to the film's other themes. Even the little boy asks for privacy when he goes to the bathroom and he won't allow a stranger to help him take his trousers off. The woman in the taxi also values her own personal space and doesn't want anyone getting too close to her. People don't like it when others stand over their shoulder while they're using their mobile phone. The subject of personal privacy and its place in our lives today is very important to me, especially in our society, where invading the privacy of others is not as frowned upon as it should be. Sometimes we don't appreciate how invading the privacy of others, whether through our words or our actions, can have damaging consequences—especially with the rise of the internet and social media.

Notes

1. Iranian modernist poet (1925–2000).

2. Iranian film director.

3. Iranian singer (1907–2000) of Persian classical music.

4. Iranian cult rape-revenge drama from 1969, directed by Masoud Kimiai.

5. Iranian psychiatrist and writer (1936–1985) who wrote novels, plays, and film scripts. His most famous screenplay was for *The Cow*, which is referenced in *The Salesman*. His work faced censorship both before and after the Revolution. He died in exile in Paris.

6. This is the original Swedish title for this 1968 Bergman film starring Liv Ullmann and Max von Sydow; the English title is *Shame*.

No One Knows What the Past Holds

Amir Pouria / 2018

From *Film Monthly* (Tehran), Vol. 36, No. 552, December 2018.[1] Translated by Ehsan Khoshbakht.

Amir Pouria: The first reaction to the title of your new film, *Everybody Knows*, is that it assures us there's a secret known by many but never spoken. Let's start with the title of your film.

Asghar Farhadi: *Everybody Knows* was one of those films whose title was confirmed very late in the production. Maybe you'd heard that first it was called *No One Knows*. In the past five years, one of the things that changed in proceeding from synopsis to shooting script was the title of it. I started working on it five years ago, and it was advanced to a certain stage when I returned to Iran and capriciously decided to make *The Salesman*. When I returned to Europe, the Spanish film team thought I had given up making it. Anyway, the title came later. The thing about the title of the film is that it has ambiguity and is more intriguing because when we say, "Everybody knows," the question becomes what is it that everybody knows? This, in fact, comes from a line in the film spoken by Alejandro. The reason for staying with this title was to play with revealing, uncovering, and exposing elements of the story, and as you said this choice of title was somehow different from my previous approach.

One other factor in choosing a title is that it should be easily translated into different languages, such that in each language it remains appealing so the distributors don't change it themselves. For instance, *About Elly* was changed to *A Girl on the Beach* in some Asian country! Or *The Salesman* in Brazil became *The Apartment* and in France, *The Costumer*. In these countries, because it went by a different title, people couldn't associate it with Miller's play. This time I wanted to avoid that confusion, although in Germany they still changed the title. In any case, first it was *No One Knows*, which was more ambiguous and mysterious, but then I decided to avoid alluding to the mysterious nature of the film in the title and go for quite the opposite: addressing the theme of revelation.

AP: The first film you directed outside Iran was *The Past*, and everything in it was arranged in such a manner that if the film had been made in Iran, you wouldn't have had to alter it a bit. After all that caution in *The Past*, now *Everybody Knows* shows you have freed yourself from the limitations you had imposed on yourself, as if you've decided to disregard those guidelines set by officials in Iran.[2]

AF: No, it was impossible to work in Spanish culture with those limitations in mind. I decided that I shouldn't limit myself or adjust the film with any guidelines in mind. I needed to first make *The Past* in order to get to this point where I felt that if this film is going to be seen by a Spaniard, it shouldn't look unfamiliar. Everything, from the accents to subtle details, needed to be thoroughly Spanish. This meant I didn't have to think of those specifications that have nothing to do with cinema, which you abide only if you want to have your film shown in Iran. *Everybody Knows* was an act of liberation from many things, even freeing myself from the narrative style of my previous films. This is why you see less indirectness and hinting in this film. During the production, whenever the crew members asked whether this film would get distribution in Iran and I was answering, "No, it won't," they were surprised why. In their view there was nothing indecent or immoral in the film. To them, what we see in the film is part of their daily life. If I wanted to make it discreetly, I would have lost the essence of this experience. *The Past* was set in a season of the year when people's clothing is covering them, which means it can't pose an issue when it came to showing the film in Iran. But Spaniards show their emotions more than the French do. Physical contact is part of their culture, especially in villages. That's why we see more hugging and embracing in this film. So from the first day I decided to put aside any discretion, even if it was partly unconscious.

AP: You once said *About Elly* could have taken place anywhere, even in the Alps and at a ski resort instead of a beach. Does this apply to *Everybody Knows*, too? The Spain in the film, does it afford the film certain characteristics, or is the setting here just for the sake of the story?

AF: It's the outer layer only, meaning that it's the surface of the story, the evident logic of the events, the structure and means of the narrative to give the film a native flavor. But reaching this level in which a Spaniard could watch and believe the story doesn't mean it couldn't be set just anywhere. It was important how the audiences would react to the film in Spain. Fortunately, the film got the best feedback from the Spanish audience. If the film were set in another culture, the conversation at the end of the film couldn't be the same, with the characters speaking so openly about their past and their private issues. Spaniards don't hide their feelings, which makes it hard to believe the country was under a dictatorship until a few decades ago. They have many cultural similarities with Iranians, but in certain things, because of that freedom that they don't take for granted, they are different from us.

AP: When did it become known that the film would be made in Spain?

AF: Since the idea came to me, I said if I make it, it should be made in Spain. The first spark was when I was traveling in southern Spain, and everywhere I went, on the walls of the city, I saw images of a disappeared girl. I guess it was after *Beautiful City* or *Fireworks Wednesday*. Years later, I returned to this initial idea and thought a lost child could be the right kind of crisis for getting into the past of the people who are caught in it. After *The Past*, the plan was to make a French-produced film in the US. I went to the US to research the story in a prison in San Francisco. The atmosphere of the prison was so heavy that I couldn't continue. After abandoning that project, I decided to make this film with the same producer. At first it was about a middle-aged American and his family visiting Spain to attend a wedding. The actor was meant to be Tom Hanks, and we had some sessions working on the script and later developing the character together via emails. When I came to Iran to make *The Salesman*, one of the things that gradually changed was the nationality of that character from American to Argentine, and he became Alejandro. Therefore, the film didn't need to be bilingual. I didn't like the idea of a bilingual film. Making it in Spanish only made things relatively easier.

I wrote the synopsis with the collaboration of a consultant. All the intricate questions related to the cultural details were discussed with him and a couple of other crew members, and we had many meetings over the course of several months, working out these details.

AP: Who was this consultant?

AF: David Trueba, a well-known Spanish novelist and journalist who has made films, too. His brother is a great filmmaker in Spain.[3] The fact is, when the synopsis was written I was still not sure how native the story would feel. At that point Pedro Almodóvar was still the producer of the film. We had a meeting after he read the synopsis, during which the first question I asked was about how Spanish he felt the story was, and he joked that it felt Spanish enough that if I weren't to make it, he'd make it himself. That eased my mind. Later on whenever I gave the script to the team, I always asked the same question first. When Penélope Cruz read the script, she was surprised that it was written by someone who hadn't lived in Spain before. She had found the story perfectly adjusted to the cultural traits of Spain. Part of it is because we have many things in common with them.

AP: The wedding sequence feels very long. My question concerns the editing. The editor of the film, Hayedeh Safiyari, is the only person from your Iranian films that you kept on for this one. How important was it to have a fellow Iranian you'd worked with—someone who's very professional in her job—be a kind of last filter for this production?

AF: The wedding scene was much longer and was shortened in the final cut. Now, the main wedding scene in the courtyard doesn't last more than three or four minutes, but the variety and volume of shots make us feel as if we have seen an elongated ceremony. Because the course of the story shifts in this scene, if it was too short, it could have felt like it was there just to give that twist and the crisis that follows. Meanwhile, during the wedding sequence, from the scene in the church to the time the rain starts to pour, a significant part of establishing the main characters is indirectly in process, especially that of Paco and his relationship with Laura. Maybe you could find more revelatory signs about the characters if you view this sequence again. In *About Elly*, too, there were many characters, though perhaps not as many as in this film. But in that film, I spoke very little about the past of the characters because the story didn't need it. Here, a collective past is made out of all the characters, which has a particular function as the story develops.

As for collaborating with Ms. Safiyari, I believe the editor is the second director of the film. Ms. Safiyari, after five films that we did together, is now an extension of my mind. She enters the project from the synopsis-writing stage and is kept in the loop on every change made. She stays with the film from beginning to end. What she has done in this film is quite amazing. She has edited a film in Spanish with many characters and a great number of shots. It was not surprising to me that the Spanish Academy nominated her for a Goya[4] for her work on this film.

AP: To what extent do you try to make invisible your directorial hand?

AF: A great portion of work is directed by the filmmaker's unconscious, of course, an unconscious which has been cultivated and has gained more layers by experience. If we return to the unconscious, sometimes it works better than when things are done consciously. If you ask a writer or director on the spot about the reasons behind their artistic decisions, they can't explain straightaway, which usually means the unconscious is at work. The obvious example is learning to drive; we learn the rules before sitting behind the wheel and then we practice, but when we become a driver, we don't consult the book every time we want to put our foot on the brake or turn the wheel—our hand and foot do it automatically. But one should note that sometimes it's inevitable that the unconscious becomes conscious, in both the director and the spectator.

In my previous films, there have been scenes where you could see the direction slightly more pronounced, such as the kite-running scene in *About Elly*. Throughout these years, even regular moviegoers have identified my methods, which is a precious thing. This, however, means that no matter what I do, even when hiding my directorial marks, the audience feels my presence. I don't think I can do anything about it, unless I go make an entirely different kind of cinema and distance myself from it, in which case it will no longer be me. As far as conscious work good, I try to eliminate my presence in the film or at least make it as invisible as possible. But trying to completely eliminate my presence could result in another form of artificiality.

Unlike the way it might look from the outside—that in my writing everything is arranged—I must say I write intuitively. It's in the rewritings that I work on signs, characters, connections, and colors and add and remove elements.

In any case, the outward aspect of this new film is a continuation of my previous films, but what's new here is the expansion of certain themes and subjects we had previously seen in a different form.

AP: Such as the theme of love and possession, which exists in your first film and is seen here in a different light.

AF: Once, in my student days, I read in a book by Erich Fromm that "Love is the child of freedom."[5] Back then I couldn't understand the meaning of it. Later I realized its exact meaning: when you love something, you don't own it. When Paco is in love with a woman he doesn't own, fathering a girl whom, again, he doesn't own, this is love that is not about possession and belonging.

AP: Here the subject of possessing the land coexists in parallel to the main story.

AF: Yes. We have two parallel stories. One is the story of a land that had once belonged to a family and that someone else has cultivated and turned into a farm. The other is the story of a girl who's been raised by a family and a man other than her biological father. These two stories proceed in contrast. Put another way, what Alejandro's daughter means to him, the land means to Paco.

AP: I feel that the part concerning the land, both its role in the film and the amount of time dedicated to it, is not on par with that of the girl. Even when they say Paco has been the son of the caretaker of the house, you don't stay on it too much. Why? Is it because you didn't want to impose on the film class division and conflict?

AF: In fact, one of the side themes of the film is that of class contempt, which has been in my previous films, too; in A Separation it was a major theme, in fact. Had I emphasized it more here, it would have become the dominant theme of the film. It means the film could no longer be as multisided as it is now, which allows the spectator to see and understand the film from an angle that means more to him or her. Otherwise, the dominant theme becomes the one that is discussed more in the debates following the film. For example, in The Salesman the theme of honor became dominant and many comments hinged on that, whereas for me it was never the main theme of the film.

AP: Of the themes we discussed in Everybody Knows, which is the main one for you?

AF: When writing Everybody Knows, I heard a Cuban proverb that went "No one knows what the past holds." It was intriguing because we typically use "no one knows" only for the future, but here it's about the past. I take it to mean that things to come are not our future but rather our past whose consequences are yet to be realized, thus forming our future. With some clues in the film, this "past" has been designated as the major theme in the film—or at least one of them. All the characters in this film know they have a past that they haven't fully come to terms with. Alejandro, for instance, has become a very religious man after being an alcoholic. . . .

AP: . . . And then we have Paco's past.

AF: I remember Javier Bardem said something interesting before we began filming. He asked, "What's the main reason behind Paco selling his land?" to which I replied, "He has different reasons, including saving the life of the girl to whom he feels like a father, and for the love that he still feels for Laura, and because he is not a calculating type of person." But Javier argued that the main reason was Paco's inferiority complex toward the family. It's true that the family has lost its past grandeur and everything in the house is decaying and falling apart, but Paco, in order to prove that now it's the family who needs him and it is he who can resolve this issue, sells the farm. In other words, to compensate for the past's degradation, he wants to proves himself a hero. This is how Javier saw that character.

AP: I think Laura's detailed recollection of what went on in the night en route to the airport is unnecessary. She could have simply asked Paco whether he remembered that night and then told her story about Irene. Why does she tell everything in detail? It feels as if she's explaining all this to the viewer and not for the sake of the film's drama.

AF: In that scene we are supposed to say something that the spectators more or less have already guessed. There are signs given throughout the film to help the audience develop a trace of doubt. If you reveal this in one line and without prior notice, it could shock the viewer. Whereas here the viewer kind of guesses what is going on. The secret is revealed rather slowly and with a lengthy introduction, so that before reaching the last line of that scene, the viewer's guess, like Paco's, could turn into certainty. With this type of game played, this mise-en-scène, and the introductory dialogues, the expectation of shock is quashed. Before the last bit of dialogue, which reveals that the secret is spoken, the audience gets the answer.

AP: In this film, your narrative is omniscient, such that the criticism directed at you for not showing Razieh's falling down in *A Separation* or the man, played by Farid Sajjadi Hosseini, entering the apartment on the night of the incident in *The Salesman*, no longer applies. Yet, even as you employ an omniscient narrative, when in the process of unraveling the story you decide to show who was kidnapped the girl, one feels "taken hostage," to quote Abbas Kiarostami. Viewers may ask themselves, "Farhadi wants to show us this now. But why now?"

AF: That revelation has a precursor, of course, when the wedding video is rewatched by Alejandro and the rest of the family. The seed is planted in the few shots we see there from the wedding, with pauses on some of the images and seeing that Rocío is also watching. It functions as the introduction to the next scene. There it occurs to Rocío that the circle of suspicion is getting smaller and soon she might get exposed. This is enough for Rocío to feel threatened and tell her husband that she regrets the kidnapping. With this introduction, we move to Rocío's side of the story. In my view, it's not like the director can go anywhere and show anything he likes. The suspicion, which at first is very broad, gets narrower and falls on a couple of characters. Now after viewing the wedding video in which Rocío, unlike other dancing guests, looks very anxious, she fears that this will give her up, so she goes to the forest. I could avoid showing the kidnappers' scene and leave their identity unexplained, but that could leave the viewer with what I feel is the wrong question: "So, who did this after all?" This was not my point in making the film. By showing their identity, I solved that problem and didn't let it become the main question popping up in the viewer's mind after the film is finished.

On the other hand, what the audience might get a shock from is how far from the stereotypical image of kidnappers these people are, and I liked that effect. If you remember, I was also criticized for the sudden revelation at the end of *Fireworks Wednesday*. Although we have a mystery in this film, it doesn't mean that I have to follow the textbook of Miss Marple or Hercule Poirot. On the contrary, I am deliberately trying to eschew the expectation that I am making a detective movie.

Essentially, in this film there's less concealing, hiding, and ambiguity compared to my previous films, and it comes principally from the experience of being in Spain. The narrative is more open here and that's new for me, especially after *The Salesman*, which is structured in a way so that its dramatic weight is never on display for all to see. Here, I tried to show more.

Notes

1. This is an abridged translation of the original interview.
2. The question refers to abiding by the rules of Iran's Islamic regime in regards to sex and nudity, which made the screening of *The Past* in Iran impossible. For that same reason, *Everybody Knows* couldn't be publicly screened in Iran.
3. Fernando Trueba, fellow Academy Award winner for Best Foreign Language Film (*Belle Époque*, 1992).
4. The Goya Awards are Spain's annual national film awards. *Everybody Knows* was nominated for eight Goyas, none of which it won.
5. The full quote: "Love is the child of freedom, never that of domination" (*The Art of Loving*, 1956).

A Country without Heroes

Ehsan Khoshbakht / 2021

Conducted November 14, 2021. Translated by Ehsan Khoshbakht.

For this exclusive interview Farhadi answered my questions via voice message, which were then transcribed by his assistants. This interview was given shortly after Farhadi had returned to Iran from a promotional tour abroad for his latest film, *A Hero* (2021).

Having earlier premiered at Cannes, where it took home the Grand Prix, *A Hero* became a curious case in Iran. Even before the film had been screened, word quickly spread that it lacked any overt reference to the country's political crises. In response, Iranians flocked to the internet to pan the film and Farhadi himself. This speaks to a highly reactionary, volatile climate in Iran today, but also to the expectations placed on Iranian filmmakers to make politically critical, relevant films. With the country fractured by the government's woeful response to the COVID-19 pandemic, the suffocating censorship, the tragic impact of US sanctions, and more importantly the major crackdowns on protests—in November 2019 more than three hundred protesters were killed in the streets—it seems that Farhadi, at least at this stage, may not be able to satisfy the needs and emotions of the class that once cherished him as a national hero. Farhadi is shrewd enough, however, to make the impossibility of being a hero in contemporary Iran the subject of his new film.

—Ehsan Khoshbakht

Editors' note: On November 15, 2021, one day after giving this interview, Farhadi finally broke silence on the controversy swirling around him and his latest film. In reaction to those who have accused him of being either too close to the regime or too close to enemies of the regime, he released a rare statement on Instagram. Farhadi aimed his attack at Iran's regime and state-controlled media, but also at Davoud Moradian, who runs the Revayat-e Fath institute for documentary films on the Iran-Iraq War. Moradian, a stooge for the regime, had earlier made the accusation that Farhadi enjoys the company and support of both sides, provoking this reply from the filmmaker:

> Let me be frank: I loathe you! How deceitfully you associate me with a regime whose extremist media has spared no effort to destroy, marginalize, and stigmatize me in past years. A government to which I have made my views clear on the suffering it has caused over the years: from the protests in December 2017 and November 2019 to the bitter, unforgivable murder of Ukrainian plane passengers; from the cruel discrimination against women and girls to how this government has allowed coronavirus to slaughter its people. How can you call me one of yourselves when at the airport you have confiscated my passport many times and held me for interrogations? How can you call me pro-regime when this regime sends messages saying, "It's better if Farhadi never returns to Iran."

Ehsan Khoshbakht: Which films and filmmakers, if any, encouraged you to leave the world of theater behind and become a full-time filmmaker?

Asghar Farhadi: My migration from theater to cinema wasn't a direct journey. When still in theater, I was invited by a friend to write radio plays, which became my occupation for a while. It was through these radio broadcasts that someone heard my work and invited me to write for television. I worked in television before moving to cinema. As you see, my move from theater to cinema was not a simple one. Before theater I had made a short film, and for me cinema and theater were concomitant. My time in theater was such a pleasant experience—I thought I would never leave that world. The films that influenced me before joining the theater group were mostly realist films along with novelists and playwrights that belonged to the realist tradition.

EK: And when working in television, were you closer to the traditions of television storytelling or rather looking at each episode as a "film"?

AF: In television, for different series I had different approaches. Some were done in the tradition of television series, where a story is told through multiple episodes. This type of work was meant to appeal to the viewer. In the TV series that I directed myself, including *Tale of a City*, I got away from that tradition. In that series each story is told in one or two episodes, or a maximum of three. In terms of form, I have tried to break away from common trends in television. This was achieved in some episodes, while other episodes followed the more familiar format of television. From that series, I only like a few episodes that I think are worthwhile.

EK: The history of Iranian prerevolutionary cinema is being rediscovered outside Iran, mostly thanks to new restorations. Were you at all influenced by that period of Iranian cinema, especially considering that in *The Salesman* you refer to Dariush Mehrjui's *The Cow*?

AF: Yes, totally. Not only me but a great number of Iranian filmmakers have been influenced by these figures who worked before the Revolution and tried to make a new kind of cinema—people such as Dariush Mehrjui, Nasser Taghvai, Sohrab Shahid Saless, Parviz Kimiavi, Masoud Kimiai, Bahman Farmanara, Bahram Beyzaie, Fereydoun Goleh, and others. In fact, my first influences in cinema and my understanding of what constitutes good cinema were through these filmmakers. For me, they are in a different class. They were the trailblazers who continue to impact our filmmaking today.

EK: Has it ever occurred in working with your usual editor, Hayedeh Safiyari, that the film drastically alters from what was written or even what was shot? And do you edit the film as you shoot it or wait until the end of the shoot?

AF: It hasn't happened that the structure of the film changes during editing. My scripts are not the kind where you could move one entire segment and shuffle it around. Maybe we could do it when it comes to details but not the overall outline. As for the other question, some of my films see their editing start halfway through the shoot and some only after the shoot is wrapped. But the main editing process happens only once the shoot is over.

EK: How do you arrive at the designated pace of each film? Is it something you work on during the shoot or mostly work out in the editing phase?

AF: The rhythm of each film is in the script. It doesn't happen on the set. But the rhythm hidden in the script comes to life during the execution of that scene, and it is in the editing phase that it finds the harmony it needs. Often on the set the desired pace has some flaws and looks uneven, but the editing can make it look even. Essentially, though, the rhythm of each film is dictated by the script.

EK: Compared to your earlier films, the pace has dramatically picked up. Why is that?

AF: I think it's in the stories. The type of story that is selected gives way to a certain narrative. These narratives have the form of mystery and involve revealing a truth or a hidden element that, in turn, asks for a different rhythm and pace. In some of my films, like *The Past*, which is set outside Iran, the tempo is internal and more covert. In some films, like *The Salesman*, it is external and the film has a faster pace. This derives from the form of narrative that is inherent to the story.

EK: Social media becomes part of *A Hero*'s story toward the end, but it essentially seems like a reaction to the chaos of the online world in Iran and the speed with which good and bad can swap places in that world.

AF: Through the long period I was busy writing *A Hero*, I never saw social media as the film's main theme. However, the story of an ordinary man becoming a celebrity needed the devices that could facilitate that change, such as newspapers and television. Obviously, today social media also have a share in that.

When writing the script, it wasn't my intention to criticize social media. I was mostly thinking in terms of my own usual concerns and questions, and social media was only a subsidiary theme. I didn't want to reject it, nor to endorse it, only flesh out that one dimension of social media to the story.

EK: In *A Hero*, language and communication have lost their power because lying, concealing, mendacity, misunderstanding and even a state of being inarticulate have overcome them. Characters talk on behalf of each other and make decisions for each other. It seems that the film is extending this phenomenon to the entire Iranian society. Is this, for you, Iran's main crisis today?

AF: I have said many times that no film can claim to illustrate the whole of a society, especially a complex society such as ours. Any film, at least if it wants to be honest, can claim to illustrate a small part of society. In my films, I do not generalize the situations, the characters, and the story to extend them to the whole of that community.

EK: In many key scenes in *A Hero*, a character enters a space twice. He or she enters first, leaves in despair or hesitation, and enters again with more confidence to speak his or her mind and reveal a secret. How do you employ the elements of delay and repetition in your filmmaking?

AF: This usually happens in the scenes involving Rahim's character. Rahim is, after all, a man always in doubt. With the exception of the film's end, it is others who make decisions for him. One way to show his indecisiveness was to bring it into the mise-en-scène, to show that he doesn't believe in himself and isn't sure whether what he wants to say is right or wrong. These back-and-forth movements were part of his characterization.

EK: Could it be the case that puzzle and mystery in *A Hero* have partly substituted for drama? Is it possible that the human depth of characters and the complexity of situation have been sacrificed for giving clues and tying together the knots of mystery, so to speak?

AF: The viewers who watch films without preconceptions don't think of these questions. Some of the viewers who are familiar with narrative techniques, especially those that have become worn out due to overuse, might watch the film with certain expectations. But when people follow the film and enter its world they forget that it is a film that doesn't want to follow the rules they're already familiar with. The film is engineered to make the audience forget they are watching a film and to feel, instead, as if they are viewing a piece of real life. Those worn-out rules are the rules of cinema and not the rules of life. I therefore don't believe in these technical divisions. Filmmakers don't make movies to endorse the old techniques. They make films and the rules emerge from within the film. Incidentally, in *A Hero* the main difference compared to my other films is the more minute attention to developing character and their inner layers instead of focusing on drama. It seems to me that this film, more than my other works, is dependent on character study more than mystery.

EK: Why did Iranians respond negatively to *A Hero* and reject it before even having seen the film? Isn't it a reaction already anticipated in your film, which itself comments on the unpredictability of public reaction?

AF: This has happened to my previous films, too. It started after *About Elly* and *A Separation*. There are always some people who attack the film, whether they've seen it with certain preconceptions or not seen it at all. Gradually, though, the excitement dies down and what remains in focus is the film itself. I'm used to it now, even though this time the reactions were stronger because of the anger and desperation people feel in a society fraught with problems. Rather unconsciously, this theme has crept into *A Hero*.

EK: Have you ever considered making a film that isn't set in present time, that takes place, for instance, in one of the earlier periods of Iran's history, especially given that Iranian period films are always so ideologically biased and devoid of any proper character study?

AF: Yes, I always think of making a film like that. I wish one day to make a period piece—and this would be one of my last films—inspired by a classic of Persian literature. Whether this is going to happen or not, I'm not sure, but I'd love to do it and I hope one day the opportunity arises.

Index

Abadan (Mani Haghighi, 2002), 30, 31
Abar, Saber, 64, 69
A/B/C plotting. *See* plotting
Abdolvahab, Mohsen, 86, 96
About Elly (*Darbare-ye Elly*) (Farhadi, 2009), xiv, 53–69, 82, 89, 90, 111, 114, 117, 127, 149; alternate possibilities, 58; atmosphere during shooting, 53; audience, 58, 90, 91; backstory, 64; bathroom, 60, 61, 62; casting, 80, 81; characterization, 58, 62; class relations, 150; compared with *A Separation*, 72; compared with *The Past*, 99; contrasted with *Beautiful City*, 64; contrasted with *Canaan*, 64; contrasted with *Fireworks Wednesday*, 64; contrasted with *Tambourine*, 64; costume, 67; difference from previous films, 57; directing, 82; distribution, 95; domestic violence, 63, 66; ending, 136; family dynamics, 125; filming, 77; foreshadowing, 60; gender roles and relations, 66, 67, 68, 127; hairstyling, 53, 67; international reception, 95; kite-running scene, 149; lies and lying, 62, 63, 68, 92; marriage, 125, 126, 127; morality, 92; observer's viewpoint, 59; optimism, 143; origins and sources, 56, 64; outsider status, 65; problems during shooting, 53; production design, 53; reception in Iran, 157; rehearsals, 53; repetition, 68; settings, 59, 147; structure, 57, 112; themes, 74; title, 146; violence, 63; volleyball, 62
Abu Dhabi film seminar, 97
Academy Awards, ix; *A Separation*, xiv
accountability, 144
Acid (sketch by Farhadi), 19
actors and acting, 35, 36, 38; attitudes of French vs. Iranian, 118; characterization, 80, 82; child, 36; energy, 115–16; ensemble, viii; extras, 84; improvisation, 34–35, 65, 112; nonprofessional, 9, 50, 83; personality traits, 80; professional, 22, 23, 83; rehearsals, 53, 78, 80, 81; roles' effects on, 141; rumors, 53; style, 46. *See also* casting; improvisation
adultery. *See* infidelity
Adventures of Mr. Filmmaker, The, xiii
Afshar, Mahnaz, 51
Aghighi, Saeed, x
AIDS, 4, 7
alcoholism, 151
Alidoosti, Taraneh, viii, 22, 23, 34, 35, 36, 44, 49, 52, 53, 64, 82, 141; interviews, 49; personal life, 49, 52
allegory, 15
Almodóvar, Pedro, 148
Alzheimer's disease, 74
Annual Book Awards, Islamic Republic of Iran, xiv
Ansari, Anousheh, ix
Antonioni, Michelangelo, ix

architecture, 39

Aristotle, 77

arthouse films, viii, ix

Artist, The (Michel Haznavicius, 2011), 113, 120

artistic passion, 118–19

Asghar Farhadi: Life and Cinema (Tina Hassannia, 2014), xi

Asghar Farhadi: Poetics of Disintegration (Maziar Eslami, 2016), xi

audience, 23, 111, 151, 156; anticipating the plot, 44; deceiving, 55–56; expectations, 55; festival, 22, 71; as filmmaker, 131; general vs. cinephiles, 12, 22, 104; imagination, 64; international, 22; Iranian, 22, 74; judgements made by, 143; leading, 110; manipulating or deceiving, 55, 89; participation, 90; perceptions, 58; preparing, 55; previews, 90; reaction to *A Separation*, 72; respect for, 6, 90; television, 17; the unconscious, 149

Azadivar, Rana, 60

Azeri ethnicity, viii, xii

background. *See* locations

backstory, 8, 31–32, 64, 117. *See also* characterization

Bahram, Pantea, 34, 50, 51, 56

Bakhtavar, Parisa, xiv, 69

Banietemad, Rakhshan, 86, 96

Bardem, Javier, 151

bathroom scenes, 45, 50, 60, 61, 62, 131, 134

Bayat, Sareh, 80

Bayzaie, Bahram, 50, 52, 59, 69, 139, 155

Bazrafshan, Ali, 15

BBC Persian, x

Beautiful City (Shahr-e Ziba) (Farhadi, 2004), viii, xiii, 11, 19–28, 29, 30, 35, 46, 83, 104, 114; alternate endings, 25–26; class relations, 132; origins, 19; structure, 57

Bejo, Berenice, 100, 113

Bergman, Ingmar, 142

Berlin International Film Festival (Berlinale), 70; *About Elly* wins Silver Bear, 2009, 74; *A Salesman* wins Golden Bear, 2011, xiv; *A Separation* wins Golden Bear, 2011, 72–73

Bernal, Gael Garcia, 113

blocking, 86

bourgeoisie, Iranian. *See* class relations and values

boycott of Oscars, ix, xiv

budgeting, 25

Busan International Film Festival, xiii

butterfly effect, 112

camera work. *See* cinematography

Canaan (Mani Haghighi, 2008), xiii, xiv, 51, 64

Cannes International Film Festival, x; *Everybody Knows* premieres at, 2; *A Hero* ties for Grand Prix 2021, xiv, 153; *The Past*, 99; *The Salesman*, xiv, 141

capital punishment, ix

Carrière, Jean-Claude, 100

casting, 33, 44; *About Elly*, 81; *Everybody Knows*, 148; *Fireworks Wednesday*, 44, 50, 81; *The Past*, 113; *A Separation*, 81

censorship, vii, ix, 3, 12, 48, 71, 87, 148, 152, 153

Center for Intellectual Development of Children and Young Adults, xii

Chaharshanbeh-soori (Fireworks Wednesday). *See Fireworks Wednesday (Chaharshanbeh-soori)*

Channel 5 (Tehran Channel), vii, xiii, 3, 4

characterization, ix, 8, 20, 41, 46, 51, 59, 71, 80, 81, 82, 151, 156; backstory, 31–32, 117; women, 126

Chashm Be Rah (The Expectant), xiii

Cheshmeh (publisher), xiv
Chicago International Film Festival, xiv
children, 117
cinephiles, 12
cinematography, 34; close-ups, 42; digital
    camera, 85; *Fireworks Wednesday*, 46;
    Hossein Jafarian, 41, 139; *In This World*,
    86; Mahmoud Kalari, 84, 85, 139; *The
    Salesman*, 139, 142; *A Separation*, 78, 86
class relations and values, viii, ix, 20, 31,
    66, 111, 124, 131, 150
close-ups, 42
collaboration, 30
College Bridge, 49, 52
color, 41
comic relief, 12
communication, 125
Compartment, No. 6, x
costume, 35, 67; *A Separation*, 78
costume drama, 157
COVID-19, x, 153
Cow, The (Dariush Mehrjui, 1969),
    135, 154
creativity, 54
crime, 3, 9
critics, 12
Cruz, Penélope, 148
cultural differences among nations, 103
cutting. *See* editing

Dancing in the Dust (*Raghs dar Ghobar*)
    (Farhadi, 2003), xiii, 11–18, 29, 35, 46,
    114; the car, 16–17; class relations, 132;
    desert setting, 59; the finger, 15; recep-
    tion, 13; snakes and snake catchers,
    15–17; structure, 57
Darbare-ye Elly (*About Elly*). See *About
    Elly* (*Darbare-ye Elly*)
Dastan-e Yek Shahr (*Tale of a City*). See
    Tale of a City (*Dastan-e Yek Shahr*)
Dayare Zangi (Parisa Bakhtavar, 2008), xiv

Death of a Salesman (Arthur Miller),
    123–24, 130, 138, 139, 140; similarity to
    Farhadi's work, 124
desert setting, 11, 14, 59
design. *See* production design; set design
dialogue, 33–35, 62. *See also* improvisation
digital camera, 85
directing, 23, 36, 77, 152; blocking, 86; char-
    acterization, 81; children, 36; directorial
    style, 49; director's duty, 12; director's
    presence, 150; philosophy of, 115; pro-
    duction crew as minisociety, 106;
    rehearsal, 78, 80; respect for actors,
    84; techniques and tricks, 36, 37, 46, 53,
    80–84, 115–17, 141; the unconscious, 149
distribution, 23
divorce, 67, 98, 111, 136
Divorce, Iranian Style (Kim Longinotto
    and Ziba Mir-Hosseini, 1998), 86
documentaries, 9, 85, 91, 153
Dolatshahi, Sahar, 34
domestic violence, 63, 66
Dreamlab Films, 95

Ebrahimi, Zanyar, xi
economics, 105, 106
editing, 41, 142, 155; *Fireworks Wednesday*,
    50; Hayedeh Safiyari, 88; jump cuts, 42,
    50; long takes, 42; reaction shots, 42;
    realism, 50; *A Salesman*, 143; *A Separa-
    tion*, 86, 88, 89, 90; the unconscious, 149
8-millimeter film. *See* Super 8 film
Emad (name), 127
endings, 43, 44, 45. *See also* screenwriting;
    individual films
Entezami, Ezzatollah, 46, 52
Escape from the Trap (Jalal Moghadam),
    46, 52
Eslami, Maziar, x
ethics, 92, 101
Europeans contrasted with Asians, 103

Everybody Knows (*Todos lo saben*) (Farhadi, 2018), 146–60; alcoholism, 151; audience, 149, 151; Cannes (Grand Prix), xiv; casting, 148; censorship, 147, 148; characterization, 149, 151; class relations, 150; directing, 149, 150, 152; editing, 148, 149; ending, 152; farm, 150; freedom, 148; narrative style, 147; panel discussions, 150; past, present, and future, 151; plotting, 150; political climate, x; religion, 151; *The Salesman*, 151; screenwriting, 149, 150, 151; setting, 147; structure, 147; themes, 150; title, 146; wedding video, 152

Expectant, The (*Chashm Be Rah*), xiii

extras, 84

Face to Face with Asghar Farhadi (Esmaeil Mihandoust, 2018), xi

Facts about Idris's Daughter, Leila, The, (screenplay, Bahram Beyzaie), 139

Fajr Film Festival, xiii, xiv, 29, 50

Famanara, Bahman, 155

family: definitions of, 104–6; dynamics, 126; effects of economy on, 105–6; in *The Salesman*, 123–24

Farahani, Golshifteh, ix

Farahani, Shaghayegh, 10

Farahzad, Tehran, 57

Farhadi, Asghar: academic career, 6, 11; biography, xiii–xv, 154; commercial success, 24; directorial style, 49; future plans, 157; motivation, 73; personal life, 74, 122–23; political statements and opinions, ix, x, 153; popularity, 121–23; progress through career, 55; reception outside of Iran, xiv, 12, 22, 95, 99, 121; reception within Iran, ix, x, xiv, xv, 22, 121; scriptwriting, xiii; theater, xiii, 6, 11; university years, 6, 11, 19

Works by: *Acid* (sketch), 19; *The Adventures of Mr. Filmmaker* (juvenilia), xiii; *Canaan* (script, 2008), xiii, xiv, 51, 64; *Doctors* (*Pezeshkan*) (script, 1998), 11; *The Expectant* (*Chashm Be Rah*) (1998), xiii; *The Kind Moon* (*Mah-e Mehraban*) (script, 1997), xiii, 11; *The Last Heroes on Earth* (play, 1999), 6; *Low Heights* (*Ertefa-e Past*) (script, 2002), xiii, 11, 47, 52; *Tambourine* (*Dayere Zangi*) (script, 2008), xiv, 55, 64; *Time of Youth* (*Roozegar-e Javani*) (script, 1998), 4, 7, 11; *Trial on the Street* (script, 2008), xiv; *Vagabonds* (play), 6; *The World of Walls* (juvenilia), xiii. See also *About Elly* (*Darbare-ye Elly*); *Beautiful City* (*Shahr-e Ziba*); *Dancing in the Dust* (*Raghs dar Ghobar*); *Everybody Knows* (*Todos lo saben*); *Fireworks Wednesday* (*Chaharshanbeh-soori*); *Hero, A* (*Ghahreman*); *Past, The* (*Le Passé, Gozashteh*); *Salesman, The* (*Forushande*); *Tale of a City* (*Dastan-e Yek Shahr*)

Farhadi, Sarina, 84–85

"Farhadism," x

Farrokhnezhad, Hamid, 35, 36, 83

Fazeli, Mohammad Reza, 15

"festival films," x

Field, Syd, 61, 76, 77

film festivals, 71, 74; panel discussions, 150 *See individual film festivals*

Film Monthly, xi, xii, 53; interviews appearing in, 3–5, 6–10, 11–18, 19–28, 53–69, 70–96, 121–45, 146–60

Film Today (*Film-e Emrooz*), xii

filmfarsi, viii

Filmnegar magazine, 19

Fireworks Wednesday (*Chaharshanbeh-soori*) (Farhadi, 2006), vii, xiii, 29–52,

58, 64, 75, 111; acting styles, 35; actors and acting, 44; audience participation, 91; audience reaction, 44; bathroom scenes, 45, 50; beginning, 45; broken glass, 45; casting, 44, 50, 80, 81; censorship, 48; characterization, 46; child actors, 36; cigarettes and smoking, 45; cliché gestures, 45; College Bridge, 49; costume, 35; directing, 36; editing, 50; elevator, 46; ending, 43, 44, 45, 55, 56; family dynamics, 125; gender roles and relations, 126; hairstyling, 36; home environment, 125; infidelity, 47, 48, 126, 144; lies and lying, 92, 110; makeup, 35; marriage, 47, 126; mirrors, 50; motorbike, 45; music, 44, 48; narrator, 45; nonprofessional actors, 50; pacing and rhythm, 46; realism, 50; setting, 125; sources and origin, 57; sound recording, 36, 38; symbolism, 125; themes, 74

Forushande (*The Salesman*). See *Salesman, The* (*Forushande*)

framing. *See* cinematography

France, xiv, 99; French culture contrasted with Iranian culture, 100–107; Paris, 102, 120. See also *Past, The* (*Le Passé, Gozashteh*)

freedom, 148

French language, 114

Fromm, Erich, 150

Gainsbourg, Charlotte, 113

gender roles and relations, 66, 67, 68, 71, 72, 91, 92, 93, 105, 126. *See also* marriage

genre films, viii

gestures, cliché, 46

Ghaemian, Farhad, 23

Ghahreman (*A Hero*). See *Hero, A* (*Ghahreman*)

Gharibian, Faramarz, viii, 12, 17, 18, 22, 35, 36, 114

Gheisar (Masoud Kimiai, 1969), 134

Ghorbanzadeh, Ali, 7

Ghotbizadeh, Saeed, 53–69

Goleh, Fereydoun, 155

Golmakani, Houshang, xii, 29–52

Goya award, 149, 152

Gozaresh. See Report, The (*Gozaresh*)

Gozashteh. See Past, The (*Le Passé, Gozashteh*)

Grand Prix. *See* Cannes International Film Festival

Grant, Phillip, 70–96, 97–120

Gray, James, 113

Haghighi, Mani, xiii, xiv, 29–52, 53, 75; *Canaan*, 51; judgment on actors, 50; meeting Farhadi, 29–30; *Men at Work*, 48, 51, 52

hairstyling, 36, 53, 67

Hamlet, 108

Hamoun (Dariush Mehrjui, 1990), 120

Hamshahri newspaper, 49

Hanks, Tom, 148

Hassannia, Tina, xi

Hatami, Leila, viii, 79–81, 97, 115

Hatamikia, Ebrahim, vii, viii, 11, 18, 47, 52

Haznavicius, Michel, 99, 120

Hero, A (*Ghahreman*) (Farhadi, 2021), 153–57; audience, 156; Cannes International Film Festival, xiv; characterization, 156; editing, 155; IMDB listing, xiv, xv; lies and lying, 156; mise-en-scéne, 156; mystery, 157; pacing, 155; plagiarism charge, xv; reception in Iran, 157; reception within Iran, x, xiv, xv; repetition, 156; rhythm, 155; screenwriting, 156; social media, 155; structure, 155

Hitchcock, Alfred, 43, 110

HIV, 4, 7
Homayoun Shahr, Iran, xiii
homosexuality, 105, 106
honesty, 22. *See also* lies and lying
honor, 133, 134, 144
hope, ix, 137
Hosseini, Farid Sajjadi, 141, 151
Hosseini, Seyyed Majid, x
Hosseini, Shahab, viii, 53, 81, 82, 86, 114,
    140, 141

ideological cinema, 109
IMDB.com, xii, xiv
Immigrant, The (James Gray, 2013), 113
improvisation, 34–35, 65
In the City (Tehran Channel news
    program), 3, 4
In This World (Michael Winterbottom,
    2002), 86, 96
independent filmmaking, 25
infidelity, x, 47, 48, 144
Instagram post, x
international reception, xiv, 12, 22, 95, 99
Ionesco, Eugene, 140
Iran: capitalism in, 124; France, contrasted
    with, 100–105; international view of,
    101; political situation, 153; protests and
    massacres, 153; reception in, xiv, xv,
    157; similarities to America, 124; social
    change in, 105, 106, 124; "tourist gaze"
    of, 101; US sanctions, 153
Iran (newspaper), 9
Iranian film: international reception, 71;
    prerevolutionary, 154
Iranian government, ix, xiv, 52, 71
Iranian literature, 132
Iranian revolution, ix, 85
Iranian social realism. *See* realism
Iranian society, 71
Iranian Youth Cinema Society, xiii

IRIB (Iranian national television), vii.
    See also Channel 5
Isfahan, Iran, 6
Islam, 27, 28
Islamic jurisprudence, 137
Italian neorealism. *See* neorealism

Jafarian, Hossein, 39, 40, 139
Jahangir, Abbas, 15
Jaoui, Agnes, 101
Jodaeiye Nader az Simin (*A Separation*).
    See *Separation, A* (*Jodaeiye Nader az
    Simin*)
Journey of Stone, The (Masoud Kimiai),
    46, 52
jump cuts, 42, 50
justice, 132, 133, 143

Kalari, Mahmoud, 84, 85, 139
Karimi, Babak, 80
Karimi, Nosrat, 80
Kavousi, Houshang, 134
Khandan, Reza, 10
Khomeini Shahr, Iran, xiii
Khoshbakht, Ehsan, 153–57, 169
Khosroshahi, Zahra, 11–18
Kiarostami, Abbas, vii, x, 34, 151
Kieślowski, Krzysztof, 108
Kimiai, Masoud, vii, viii, 155; *The Journey
    of Stone*, 46, 52; *Verdict*, 46, 52
Kimiavi, Parviz, 155
Kind Moon, The (*Mah-e Mehraban*), xiii

Lahiji, Masoumeh, 114
Last Heroes on Earth, The (play by
    Farhadi, 1999), 6
Leila (Dariush Mehrjui, 1997), 34
lies and lying, x, 41, 62, 63, 68, 92, 95, 107,
    110, 144, 156
lighting, 39

Locarno Film Festival, xiv
locations, 15, 33, 54, 102; College Bridge,
 49, 52; courthouse, 87; desert, 11, 14, 15;
 The Salesman, 125; *A Separation*, 86;
 Tehranpars, 50; urban, 15. *See also*
 setting
long takes, 42
Longinotto, Kim, 86
Lost (TV series), 59

Maadi, Peyman, viii, 80, 81, 83, 97
Maham, Mehran, 23
Majid's Tales (TV series), 6,
 40, 52
makeup, 35
Makhmalbaf, Mohsen, ix
Marceau, Sophie, 113
marriage, 47, 92, 105, 125, 126
Masihzadeh, Azadeh, xv
Mehrabi, Massoud, xii, 70–96
Mehrjui, Dariush, 34, 86, 155
Memento distribution company, 95, 98
Men at Work (Mani Haghighi, 2006), 48,
 51, 52
metaphor, 59
middle class. *See* class relations and values
Mihandoust, Esmaeil, xi
Miller, Arthur, 123, 130
Ministry of Culture and Islamic Guidance,
 xiv, 52
Mir-Hosseini, Ziba, 86
Mirkarimi, Reza, 122
mirrors, 38, 50, 61
mise-en-scène, 33, 36, 151, 156
Moazezinia, Hossein, 97–120
Modarres-Sadeghi, Jafar, 56
modernization and modernity, ix, 124
Moghadam, Jalal, 46, 52
Moghaddam, Keyvan, 87
Moradian, Davoud, 153

morality, 92, 95, 101, 143
Mosaffa, Ali, 97, 110, 113, 114
Motamedi, Alireza, 6–10
Mo'tamen, Farzad, 47, 52
motivation, 73
multistory plotting. *See* plotting: A/B/C
murder, 28
music, *Fireworks Wednesday*, 44, 48

Naderi, Amir, vii
Najafi, Yadolah, 142
Najvan, Omid, 11–18
neorealism, viii
nonprofessional actors. *See* actors and
 acting: nonprofessional

open endings, 43
optimism, 143
orientalism, 101, 102, 104
Oscars. *See* Academy Awards
outside status, 65

pacing, 14, 31–33, 50, 59, 61, 133; *The Salesman*, 141; *A Separation*, 89. *See also*
 rhythm
Panahi, Jafar, ix
panel discussions, 150
parallel narratives. *See* plotting: A/B/C
Paris, France, 102, 105, 120
past, present, and future, 104, 151
Past, The (*Le Passé, Gozashteh*) (Farhadi,
 2013), 97–120, 138; advisors, 112; apologies, 107–8; budget, 119; Cannes Best
 Actress Award 2013, 99; casting, 113;
 cleaning, 127; confession, 107; costumes,
 147; family dynamics, 125; French vs.
 Iranian modes of relating, 107; gender
 roles and relations, 105, 127; improvisation, 112; lies and lying, 107; locations,
 102; marriage, 125, 126, 127; origins, 99;

pacing, 155; painting the walls, 125, 127; political climate, x; production conditions, 118; production crew, 119; revisions, 112; setting, 125; structure, 111, 127; suicide, 112; symbolism, 125

Pear Tree, The (Dariush Mehrjui, 1998), 86, 96

Persian language, formal vs. informal, 54, 69

Pinter, Harold, 140

plagiarism charge, xv

plotting, 4, 12, 27, 30; A/B/C, 4, 20; *About Elly*, 56; *Fireworks Wednesday*, 56; foreshadowing, 23, 60; origins of stories, 9, 10; surprise, 23, 56; suspense, 60; *Tambourine*, 56

Polanski, Roman, 139

police, 134

popular films, viii

Pourahmad, Kiumars, 6, 40, 52

Pouria, Amir, 146–60

poverty, 20

primary/secondary plotting. *See* plotting: A/B/C

privacy, 144

prizes. *See* film festivals

production design, *A Separation*, 87

profit motive, 25

props, 16. *See also* mirrors

radio, 154

Radio (Farhadi juvenilia), xiii

Raghs dar Ghobar (*Dancing in the Dust*). See *Dancing in the Dust* (*Raghs dar Ghobar*)

Rahim, Tahar, 98, 100, 116, 120

Rana (name), 127

Rashidi, Davoud, 46, 52

Rasoulof, Mohammad, ix

Rastin, Shadmehr, 19–28

reaction shots, 43

realism, viii, 9, 15, 20, 22, 34, 50, 109, 154

redemption, 94

rehearsal, 34–35, 41, 53, 78–81, 101, 113–17, 140

relativism, 110

religion, 27, 94, 151

repetition, 68, 156

Report, The (*Gozaresh*) (Abbas Kiarostami, 1977), 34

retaliation and revenge, 27, 133

Revayat-e Fath institute, 153

revelation, 146

Revolutionary Guard, 20

Reza, Yasmina, 98, 99, 120

rhythm, 50, 133, 142, 155. *See also* pacing

romance, 12

Säedi, Gholam-Hossein, 135, 140

Safiyari, Hayedeh, 33, 50, 88, 89, 142, 148, 149

Salesman, The (*Forushande*) (Farhadi, 2016), xi, 121–45; accountability, 144; acting and actors, 141; anger, 137; art school, 135; atmosphere, 136; audience, 131, 138, 143; bathroom, 131, 134; betrayal, 144; Cannes International Film Festival, xiv, 141; characterization, 130, 137; cinematography, 138, 139, 142; class relations, 131, 150; cracks in the walls, 125; *The Cow*, 135; *Death of a Salesman*, 123–24, 130, 138, 139, 140; decoupage, 142; directing, 141; economics, 133; editing, 138, 142, 143; Emad, 127; ending, 136, 137, 143; family, 123–26; farm, 150; gender roles and relations, 126, 127; honor, 133, 134, 144, 150; hope, 137; Iranian literature, 131; Islamic jurisprudence, 136, 138; justice, 132, 133, 134, 137, 143; law, 138, 144; lies and lying, 144; marriage, 125; mise-en-scène, 143; morality, 123, 131, 137, 143; music, 129; pacing, 133, 141, 155; point of view, 138; police, 134, 138, 144; privacy,

144; the prostitute, 138; Rana, 126, 127; revenge, 133; rhythm, 133, 141, 142; *A Separation*, 140; screenwriting, 126; set design, 139, 141; setting, 125, 135; sexuality, 131; the slap, 144; social change, 124; sound, 142; sources and origins, 127; storytelling, 131, 143; symbolism, 125, 127, 131; screenwriting, 133, 138, 143; structure, 142; theme, 131, 150; title, 146; tone, 136, 143; violence, 144; women, 127

Sartre, Jean-Paul, 57

screenwriting, 15, 23, 25, 30, 39, 62, 94, 131, 138, 143; advisors, 112; backstory, 31–32, 117; beginnings, 75; classic narrative form, 110; collaboration, 31; conventions, 156; dialogue, 33, 34; dramatic writing, 110; endings, 43, 44, 55, 75, 76, 136, 137, 152; Farhadi's approach, 54; themes, finding, 108–9; foreshadowing, 23, 60, 151; form vs. content, 110; improvisation, 34, 65, 112; intuition, 150; process, 4, 75, 106–8; revisions, 78, 86, 112, 150; rules and formulas, 54, 61; story-based vs. ideology based, 109–10; structure, 32–33, 75, 76, 111; surprise endings, 55; television, 154; the unconscious, 149; vs. filming, 77. *See also* pacing; plotting; rhythm

secondary plotline. *See* plotting: A/B/C

Secrets of Separation, The (Saeed Aghighi, 2017), x

Separation, A (*Jodaeiye Nader az Simin*) (Farhadi, 2011), xiv, 70–96, 99, 103; Alzheimer's disease, 74; audience, 72, 89, 90, 91; bath, 74; beginning, 75; Berlin Film Festival, 70, 72; Cannes, 99; casting, 80, 81; censorship, 71, 87; characterization, 71, 80, 81; cinematography, 78, 85, 86; compared with *About Elly*, 72; compared with *The Past*, 99, 100; costume, 78; delayed by government, ix, xiv; digital camera, 85; directing, 80–84; distribution, 95; documentary structure and style, 85, 86; editing, 86, 88, 89, 90; ending, 75, 76, 136, 137; extras, 84; the fall, 151; family dynamics, 125; filming, 78; gender roles, 71, 72, 91, 92, 93; glass breaking, 87; international reception, 95, 96; lies and lying, 92, 95; locations, 86, 87; marriage, 92, 93, 125; miscarriage, 92; morality, 92, 94, 95; pacing, 89; previews, 90; reception in Iran, 157; redemption, 94; rehearsal, 80, 81; religion, 94; revisions, 78; sets, 87; sound, 89; structure, 75, 76, 85, 91, 93, 112; suspense, 91; themes, 74, 75; truth, 95; women, 71, 72, 92, 93

set design, 39, 41, 86, 135, 139, 141, 142. *See also* production design

setting, 15; desert, 11, 14, 15, 59; home, 125; sea, 59; urban, 15. *See also* locations

Seven Scripts by Asghar Farhadi, xiv

sexuality, 131

Shahid Saless, Sohrab, 155

Shahr-e Ziba (*Beautiful City*). See *Beautiful City* (*Shahr-e Ziba*)

Shahsavari, Saeed, 18

Shakespeare, William, 108

Shakibai, Khosrow, 116, 120

Shame (*Skammen*) (Ingmar Bergman, 1968), 142

Shamlou, Ahmad, 122

sharia. *See* Islamic jurisprudence

Skammen (*Shame*) (Ingmar Bergman, 1968), 142

snakes and snake catchers, 14–17

social impact of film, 95

social media, 155

social realism. *See* realism

socialist filmmaking, viii

Soltani, Amir, 3–5, 6–10

sound recording, 36, 38, 89, 142

soundtrack, 43

Spain, x, 152. See also *Everybody Knows* (*Todos lo saben*)
Spanish Academy, 149, 152
stereotyping, 20
storytelling, 3, 6, 9, 12, 54, 61, 62, 75, 91, 92, 99, 105, 131, 143
structure, 32–33, 75, 85, 111, 142, 147
subterfuge. *See* lies and lying
Super 8 film, xiii, 6
Suri, Chaharshanbe, 50, 51
suspense, 60, 91
symbolism, 15, 125, 131

Taghvai, Nasser, 155
Tale of a City (*Dastan-e Yek Shahr*) (Farhadi, 1999–2001), xiii–xiv, 3–5, 11, 154; censorship, 4; ending, 4; origins, 3; origins of *Beautiful City*, 19; plotting, 4; reception, 53
Tambourine (*Dayere Zangi*) (Parisa Bakhtavar, 2008), 56
Tarbiat Modares University, xiii, 11
Tehran, Iran, vii; modernization of, 124
Tehran Channel. *See* Channel 5
Tehrani, Hedieh, viii, xiii, 34, 35, 36, 44
Tehranpars, 50, 52
television, 17, 18, 154
tempo. *See* pacing
Tenant, The (Roman Polanski, 1976), 139
theater, 23, 38, 77, 93, 110, 139, 140, 154. See also *Death of a Salesman*
themes, 75, 131, 150
threading. *See* plotting: A/B/C
time, 54; passage of, 42
Time magazine, *Time* 100, xiv
titles, 146
Todd, Drew, 169
Todos lo saben (*Everybody Knows*). See *Everybody Knows* (*Todos lo saben*)
Tohidi, Farhad, 47, 52
tone, 12, 143

"tourist gaze," 101, 102, 104
tradition, 66
Trauma (Seyyed Majid Hosseini and Zanyar Ebrahimi, 2016), x
travel ban by Donald Trump, ix, xiv
true crime, 3, 9
Trueba, David, 148
truth, 95, 110
24 Monthly, 97–120

Under the Skin of the City (Rakhshan Banietemad, 2001), 25, 28
unfaithfulness. *See* infidelity
United States of America, similarities to Iran, 124
University of Tehran College of Fine Arts, xiii

Vaezzadeh, Shahab, 53–69
Vagabonds (play by Farhadi), 6
Vaziri, Qamar-ol-Moluk, 129
village residents. *See* class relations and values
violence, 63, 66, 144, 153
Vossoughi, Behrouz, 46, 52

Warsaw International Film Festival, xiii
Willy Loman. *See* Miller, Arthur
Winterbottom, Michael, 86, 96
women, 71, 72, 92, 93, 126. *See also* gender roles and relations; marriage
working class. *See* class relations and values
World of Walls, The, xiii

Yari, Abbas, 29–52
Yazd, Iran, 11
Yazdanian, Peyman, 48
Youth Cinema Society, 6

Zarei, Merila, 60
Zarrabi, Moluk, 129

About the Editors

(c) Noemi Usai

Ehsan Khoshbakht is codirector of Il Cinema Ritrovato film festival, held an-nually in Bologna, Italy. He is a noted film curator whose series have traveled the world, a film critic, and a documentarian.

Photo by Michela Martini

Drew Todd teaches film studies at San José State University and has published n various journals in his field. He is editor of *Jafar Panahi: Interviews*, published y University Press of Mississippi.

Printed in the United States
by Baker & Taylor Publisher Services